Denmark

Copenhagen·

BALTIC SEA

Danzig·

Altona· ·Lübeck
·Hamburg

rdam

Brunswick·

Hameln·

H o l y

·Leipzig

·Lützen   *Friedland*

Bohemia   ·Breslau

R o m a n

·Frankfurt   ·Prague

·Mainz

E m p i r e   *Moravia*

·Worms

Nuremberg·

Bavaria

·Augsburg

·Constance   ·Munich   Vienna·

·Zurich

·Cadore

lais   Trent·

·Bergamo   ·Venice

an   Padua·

Mantua· *Modena*

·Parma

a·   *Tuscany* ·Bologna

Pisa·   Florence·

·Arezzo

Italy   A D R I A T I C

S E A

·Rome

·Naples

S E A

With *Renaissance Lives,* Theodore K. Rabb revives a tradition of writing that was often practiced by the historians of that astounding era: to tell the story of an age by examining the lives of those who lived it.

Rabb gives us here the stories of fifteen men and women of the Renaissance. Some are familiar: Catherine de' Medici, Titian, Galileo, Montaigne, Milton—others less so: Thomas Platter, a student and teacher; Glückel of Hameln, a woman merchant; Ralph Josselin, a simple religious man. He makes us see anew the profound transformations of society that cut across and remade the realms of human conduct and custom, and see why this entire era took for its name a word meaning "rebirth."

For Rabb's subjects are all people who felt change gather speed around them: whether it be Jan Hus at the heart of a violent conflict with the papacy; Titian relishing Venice in her golden age; Thomas Platter fighting off starvation; Catherine de' Medici and Michel de Montaigne agonizing through civil war; or John Milton challenging satanic forces. In their stories we see the church being displaced by the university; the commercialization of art as patronage is replaced by market demand; the economic considerations that changed the practice and motive of warfare; the power of faith to gird both the skeptic and the scientist; and above all, the power of ideas to liberate, to enthrall, to provoke, and to resolve conflict.

Renaissance Lives shows us the struggle—with its grave disappointments but also its extraordinary achievements—that accompanied the creation of the world we recognize as our own.

Renaissance Lives

Also by Theodore K. Rabb

Enterprise and Empire: Merchant and Gentry Investment
in the Expansion of England, 1575–1630
The Struggle for Stability in Early Modern Europe

Renaissance Lives

Portraits of an Age

Theodore K. Rabb

PANTHEON BOOKS   NEW YORK

Library of Congress Cataloging-in-Publication Data

Rabb, Theodore K.
Renaissance lives : portraits of an age / Theodore Rabb.
p.   cm.
ISBN 0-679-40781-2
1. Europe—Biography. 2. Renaissance. I. Title.
CT759.R32   1992
920.04—dc20
[B]   92-54121

BOOK DESIGN BY FEARN CUTLER

Manufactured in the United States of America
First Edition

For Tamar

 Contents

Foreword   *ix*

PART I The Assault on the Past   *1*

Two Dissenters   *3*

Petrarch   *4*

Jan Hus   *18*

PART II The Creation of a New Vision   *33*

Two Artists   *35*

Titian   *36*

Albrecht Dürer   *52*

PART III The Enthusiasm for Change   *73*

A Student   *75*

Thomas Platter   *76*

PART IV The Response to Change   *93*

A Believer and a Dissenter   *95*

Teresa of Avila   *96*

Michel de Montaigne   *109*

PART V The Search for Order *123*

    A Prince *125*

    Catherine de' Medici *126*

PART VI The Discovery of New Worlds *139*

    An Explorer and a Scientist *141*

    Walter Ralegh *142*

    Galileo Galilei *155*

PART VII The New Professional *175*

    An Artist *177*

    Artemisia Gentileschi *178*

PART VIII The Mastery of Power *193*

    A Warrior *195*

    Wallenstein *196*

PART IX The Pragmatist in Changing Times *211*

    A Merchant *213*

    Glückel of Hameln *214*

PART X The Response to Revolution *227*

    A Believer and a Dissenter *229*

    Ralph Josselin *230*

    John Milton *241*

    Afterword *255*

    Acknowledgments *257*

    Illustration Credits *259*

Foreword

THE dilemma I faced as I began working on this book, and on the television series to which it is related, was straightforward. Stripped of the details, the nuances, and the qualifications that normally shield the scholar, how was I to convey the fascination and importance of the distant past without affronting either the lords of modern mass communications or the guardians (myself included) of academe?

It was not hard for me to decide which of these two sentinels seemed the more formidable. After all, I had found quite reassuring, and only slightly uncomfortable, the experience I once had of being shown to a dust-laden archive, deep in the cellars of an ancient London organization, only to have the archivist slam a huge metal gate behind me, lock it elaborately, and then leave me for nearly a day to read documents that can be consulted only in the security of a dungeon. Those documents, crucial evidence of the activities of Renaissance merchants, remain the property of a company that was once a powerful guild and now guards its past like a mother her child. Although the scholar has to enter the world of the man in the iron mask in order to read those records, that life can seem tame in comparison to the demands of the twentieth-century media.

The very thought of a more general readership raises the specter of compromise, dilution, and the gamut of scholarly sins. And yet, how can anyone who devotes himself to animating people long dead—and arguing for the need to understand them if we are to understand ourselves—resist the opportunity to do the resurrecting for an audience far larger than the historian's normal company of students and specialists? How is one to evoke, without complex narrative, the flavor and the dynamic of a time long gone?

The answer both here and in the television series has been to focus on a representative group of social types—the Dissenter, the Artist, and so forth—who typified the age and shaped its development. Through these exemplary figures, we can follow the transformations that marked the Renaissance, with consequences we still feel. To see social types in action, however, free of the abstractions that quickly engulf grand concepts like power or art, we need a shaft of light that is even narrower: the individual life. The microcosm is, after all, an old device—the head of a pin that embodies an entire world.

If one tries to picture dissent in the twentieth century, for example, eyes soon glaze over as the movements, the isms, and the fine distinctions multiply. Far more will be understood, and the ideas will have concrete meaning, if we can find the summary individual who can typify dissent in our times. The leader of Solidarity in Poland, Bronislaw Geremek, for instance, conveys more of the essence of the changes in Eastern Europe in the 1980s, and the dissent on which they were based, than a dozen historical or philosophical tracts. Himself a historian of fringe groups, like the poor, in the Middle Ages and the Renaissance, Geremek ended up in prison for his criticisms of the Communist regime; he became a prime advisor to Solidarity; and he served as one of the party's major figures in the Polish Parliament, though still uneasy at his role in the Establishment, and sympathetic to the students who now protested against him. The story of his career brings a major revolution, and the dilemmas of dissent, vividly to life.

The burden that the fifteen people chosen for this book carry is that they have to represent, not just one episode, but an entire era—they must make personal and accessible the profound struggles that eventually created the modern world. And they have to range across many realms: politics, the military, religion, philosophy, learning, art, and the economy. There is a splendid model from the period itself: John Aubrey's *Brief Lives*. Our subjects, however, cannot stand on their own, as do Aubrey's delightful embodiments of high-class gossip. They must offer a sense of the variety and progression of Renaissance times. It may be helpful, therefore, to outline at the start the larger history in which their lives belong.

The first hints that corrosive forces were at work on medieval society came in the late fourteenth and early fifteenth centuries, in the wake of the terrible blows visited on Europe by the Black Death, by the political and economic disorder that followed, and by the crisis in the Church when the papacy moved from Rome and was then rent by schism, with two or more candidates claiming to be pope. Out of this period of upheaval emerged two movements fraught with consequence: humanism, a program of educational and moral reform, based on an admiration for antiquity, which swept from Florence throughout Italy and then all of Europe; and the demand for religious change which, though suppressed, eventually bore fruit when it inspired the Reformation.

The influence of humanism during its first two hundred years transformed much of Europe's intellectual and creative activity. New inspirations were found, in fields as different as political theory and epic poetry, among the writers of Greece and Rome. Military strategy was rethought; universities changed their curricula. But the most spectacular impact was on the visual arts, whose radiance and originality have come to represent the era as a whole. The very appreciation of genius was a by-product of humanist thought and helped transform the artist into one of the most honored and admired figures in society.

By the beginning of the sixteenth century an extraordinary succession of changes was under way. Newly aggressive governments; a resumption of economic and population growth; stunning discoveries overseas; and the radical ideas associated with Copernicus and Machiavelli—all had made their disturbing entry onto the European scene. None of these momentous events, however, had an impact to compare with the Reformation, which also gathered force during the decades following 1500. For some, vitality, excitement, and unbounded opportunity seemed the order of the day. For others, especially as religious dispute erupted into a century of fanaticism and devastating conflict, optimism seemed misplaced. Governments battled to reimpose order, and in the world of ideas there was room for both shining belief and profound doubt.

But the pace of discovery did not slacken. By 1600, settlers as well as explorers had covered the globe. And the transformation of the study of nature that we know as the scientific revolution was about to enter its most productive years. If anything, the ability of Europe's intellectual and artistic leaders to create new styles in art and thought was coming to be taken for granted. No longer fringe figures, they had an accepted, and even respected, professional position at the heart of society.

Yet the time of upheaval was far from over. The changes set in motion around 1500 bore bitter fruit during the first two-thirds of the seventeenth century, when intolerance, battles over ideas, social upheaval and revolt, and war reached new levels of intensity. Historians have seen the middle decades of the century as a time of general crisis, when the worst period of the Thirty Years' War, and political turmoil in just about every state in Europe, threatened to descend into total anarchy. Warfare assumed a scale of destructiveness and levels of technological sophistication that had never been seen before. And in England a violent revolution spawned radical ideas that transformed basic assumptions about the nature of government and social relations.

That the mayhem did come to an end was the result not only

of weariness after decades of struggle but also of a feeling that the great disputes that had raged ever since humanists and religious reformers first challenged the old order might at last have been resolved. Science inspired confidence that truth and certainty were once again attainable; assertive governments, allied with the increasingly powerful interests of a merchant community that was fashioning the commerical revolution we know as capitalism, were imposing stability; and coexistence became the norm for previously irreconcilable religious faiths. In other words, the great changes we associate with the Renaissance had been assimilated into European culture and society. A period was over, and a new one, the era of the Enlightenment, was about to begin.

The exemplary lives—four Italian, two Bohemian, two German, one Swiss, one Spanish, two French, and three English—that serve to embody this age in the pages that follow range across all social ranks. None, however, had to suffer through dull times. Whether it be Jan Hus at the heart of a violent conflict with the papacy; Titian relishing Venice in her golden age; Thomas Platter fighting off starvation; Catherine de' Medici and Michel de Montaigne agonizing through civil war; or John Milton challenging satanic forces; these were all people who felt change gather speed around them. They were forging a new world, but to do so they battled endlessly with themselves and their contemporaries. It is the sense of struggle, with its grave disappointments but also its extraordinary achievements, that gives the period its particular sheen. And if the image of struggle and labor seems always to accompany stories of birth, that is surely appropriate for the age we call by the very name of Renaissance.

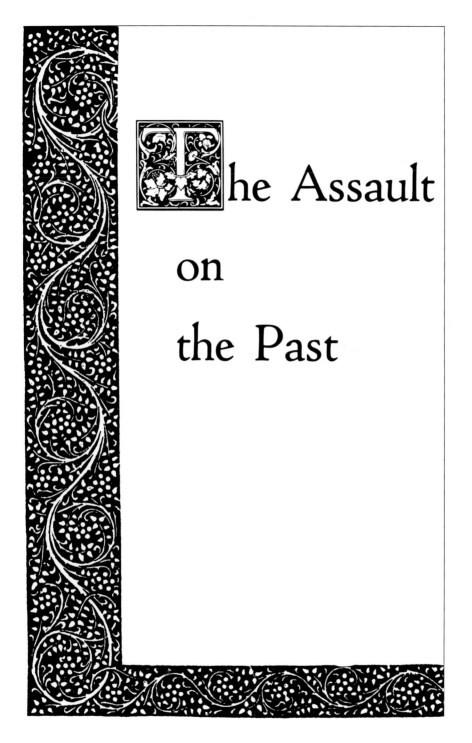

PART I

The Assault

on

the Past

Left: Lombardo della Sala, Petrarch. This portrait, drawn by a friend in a manuscript of Petrarch's last work, *On Illustrious Men*, is probably the most accurate likeness of the author that has survived.   *Right:* Jan Hus. We do not know what Hus looked like, but to the Lutherans of the following century what counted—as this engraving makes clear—was his martyrdom, his adherence to the word of God, and his faith in Christ. The goose is a reference to the meaning of Hus in Czech.

Two Dissenters

SSENTIAL TO THOSE WHO SHAPED THE WORLD of the Renaissance was their willingness to break with their predecessors. They sent European civilization off in new directions precisely because they were willing to proclaim that they knew better how to create the good individual and the good society. Their models may have come from the distant past—from ancient Rome or the age of the Bible—but that did not lessen their distaste for what they found in their immediate surroundings or in received opinion. To start anew they had to challenge their own times. ❦ The creators of the Renaissance were therefore unavoidably dissenters. The earliest advocates of new ideas, appearing as they did when there was little likelihood of change, were often alone. They did find disciples, but even so, it was no easy task to take on the powers that dominated intellectual life—scholasticism and the Church—and suggest alternative ways of seeking truth. Yet take them on they did. Two pioneers in particular, who lived in the plague- and depression-ridden later years of the fourteenth century, when few were offering messages of hope, exemplified the early stirrings that eventually were to transform their world. ❦ The older of the two, Petrarch, was a historian, philosopher, poet, and diplomat; the younger, Hus, was a scholar, theologian, preacher, and rebel. It was their versatility and determination that made them archetypes of the Renaissance, and it was the power of their example that inspired followers for generations to come.

Petrarch

THAT the small region of central Italy known as Tuscany should have been the source of so much of the inspiration of the Renaissance continues to astonish us. To its people, though, there was no mystery, for as one of its sons, the artist Giorgio Vasari, put it: "The Tuscan genius has always been pre-eminent." That pride and sense of identification persisted even when, as was often the case, these Tuscans did their greatest work far from home. After all, the two sons of Florence, the region's principal city, who had made the area famous in the early fourteenth century, the poet Dante and the painter Giotto, had spent most of their careers elsewhere. And the same was to be true of the most remarkable figure of the following generation, Francesco Petrarca, whom we know as Petrarch.

Like Dante, Petrarch's family found itself on the losing side in one of the vicious feuds that rent Florence apart in these years, and was forced into exile by the victors. And yet, even though he spent little time in the city, both Petrarch himself and the Florentines always considered him a native son. The family was already in exile when Francesco was born, in the nearby town of Arezzo, in 1304. He came from a long line of successful notaries—men who dealt in documents and legal records, and whose literacy led them, at least in the case of Francesco's father Pietro, to an interest in poetry and fine writing.

It was thus at home that the boy first received an introduction to two of his later heroes, Cicero and Vergil.

From an early age Francesco became used to life on the road. When he was seven, the family moved to Pisa, and the next year, still unable to return to Florence, they went on to Avignon, in what is now southern France. Here the papacy, fleeing Italy, had set up its court, and this bustling center was a natural place for the notary to find work. Although Pietro had to live in the city, he settled his family (now enlarged by a second son, Gherardo, who long remained Francesco's closest companion) in the village of Carpentras, some fifteen miles away. The next four years were an idyllic time for the young Petrarch. In contrast to Avignon which, as he wrote later, was "at that time a constricted spot, ill provided with houses and over-flowing with inhabitants," Carpentras seemed perfect.

> Do you remember those four years? What happiness we had, what security, what peace at home, what freedom in the town, what quietness and silence in the countryside!

It was here, in Provence, that Petrarch was first moved by the love of nature that he was to express so warmly throughout his life.

When he was twelve, however, the idyll came to an end. He was sent off to the University of Montpellier, some fifty miles away, to study law. Family tradition notwithstanding, it was not a subject he was ever to enjoy, and soon he was spending his time reading Latin classics instead. Fearful that his neglect of his studies would be discovered, he hid the books when his father came to visit, but Pietro found them. As punishment, he burned them, but rescued works of Vergil and Cicero when he saw his son's torment at the loss. It was while Francesco was at Montpellier that his mother died, and his grief inspired his first poem, a delicate elegy about memory in Latin hexameters that echo Vergil.

At the age of sixteen, the boy was sent to the principal law school of Europe, the University of Bologna, to complete his studies. He remained there, with interruptions and home visits, for the next six years, until he returned to Provence following the death of his father in 1326. With parental demands gone, Petrarch lived the life of a man-about-town during the next four years. As he later reminded his brother in a nostalgic letter, they had consumed their father's estate as classic wastrels. They had cultivated their looks with the latest fashion in curling irons (occasional accidents notwithstanding), perfumed gowns, and tight shoes, and had even been reluctant to venture forth in high winds that might ruin their hair. When the money ran out, a reputation as a fop and versifier had little value, and it was clear that, with his excellent education, he ought to take up a profession. Neither law nor medicine appealed to him, and so he turned to the only other possibility at the time, the Church.

It was at this time, in 1327, that Petrarch was smitten, in church, with a woman he called Laura. Although his love poetry now abandoned frivolity and lightness for real passion, his vow of celibacy (or perhaps her rejection) left her always beyond his reach, a situation that seems to have made even more delicious the agonies of love he recounted in the poems. For it was not as if his clerical vows kept him chaste: we know of at least a son, Giovanni, and a daughter, Francesca, whom he fathered during the next twenty years.

As his family's fortune dwindled, Petrarch finally decided, at the ripe age of twenty-six, to seek a clerical position that would give him both an income and an anchor. Not that he ever had much interest in wealth per se. Among his many comments about himself, usually made for their effect, few have so clear a ring of truth as:

> I have always greatly despised riches—not in themselves, but because of my hatred for the toils and cares that are their inseparable companions.

The leisure to do as he wished was what counted. Even when appointed as a chaplain in the household of a cardinal, as he was in 1330, he insisted on the time he needed to pursue the scholarship and literature that he increasingly saw as his life's task. And indeed, the various Church appointments he received over succeeding years gave him exactly what he wanted: an income without obligations, and the freedom to do his work.

By day and night I read and write, relieving each task with the solace of the other. I know no pleasure and no sweetness except in such toil, and I am so absorbed in it that I am not aware of any other labor or peace. So new works are constantly pressing upon me. Yet the years are passing, and when I consider the brevity of life I am filled with dismay at the amount of work I have begun. Meanwhile, I pant, keep vigil, sweat, and struggle onward.

Workaholic that he was, he had no trouble refusing the bishopric and the high office at the papal court he was offered in the 1340s and again in the 1350s, because posts at that level would have interfered with his writing.

By then, however, he was already a famous man. For he had been writing since his twenties the lyric poems in his native Italian —notably fourteen-line sonnets that became an inspiration for centuries of reflective poetry—that marked him as the heir, for his generation, of Dante.

> If this should be Love, O God, what shakes me?
> > If Love it is, what strange, what rich delight!
> > If Love be kind, why has it fangs to bite?
> > If cruel, why so sweet the barb that rakes me?
> If Love I crave, why this lament that breaks me?
> > If not, what tears or sighs can mend my plight?
> > O Death in Life, dear pain, where lies thy might
> > If I refuse the doom that overtakes me?
> If I consent, without a cause I grieve;
> > So in a tempest do my fortunes heave,
> > By winds contrary and by waters tost;
> So, in a stupor, like a blind man lost
> > In mischievous error, lured from doubt to doubt,
> > June freezes, January thaws me out.

Petrarch's distinction as a scholar—as editor of Livy, collector of the writings of ancient authors, especially Cicero, and author of a series of brief biographies of Roman heroes—may have made him a considerable figure in the intellectual circles of the day, but it was his verses that set him apart. Taking the troubador tradition that sang of sadness only at the dawn farewell, he deepened and expanded the ability of poetry to juxtapose anguish with ecstasy at every turn. Only his attempt to follow Dante into the epic mode, with an enormous Latin poem on the exploits of the Roman general Scipio Africanus, proved a disappointment, even though the promise of that epic earned him the reward of a ceremony that may well have given him more pleasure than any of the other events of his life.

It had been the custom in ancient Rome to hold a poetry competition every five years, and to crown the winner with a wreath. The practice of awarding the wreath had reappeared in Italy, and it became Francesco's dream to receive a crown himself. He campaigned for the honor both at the University of Paris and before the king of Naples—two authorities who had sufficient standing to bestow such an honor—and finally received invitations from the two places on the same day. Naturally, he chose Italy, where, in April of 1341, he was the star of a magnificent ceremony on the Capitoline Hill in Rome. Now he could truly feel himself the heir of Vergil (PLATE I).

And yet for all the pleasure that literature gave him, Petrarch had grander themes he wanted to pursue. He may have loved the peace of the Provençal countryside, but he never hesitated to throw himself into the great events of his day. He traveled astonishing distances: over most of Italy, much of France, and parts of the Netherlands and the Rhineland. And he did not hesitate to offer his advice on all sides: at one point he warned the doge of Venice against going to war, at another he urged the Holy Roman emperor to reestablish his authority in Italy. Since it was a time of turbulent, even anarchic politics, he often found himself deploring what he saw, especially the wars that "hardened and shut" men's hearts. Yet when they caught up with him, he did not flinch. Just three years after the coronation in Rome, he was trapped by a siege in the city of Parma, and he determined to escape. As he recalled two days later:

> I started out with a few companions, and we made our way between enemy positions. About midnight, a band of marauders broke out of an ambush, shouting noisily, and threatening to kill us. There was

The most famous depiction of Renaissance Rome was this woodcut in *The Nuremberg Chronicle* (see page 54), which, though produced over a century after the time of Cola di Rienzo, probably gives a good sense of the city as it was in Petrarch's day. We can see the fortified walls, monuments such as the semiruined Colosseum, and the Tiber River, all recognizable to this day.

nothing for it but to flee. But after we were safe my horse stumbled in the darkness and fell, injuring me and knocking the breath out of me. Gathering all my strength, I got to my feet, and although today I can hardly lift my hand to my mouth, I managed to get on to my horse again. Meanwhile a thunderstorm was raging, and rain and hail were coming down. We spent that hellish night on the bare ground; and the arm hurt in the fall was swelling and paining me severely. In the first light of dawn we came to a friendly town, where we learned that the enemy troops abandoned their search for us because of the storm. That day, with a rough bandage on my arm, we went by a mountain road to Modena.

Three years after this escape, in 1347, Petrarch's political dreams of a return to ancient ideals seemed to come true. A friend from Avignon days, a firebrand named Cola di Rienzo, overthrew Rome's aristocratic government and tried to reestablish the Roman republic. Francesco called Cola "the unique champion of liberty," and he was bitterly disappointed when his hopes proved misplaced. The liberator proved to be a demagogue; his power, though supported by the pope, soon collapsed, and Cola himself was killed by a Roman mob. Despite what proved to be one frustration after another, however, Petrarch maintained his fascination with politics.

A few months later he undertook a diplomatic mission for the papacy, even though 1348 was the gruesome year of the Black Death. The plague killed his beloved Laura, and many relatives and friends, but he traveled through Italy undaunted and unharmed. In the mid-1350s he was still at it, making a long journey from Milan to Basel and Prague in the hope of persuading the emperor to maintain peace in Italy, and receiving ennoblement as a count for his pains. When friends worried that he endangered his freedom by associating with rulers they regarded as tyrants, he insisted that one had nothing to do with the other:

Lay aside your fear on my behalf. While I might seem to have been subject to a yoke, I have always been the freest of men. I shall try always to be free in spirit wherever I am, even if I am subject, bodily and materially, to rulers. It is easier to stand up to a tyrannous man

than a tyrannous people. If I had not been able to live in freedom of
spirit, either my life or my contentment would have come to an end.
Nor would I serve anyone save of my free will.

With that principle to guide him, he continued, even till his last years,
to throw himself into the affairs of the day. He tried to persuade the
pope to return from Avignon to Rome, and a few months before his
death he was a member of a diplomatic mission to Venice.

Petrarch, like many an intellectual both before and since, probably hoped for more influence in the world of affairs than he ever
achieved. Yet he could never have imagined how great his impact
would be on the world of letters. The antiquarian impulse, in particular, roused his friends and followers to unprecedented action. They
roamed Europe in search of ancient manuscripts, uncovering in monastery libraries long-forgotten texts of Greek and Roman authors.
For the humanists, these were essential tools in the revival of antiquity,
and they were not above stealing especially interesting documents for
further study.

Yet the origins of the enterprise, at least for Petrarch, did lie
in politics. It was the condition of public life that was at the root of
his yearning for peace, his admiration for the Roman republic, and
his regret at the state of Italy. What could not have been foreseen,
however, was the way he combined his skill with words (the main
reason he found political employment at all) with his love of the past
and his despair at his own times to fashion a moral program that was
to be at the very heart of Renaissance culture.

Everything he did was material for Petrarch's exploration of the
question that dominated his writings: how can a person learn to be
good? Very early on, his clerical status notwithstanding, he concluded
that the Church offered only feeble guidance. Its moral standing was
hopelessly undermined by the corruptions and materialism visible in
Avignon.

You can see with your own eyes what this new Babylon really is:
seething, obscene, terrible. Whatever perfidy and fraud, whatever
cruelty and arrogance, whatever shamelessness and unbridled lust you

have heard of, whatever impiety and immorality—all this you may see heaped up there.

What, then, was the alternative?

The answer came from the joy he found in words and in the ancient classics. Petrarch was a rhetorician—a man who received diplomatic assignments because he was so adept with language. He was especially admired for his letters, which he himself was careful to preserve for posterity. Indeed, his best-known work, an account of a climb with his brother of Mount Ventoux, in Provence, was written as a letter. The form enabled him to address the reader directly, one-on-one, and to powerful effect. Yet it was not made so personal that it could not be reproduced and distributed, and it thus became a favorite means of communicating his ideas.

What the rhetoricians of Petrarch's day—the writers of letters and speeches—argued was that their profession was crucial, because the way a thought was expressed determined its impact. Without proper presentation, meaning would be lost; only if a message was conveyed well could a person teach or learn. It was this commitment to the proper use of words, and above all to the virtue of eloquence, that set the rhetoricians apart, and led Petrarch to the view that style—the manner in which ideas were conveyed—was essential to moral education, for it could "make the heart teachable."

Yet where were the models to be found? For Petrarch there could be only one answer: the Roman classics. They were written at a time when, in contrast to the sorry present, Italy had ruled the world. Clearly, the virtues they displayed were the ones to be emulated. If an example was needed, one could look to a great Roman like Cicero, who had also been a rhetorician, a master of language. And what language! Latin had a purity, an expressiveness, that modern tongues could not equal. Moreover, despite some obvious lapses, he had sought to combine the *vita activa* and the *vita contemplativa*—both the life of affairs, as a prominent politician, and the life of the mind, as a writer.

By posing urgently the question of whether the two lives could be combined, Petrarch raised an issue that humanists were to grapple with for decades. And by implying the possibility of universality, he suggested an ideal that has been associated with the Renaissance ever since. Few of its great figures in fact excelled in a multitude of skills. Michelangelo certainly mastered poetry, sculpture, and architecture as well as painting; Leonardo's versatility is legendary; Bacon combined law, science, and politics; his contemporary Ralegh was a soldier, explorer, and poet; Leibniz roamed from Egyptology to mathematics; and even an ordinary man like Thomas Platter was at various times a rope maker, a printer, and a schoolmaster. Such adaptability was possible in an age when few fields had succumbed to the specialization that now afflicts them. But one must not confuse the occasional achievement with a general goal. All that the ideal required, during the Renaissance, was equal attention to active and contemplative pursuits. And even that simple combination, as Petrarch knew, caused problems.

Might not public service interrupt or debase the quest for virtue? On the other hand, could one cultivate one's finest qualities in isolation? Was a higher virtue achieved when one combined public affairs with self-improvement? What was clear to Petrarch was that only by imitating the style of a figure like Cicero could one begin to attain such virtue. Above all, he said, one had to try to imagine oneself a Roman. He wrote letters to his ancient heroes, and even imagined Cicero visiting him in Provence, where the Roman had never been, and which Petrarch loved. As he wrote to Livy:

> I would wish either that I had been born in your age, or you in ours. I should thank you, though, that you have so often caused me to forget present evils and have transported me to happier times. As I read, I seem to be living amidst Scipio, Brutus, and Cato. It is with these men that I live at such times, and not with the thievish company of today, among whom I was born under an evil star.

Since his own times were so conspicuously lacking in exemplary behavior, Petrarch felt that the models for a moral education had to be taken from antiquity. Study the classics, imitate their style, use words as they did, and you might be able to become like them and thus partake of the virtue they attained. What this meant, of course, was that the teachings of the previous thousand years had to be ignored. Petrarch was calling for a rebirth of ancient culture; he regarded the intervening centuries, the dark period in between, as the "middle" ages. Previously, all of history had been divided into just two eras, before and after Christ's sacrifice. By establishing a three-part structure, Petrarch paved the way for a modern sense of history, and indeed for the very notion of a Renaissance.

Part of this new moral program, taking its cue from the ancients, was a love of the natural world. One's heart was not always to be fixed on the spirit; one could love God's visible creation, too. Moreover, one could admit to feeling the pangs of physical love, and the lure of earthly fame. All of this, of course, fitted Petrarch's own instincts perfectly. By finding support for his views, he was also adding luster to himself.

And yet what gave Petrarch's vision such vigor were his own doubts about it, his refusal to claim that he knew the answers; he merely wanted us to keep trying to find them. In his last years he wrote an invective accurately entitled *On My Own Ignorance and That of Many Others*, which makes, with great power, the skeptic's case against the easy assurance that knowledge is attainable.

> What is so common as ignorance? What is more abundant or more widespread? Wherever I turn I find it, in me and in others. If you gaze upon truth and disregard the noisy talk of men, you will find that they have a moderate portion of knowledge and an enormous mass of ignorance. The very greatest minds are in the same straits: they know little, and what they do not know is much. How ridiculous are the vanities of philosophers, how often they contradict themselves, how great their obstinacy and impudence! Deep and inaccessible are the caverns where truth is buried. Socrates says: "This one thing I know, that I know nothing." A glorious philosophy!

Petrarch's particular preferences and interests may have been unmistakable, but he could not insist on them, because they raised an immediate and serious problem: as a deeply believing Christian, how could he find such pleasure in the writings of ancient pagans, in love, and in fame?

He addressed that question directly in a work he entitled *My Secret*. Written in the form of a dialogue with St. Augustine, the ancient who was an even greater hero for him than Cicero, it lays bare the agonies that bedevil him. The saint, who himself had struggled to achieve worthiness and piety—in his famous phrase, he had prayed "for chastity and continency, but not just yet"—speaks as Petrarch's stern and unyielding conscience.

AUGUSTINE: You can gain your freedom only by breaking your chains.

PETRARCH: What may these chains be?

AUGUSTINE: Love and glory.

PETRARCH: You call these things chains?

AUGUSTINE: They are pleasant though they injure; they deceive you by a false show of beauty. Have you forgotten that the climax of all evils is when a man, rooted in some false opinion, grows fatally persuaded that his course is right?

PETRARCH: My principle is that, concerning the glory we hope for here below, it is right for us to seek it while we are here below. It is the true order for mortal men to first care for mortal things.

AUGUSTINE: O man, little in yourself, and of little wisdom! What shall I say of the brevity of human fame? Consider the perishing of the books in which your name is written!

PETRARCH: Is it your wish I should set all my studies aside and renounce every ambition?

AUGUSTINE: I will never advise you to live without ambition; but I would always urge you to put virtue before glory.

At all times Augustine seemed to be at Petrarch's side. When, in his account of his ascent of Mount Ventoux, Francesco finally reaches the summit—having taken the harder, more uplifting route—he looks out toward Italy to enjoy the magnificent view. But as fate would have it, he has a copy of Augustine in his pocket; he pulls it out, and it falls open precisely to a passage of apt moral warning:

Men travel about to wonder at the heights of mountains, the wide sweep of rivers, the circuit of the ocean, and the revolutions of the stars, but themselves they consider not.

Even the love of nature, Petrarch is reminded, can divert one from the pursuit of virtue. In *My Secret*, however, Augustine takes issue with much more fundamental failings. For what happens, he asks, when a person seeks earthly pleasures, particularly love and fame? It may be all very well to imitate the ancients, but surely not if their example leads one in such materialistic directions, to the detriment of one's spiritual life. Even more disturbingly, this criticism raised doubts about the value of the *vita activa*. Does not participation in matters of this world prevent adherence to high moral standards? Surely it is only by withdrawing to the *vita contemplativa* that one can guard one's soul from temptation (PLATE II).

It was precisely because Petrarch did not—felt he could not—answer such questions that he was so appealing to his own and subsequent generations. Through his great friend the poet Boccaccio and other connections, he became the inspiration for a new intellectual and artistic movement that was to set Florentine culture apart and ultimately make it a model for all Europe. If this movement, known as humanism, soon dropped its founder's doubts, and confidently asserted that virtue was indeed to be acquired by imitating the ancients and engaging in public service, that was perhaps only to be expected of a group of aggressive pioneers who were determined to prove their own superiority. Eventually, the doubts did return, and became a continuing theme of moral and political philosophy.

Petrarch would doubtless have been thrilled (though surprised) to see the effects of his ideas. For a man who proudly owned a painting by Giotto, he would have been delighted that artists, inspired by his call to look to antiquity, were soon to revolutionize painting, sculpture, and architecture, and to create a style that transformed our visual sense. And he would have been pleased that, for centuries, education revolved around ancient texts, poets embraced the sonnet, and philosophers worried about the pros and cons of the contemplative life.

Pinturicchio, Aeneas Sylvius Crowned Poet. Petrarch's coronation with the poet's wreath is echoed by this celebration of a similar ceremony the following century. The recipient, a leading humanist (and future pope), kneels in a symbolically classical setting that Petrarch would doubtless have approved.

PLATE I

Carpaccio, St. Augustine in His Study. Petrarch's hero, St. Augustine, is shown here as a fifteenth-century scholar, an exemplar of the *vita contemplativa*, in an elegant study of the time. He is interrupted by the flash of light that startles his dog and (according to legend) announces the death of St. Jerome.

Jan Hus Burned at the Stake. These two depictions of the burning of Hus appear in Bohemian manuscripts that were illustrated during the fifteenth and sixteenth centuries, and they emphasize the paper heretic's crown, decorated with devils, that he had to wear. The allegorical scene suggests that when the crown fell off at the stake, it was replaced by a crown in heaven; and the inclusion of the execution in a music manuscript reminds us that Hus went to his death singing hymns.

PLATE II

Titian, Assumption of the Virgin. Titian's heroic altarpiece of the Virgin's Assumption into heaven, with its larger-than-life figures and dazzling colors, has brought pilgrims to the Franciscan church in Venice ever since it was completed.

PLATE III

Titian, Doge Andrea Gritti. The splendor, magnificence, and rich colors of his native Venice are combined in Titian's portrait of a redoubtable doge. Gritti wears the hat of his office, and conveys an aura of strength and determination that makes him seem the embodiment of the might of the Venetian empire. If power was crucial, it was nevertheless not the only quality Titian celebrated in Venice's patriciate, as is apparent in the group portrait below.

Titian, The Vendramin Family. Although ostensibly a scene of religious veneration, at the foot of an altar, this is in fact a subtle portrait of a Venetian patrician family. The patriarch is at the center, but the current leader of the clan is slightly taller and seen at his full height, while his heir is behind and below him, and the young nephews and grandsons are subordinated to the central trio.

PLATE IV

Contrary to what he feared, the highly rational and logical theology that dominated universities and Church schools in his day did not remain in command of intellectual life. He attacked these scholastics repeatedly (the tract on the *Ignorance of Many Others* was aimed primarily at them), and he responded to their criticisms mercilessly:

> You write that an old logician is extremely enraged at my letter. With such men it is rash to contend in their own fashion, for their whole pleasure lies in such contention. Their object is not to discover the truth, but to wrangle. How shall we escape such demented folk? I did not know that such a monster had arrived, with a twice-sharpened false syllogism. It is the glory of a traveller to pass on quickly. So tell him that I condemn boyish old men. There is nothing more loathsome than an old logician. If he begins to vomit syllogisms, take to flight.

Nor was there much doubt about the pride he took in his work. He was an avid self-promoter, and the disingenuousness of his response to Augustine's criticism on this score is breathtaking:

> I have seen pride in others, but not in myself; and though I have been a man of slight value, in my own judgement my value has been still more slight.

One has to think of him, therefore, as spending his last years in some contentment—back in his beloved Italy, living in the peaceful countryside not far from Venice, and renowned throughout Europe. In the 1360s, and until his death in 1374, he saw much of his daughter Francesca, and the grandchildren she had borne. They must have been a consolation for the loss of his son, Giovanni, who had never taken to his father's educational demands, and had died young after a stormy life:

> Our Giovanni, born to my toiling and my sorrow, brought me heavy and constant cares while he lived, and bitter grief when he died. He had known few happy days. He died in 1361, in his 25th year, in the night, in the general devastations wrought by the plague.

By then, in any case, Petrarch was preoccupied, not so much with his reputation in his own times, but with posterity. In his last months he revised a long letter he had written to the future, in which he fashioned his own epitaph:

> Francesco Petrarca to Posterity, Greeting. Perhaps you will have heard somewhat about me. Perhaps, too, you will wish to know what sort of man I was. Youth ensnared me; early manhood carried me away; but old age corrected me, and by experience taught me the truth of which I had read so often—that youth and pleasures are vanity. I devoted myself to a knowledge of antiquity, for this age of ours I have always found distasteful, so that, had it not been for the love of those dear to me, I should have preferred to have been born in any other. And so I strove to forget the present and join myself in spirit with the past.

Little did Petrarch know, as he wrote those lines, how thoroughly the world was to be transformed by that attempt to join in spirit with the past.

Jan Hus

THE world into which Jan Hus was born around 1370 had not essentially changed since the invention of the plough. The fertile countryside of southern Bohemia, in the very center of Europe, had supported relatively comfortable peasant communities from time immemorial. Around their small villages they had raised animals and crops—most notably an ale famous throughout the kingdom—that had brought them a prosperous livelihood for centuries. It was not a place that anyone but the particularly gifted might seek to leave.

For the ambitious, however, the rural life could seem all too confining, dominated as it was by dependence on the two traditional authorities: the local lord and the priest. If the lord offered protection, some measure of justice, the resolution of disputes, and leadership in times of crisis, he also required deference and a broad array of services, from work on his land to enlistment in his companies of soldiers. The priest may also have taken care of needs: he provided annual rhythms of ritual, holy days, comfort, rites of passage from baptism to burial, and spiritual advice and hope. But he, too, required material support in return, in the form of tithes, fees, and gifts.

Yet the local priest may often have appeared to be barely superior, in learning or income, to his parishioners, despite his distinct and special place in this society. Moreover, since his background was usually not dramatically different from that of his neighbors, it would have been clear to ordinary peasants that, since the basic contours of their existence were not likely ever to change, the Church alone offered a route, and even then not an easy one, out of the grinding hard work that was their lot. Only for a few noticeably bright boys in each generation did such an opportunity present itself, but when it did, the moment was not to be missed.

It was Jan Hus's mother, together with a local priest and schoolmaster, who first saw the possibility that the boy might have the intellectual qualities to take him away from the toil of the fields to the more sedate and honored life of the mind. His curiosity and intelligence were unmistakable, and when the teacher with whom he studied in a nearby village realized that the pupil was beginning to outstrip the master, he arranged for Jan to enroll at the recently founded Charles University in the capital of Bohemia, Prague.

The journey from Hus's village to Prague covered little more than a hundred miles, but it could have been to another planet. The number of inhabitants, the size and multitude of the buildings, especially the great castle and cathedral on a hill towering over the Vltava River, and the sheer variety of the people, faiths, and ideas —German, Slavic, Jewish, Italian—he encountered must have overwhelmed the young student. Straddling the north-south trade routes between Italy and Germany, and at the same time, as the capital of the most western of Slavic countries, serving as a conduit between East and West, Prague was one of the great trading centers of Europe. Its agricultural fairs and markets attracted thousands of visitors, and its court made it a magnet for intellectuals and artists. Blessed with great wealth and creative talent, it was a city famous far beyond Bohemia; and, despite a nasty assault on the Jews during Hus's lifetime, it was second only to Venice as a diverse and bustling cosmopolitan place.

Yet even here, in sophisticated Prague, Hus's lively intellect soon made its mark. Although he was desperately poor, often subsisting on dry bread and earning a meager living by singing, he persisted in his studies and received his bachelor of arts degree in 1393, when he was in his early twenties. By 1397 he already had an appointment in the faculty of arts; just twelve years later, in 1409, he was to be elected rector, the highest office in the university. Within a very brief period, the country bumpkin had become one of the most admired figures of the day. And he clearly relished the role of student, professor, and favorite of the leaders of Prague society, who found him stimulating and amusing. Indeed, he eventually decided to enter the priesthood mainly to advance his career. He later recalled these years ruefully:

> Before I became a priest I often, and gladly, played chess. I wasted
> my time. I bought fashionable gowns and robes with wings, and hoods
> trimmed with white fur. I thought that I would become a priest quickly
> in order to secure a good livelihood, and dress well, and be held in
> great esteem. Alas! The goose was plucked of its virtue by the devil.

In Czech, Hus means goose, and he enjoyed having fun with the word in his early years. When he became a priest in 1400, however, at the age of thirty-one, he underwent a dramatic change.

The crucial influence, as he looked back, was the requirement that he undertake a close reading of the Bible. "When the Lord gave me knowledge of the Scriptures," he wrote, "I discarded from my mind all the foolish fun-making" of the previous years. He was still a professor at the university, but after 1400 his chief fame came from his activities as a priest. Already known as a brilliant lecturer, he now attracted attention as an extraordinarily eloquent preacher, and in 1401 he gained the prestigious appointment of confessor to Sophie, the queen of Bohemia.

Hus was being welcomed into the very highest levels of Bohemian society. And the honors continued. When a new church, named the Bethlehem Chapel after Christ's birthplace, was built in the middle of Prague—a unique structure, almost square, capable of holding a congregation of hundreds—the noblemen who were its founders and patrons asked Hus to take over its pulpit. There were new ideas in the air, one of which was that preachers should address their flocks in their native tongue. This was the major purpose for which the chapel had been built, and Hus's sermons, delivered in Czech, became major events. Even the queen of Bohemia, Sophie, came down from the royal palace across the river to hear him speak.

One source of new ideas was the writings of an English professor and priest, John Wyclif, who had died just a few years before. Wyclif, too, had been transformed by his reading of Scripture. As a result, he had attacked a number of the practices of his time for which he found no biblical support. He condemned the behavior of the papacy itself; the way the Church raised money and celebrated mass; and any doctrine that was not directly justified by the Bible. He wanted each believer to have equal access to salvation, and urged a translation of the Bible, so that it could be read by everyone. At first he had the support of important aristocrats, who used his ideas in their rivalries with powerful churchmen. But eventually his assault on Church traditions brought the wrath of the papacy, and of his own colleagues at Oxford University, upon him. When a peasant revolt broke out in 1381, which he refused to condemn, his aristocratic support evaporated. He had to leave Oxford, and a few years after his death, in 1384, his books were condemned and burned. The authorities even dug up his bones and threw them into a river.

But the ideas did not die with Wyclif. The queen of England at the time was the sister of King Wenceslas of Bohemia, and because of that connection the Oxford professor's writings found their way to Prague. The Bohemian royal family in fact played a crucial role in the stirrings of religious discontent during these years. Wenceslas himself was a choleric and arrogant figure who fought constantly with Church leaders as well as his nobility. Above all, he hated any hint of opposition, and did not hesitate to torture and execute those who defied him, whether prelates or princes. Although his conflicts with the Church were a matter of authority, not belief, he was happy to defend Hus. His sister Anne of England, and his wife Sophie, by contrast, were genuinely interested in new religious ideas. As was often to be true during the Protestant Reformation of the next century, the crucial early patronage of reform came from aristocratic women.

The first that Hus heard of Wyclif's ideas was at a university disputation in 1403. If there was one institution that was essential to the birth of dissent at this time, it was the disputation. Here almost any idea could be discussed, because the point of this basic means of instruction at the medieval university was to argue every issue against its opposite. The Church embraced a multitude of opinions about faith and religious practice, and many of these were expressed at disputations. Both Wyclif and Hus were masters of the genre, but the crucial boundary they crossed, and other disputants did not, was to take the ideas out of the classroom and use them, not merely to criticize, but to challenge the authority of, the Church.

The gathering at Charles University in 1403 concluded with a majority of the professors voting to condemn forty-five views of Wyclif as heretical, erroneous, and scandalous. Hus voted in the minority, because he agreed with the Englishman that all doctrine had to be based on the Bible:

> I am attracted by his writings, in which he makes every effort to lead all men back to the law of Christ, and especially the clergy, inviting them to abandon pomp and dominion of the world, and live, like the apostles, according to the law of Christ.

Why, he was to ask, should such writings be condemned?

> I have read and studied the works of John Wyclif, and I have learned from them much that is good. Truly, not everything I have found is

Dürer, The Last Supper. Dürer's engraving of the Last Supper illustrates the argument made by Hus (and later echoed by Luther) about the chalice of wine that Christ shared with his disciples. Indeed, the chalice is the only object that stands, untouched, on the table—a striking reminder of its symbolic importance.

> of the same weight with me as the gospel, for only to Holy Scripture will I give such obedience. But why should we not also read Wyclif's books, in which are written countless sacred truths?

Over the next few years Hus would devote himself unremittingly to those sacred truths.

Gradually, Hus worked out the nature of his dissent from the teachings of the Church. He came to believe, not only that the word of God should be accessible to all believers, and that the Bible as well as the services ought to be in Czech, but that the central distinction between priest and congregation in the celebration of the mass should be abolished. By tradition, the people shared in the wafer, the bread, which had been transformed into the body of Christ, and thus they received God's grace. But the chalice of wine, which had been transformed into the blood of Christ, was restricted to the priest alone. Hus noted that, at the Last Supper, Christ had shared both bread and wine with his disciples, and concluded that the distinction contradicted the Bible. When he spoke out, he wondered why it had taken him so long:

> I did not dare to preach the truth plainly and openly. Why are we like that? Surely because some of us are timid, fearing the loss of worldly favor and praise, while others fear the loss of church positions. We fear to be held in contempt by the people for truth's sake, and to suffer bodily pain.

Familiar with court circles, and aware of their growing sense of the autonomy of the kingdom—Wenceslas, for all his cruelties, remains something of a national hero for his assertion of Bohemian independence—Hus took up the cause of his fellow countrymen. One of the continuing problems at Charles University was the rivalry between Czech and German students. The conflict was chronic, and Hus was often the spokesman for the Bohemians. Indeed, his election as rector took place soon after Wenceslas sided definitively with the Czechs, and thousands of German professors and students left en masse (to found a new university in Leipzig, about 150 miles to the north). In the political arena, too, powerful German neighbors sought to influence Bohemian affairs, and Hus spoke out against them:

> I say that the Czechs in Bohemia, according to both divine and natural law, should be the first holders of the offices of the kingdom of Bohemia, as the French are in the kingdom of France, and the Germans in their own lands. The Czechs should rule their subjects, and the Germans theirs.

Secure in the support of aristocrats and the royal family, Hus had little hesitation in taking these bold stands, and becoming a focus both of patriotism and of religious reform. The latter was now becoming central to his concerns. He was translating Wyclif, and reaching conclusions similar to the Englishman's. But the opposition to the new ideas was also firm, and finally, in 1410, the issue was publicly joined. The archbishop of Prague, the formal upholder of orthodoxy, felt he could tolerate what he regarded as heresy no longer. Despite Hus's pleas, he ordered two hundred volumes of Wyclif manuscripts burned in public. Hus protested openly:

I call it a poor business. Such bonfires never yet removed a single sin from the hearts of men. Fire does not consume truth. It is always the mark of a little mind that it vents anger on inanimate objects. The books which have been burned are a loss to the whole people.

In response, the archbishop excommunicated him, and persuaded Pope Gregory XII to summon Hus to Rome to answer the charges against him. Hus, who by now had little respect for the pope, refused, even though the threat of a far more comprehensive excommunication—by the pope, who could exclude him from all Church rites, a terrible punishment for a believing Christian—now hung over him. His reply was characteristically blunt:

What reason have I, a man unknown to the Pope, and informed against by my enemies, to put myself to the extraordinary difficulty of going a great distance, passing through the midst of my enemies, to place myself before witnesses and judges who are my enemies? What is still worse, I would be compelled to worship the Pope on bended knee!

Fortunately for Hus, his royal protectors agreed.

Wenceslas, asserting Bohemia's independence, defended the right of his subject to remain in Prague:

If anyone wishes to accuse him of anything, let them do so in our country, before the University of Prague or another competent judge. Our kingdom does not see fit to expose so useful a preacher to the judgement of his enemies, to the great disturbance of the whole population.

The queen, Sophie, whose support for the dissenter focused on his ideas, and not on the politics of the situation, was even more outspoken in describing Hus's importance to Bohemia:

An order has recently been given which has caused upheaval among our people and confusion in our kingdom. We request that, for the honor of God and the welfare of our people, you will establish as soon as possible the liberty of Jan Hus, faithful preacher in our chapel, so as to end the popular commotion over his condemnation. We cannot endure so great an assault on the teaching of God's word in our palaces and cities. The word of God ought not to be hindered, but rather preached in the streets, from the rooftops, and anywhere it has listeners.

With such powerful protectors, Hus and his followers might now have been able to survive. He was making a real mark, for people flocked to his services, mesmerized by his preaching, and delighted to share the chalice. The singing of hymns that became the hallmark of his mass—he even composed some himself—not only widened his appeal, but had a long-term effect on Bohemia's musical culture. But, like most dissenters, he was not content merely to serve his growing flock. He had to apply his principles strictly whenever a new issue arose. And his next outburst, colored by the same self-righteousness that had doomed Wyclif, was (as in Wyclif's case) to alienate the political support that had been vital to his cause. Unlike Luther, who, a hundred years later, learned when to make the compromise that ensured the survival of his movement, Hus felt impelled to press forward, regardless of the fatal consequences.

Ironically, the issue that proved his undoing was the very one that was to make Luther famous: indulgences. Indulgences had first been used when, in order to raise money for Crusades against infidels, popes had promised the same forgiveness of sin to those who helped pay for the expedition as they bestowed on the crusaders themselves. The grace came from the treasury of excess merit that had been built up by the saints, who had not needed all their good deeds for their own salvation; yet it was clear that only sins identified by the Church, not those condemned in Scripture, could be redeemed. Moreover, the payment was supposed to be a form of satisfaction that was efficacious only *after* the sinner had demonstrated contrition and undertaken penance. But the sale of indulgences had become such a successful money-raising device that the qualifications had been steadily forgotten, and they were now bought on the assumption that, without further ado, they reduced a sinner's time in purgatory by a number of years equivalent to the amount paid.

Hus, like Luther after him, was outraged that indulgences had become a substitute for repentance. And the particular situation to which he saw them applied angered him all the more. For the papacy in the early 1400s was in turmoil, with three different candidates claiming the office. The chaos had given both Wyclif and Hus some room for maneuver, but now the pope, whom Wenceslas backed, ordered a crusade against one of his enemies within Europe. This was not the first time a crusade had been launched against Christians, but the idea infuriated Hus, and he denounced the indulgence that was proclaimed in support of the campaign. The trouble was that Wenceslas received a percentage of the sales in Bohemia, and he now ordered an end to the criticism: "Hus, you are always making trouble for me. If those whose concern it is will not take care of it, I myself will burn you."

These were fateful words, but Hus refused to back down, and he even celebrated a martyr's mass for three young men, two of them former students, who were executed for continuing the protest. He knew the fate that could befall such open dissent, especially when bereft of political support. Two hundred years before, the French heretics known as Albigensians had defied Rome, had become the object of a crusade, and had been violently crushed. Wyclif's fate was only too familiar. And yet, once convinced of his own truth, the dissenter could not hold back. The good of his soul permitted no compromise, even though the king's vital support began to evaporate almost at once. Even worse, his oldest friend and disciple, Stepan Palec, chastened by a term in prison, abandoned him, and became his most furious opponent. The pope now placed the whole city of Prague under an interdict—a general excommunication that closed all churches, ended all baptisms, marriages, and burials, and threatened every citizen with damnation. Unwilling to be the cause of such general punishment, Hus left Prague.

Wenceslas now made one last effort at compromise. He asked the Charles University faculty to find a middle ground between the papacy and the ideas of Wyclif and Hus, so that Prague could be absolved of the accusation that the entire city was guilty of heresy. But Hus would not retreat:

> Even if I should stand before the fire prepared for me, I hope that
> death will sooner remove me, either to heaven or to hell, than that I
> agree. I hope with God's grace to stand firm until I am consumed by
> fire. It is better to die well than to live wickedly. One should not sin
> in order to avoid the punishment of death. Truth conquers all.

It was the classic credo of the dissenter, and the fate it forecast soon
became all too real.

Faced by such defiance, Wenceslas felt he could go no further,
and turned Hus's case over to his brother Sigismund. Sigismund was
the Holy Roman emperor, and saw as his main task the restoration
of the unity of Christendom. In that effort, which involved the assertion
of the authority of the emperor over a papacy that was unable to
reform itself, the heresy of a single preacher was of little consequence.
Sigismund summoned a council of the Church—leading prelates from
all over Europe—to the city of Constance, in order to resolve the
problem of a papacy divided among three candidates, and in general
to restore order to religious affairs. In this context, as he made clear,
Hus did not loom large:

> The case of Jan Hus and other minor problems ought not to interfere
> with the reform of the Church and of the Empire, which is the principal
> purpose for which the Council has been convened. For myself, I wish
> to stand by the holy Church; I do not incline to new ideas.

Sigismund promised Hus safe conduct if he came to defend himself
at Constance. It is an indication of how small a matter the confrontation seemed that he repudiated his guarantee without a second
thought, and that the entire case, which to us seems the central moment
of the council, was regarded at the time as one of the lesser events
at Constance, easily overshadowed by the restoration of the unity of
the papacy.

As with Luther at Worms a century later, the investigation of
the heretic changed no minds. The difference was that Hus, betrayed
by Sigismund, had been chained in prison for months before he was
finally brought before the assembly. He felt totally abandoned:

I am surprised that Sigismund has forgotten me, and never sends me a word. Perhaps I shall be condemned before I speak with him. I am surprised that no Czechs visit my prison. Perhaps they are acting for the best. Make sure this letter is torn up at once.

Sigismund in fact left Hus to his enemies. "If he is unwilling to abjure," he said, "let him be burned." And abjure was precisely what Hus could not do. His ringing declaration, as he rejected all the accusations against him, was as stirring as Luther's "Here I Stand" speech 106 years later:

I, Jan Hus, fearing to offend God and to descend into perjury, and fearing also to betray the Truth or to speak against the opinion of holy men, am not willing to recant.

And so, on July 15, 1415, Hus was led to a field outside Constance. He smiled when he saw that his books were being burned at the stake; he smiled again when the paper heretic's crown, with its three devils, fell off his head; and he then began to sing to Christ until he himself was consumed by the flames (PLATE II).

Neither Sigismund's nor the Church's troubles were over, because the execution provoked a rebellion in Bohemia that was to last for decades. New Hussite leaders arose, and they were supported by all segments of society. Rallying around the symbol of the chalice, they managed to defeat the armies that the emperor sent against them, and they founded a tradition of Czech dissent against overwhelming odds that was to resurface over the centuries, down to our own time. Eventually, after some thirty years of fighting, demands for social change by the more radical Hussites, known as Taborites, who were largely drawn from the middle and lower levels of society, lost them the support of the nobility. They were defeated in battle, and peace returned to Bohemia. But calm could ultimately be restored only because the rebels were able to win one vital concession. In a major retreat, the papacy allowed priests of the Utraquist faith—as the Hussite Church was to be called—to give the chalice to the congregation at the mass.

The execution of Hus was a favorite subject of manuscript illuminators in Bohemia, because it could serve both as an object lesson for the orthodox and as a stimulus to patriotism for his followers. This decoration of an initial letter emphasizes both the bundles of wood in the pyre and, like the manuscripts reproduced in PLATE II, the heretic's crown that Hus had to wear at the stake.

The cost had been terrible, but nevertheless a lone dissenter had wrung from the all-powerful Church a concession that had vast symbolic implications for the ordinary Christian. It may seem trivial today, but at the time the sharing of the wine gave new worth to the individual, asserted the supremacy of the Bible over papal opinion or formal tradition, and reduced the inequality between priest and congregation. These issues were central to Hus's protest, and it is therefore appropriate that his statements about the chalice, which embodied his beliefs, should have been the ones inscribed on the wall of his beloved Bethlehem Chapel:

> How great a madness it is to condemn as error the Gospel of Christ about the communion of the sacrament of the cup of the Lord. They call it error that the believing laity should be allowed to drink from the cup of the Lord. If the priest gives them thus to drink, he is condemned as a heretic.

In this case, the heresy outlived its persecutors.

A hundred years later, a German monk wrote of his surprise at discovering the writings of Hus:

> I could not understand why they burned so great a man, who explained Scripture with so much discernment and wisdom. Inasmuch as the very name of Hus was an abomination, I shut the book with a sad heart.

But not for long. Driven to his own dissent, that monk, Martin Luther, was soon to take pleasure in being called the Saxon Hus, and openly to embrace the Bohemian's views. The struggle had not been in vain; the inspiration continued; and another phase began in the conflict between authority and the individual to which so notable a contribution had been made by Jan Hus.

PART II

The Creation
of a
New Vision

Left: Titian, Self-Portrait. The gravity and darkness of this self-portrait of the aged Titian reinforce its pensive mood, though the fine features and the rich gold chain remind us of the dignity and status he had achieved.   *Right:* Dürer, Self-Portrait. This is the Dürer who in 1498 recalls the spirit of Venice—the artist as elegant gentleman, in fashionable (almost feminine) hat, cloak, and gloves, sitting in front of the open window and distant landscape that were characteristic of Italian Renaissance portraits. He was to look very different in his Nuremberg guise two years later (PLATE VI).

Two Artists

I N THE CENTURY FOLLOWING PETRARCH'S DEATH the changes he had begun gathered momentum. Humanists, urging the imitation of antiquity, became major figures at princely courts and universities throughout Europe; and Petrarch's campaign to bring back to life the thought and culture of Rome captured the imagination of scholars, philosophers, and artists. For the latter, the message was straightforward: study the ancients, and produce works of art that reflect their style and their spirit. Starting in Petrarch's native city, Florence, but soon throughout Italy, that was precisely what painters, sculptors, and architects did. In the process, they created, by 1500, a new esthetic and a new vision of the purpose of art. ⁋At the same time, the belief that artists were particularly adept at recapturing the spirit of Rome, and that they could bestow fame on their subjects, prompted a transformation in their status. Where once they had been mere craftsmen, they now were honored by the social elite. This new role was perfectly embodied by the Venetian painter Titian, who became one of the most sought-after and admired portraitists of the age. His contemporary, the German painter and engraver Dürer, typified in a different way the artist's newly won independence. The growing appreciation for art;

the rising prosperity of Europe's cities as trade quickened around 1500; and the influence of the religious upheaval that was a delayed legacy from Hus—all had an effect on Dürer's work and career. Between them Titian and Dürer demonstrate to the full the independence, the social recognition, and the quest for new esthetic standards that characterized the artists of the Renaissance and have shaped the role of the artist ever since.

🔲 Titian

OF the many cities that claimed to have inherited the mantle of ancient Rome, none had a better case than the proud queen of the Adriatic, Venice. Called by her own citizens Serenissima, the most serene, she stood in 1500 at the pinnacle of powers whose like had not been seen since the decline of Rome. Like her ancient forebear, Venice was both a city-state and the center of a large Mediterranean and Italian empire, a tolerant ruler of polyglot peoples whose authority was maintained by naval, military, and economic supremacy. From Cyprus near the Holy Land to Bergamo on the outskirts of Milan, from Crete to the Dolomites, the Venetians held at bay such powerful neighbors as the Turks and the Habsburgs. Single-mindedly focused on commercial success, they welcomed traders of every race and religion, and fostered a relaxed lifestyle that had already made their canals a magnet for tourists in the fifteenth century.

Tiziano Vecellio was born at the northern edge of this thriving empire in the mid 1480s. He grew up in a remote mountain village, Cadore, in the Dolomites, where his artistic talents were soon recognized—as a result, so one story had it, of his using juices from crushed flowers to paint a Madonna. His parents, prominent local citizens, soon decided, perhaps when he was a mere nine or ten years old, that his future could be assured only in the great city to the south, and they probably used their political contacts to secure him an apprenticeship in an official artistic enterprise. For the workshop he joined had the task of cutting mosaics to decorate the Church of St. Mark, a state institution. Here the boy was introduced not only to the lush colors for which Venice was famous but also to its unique mixture of artistic traditions.

The use of mosaic, for example, had been associated particularly with the Greek Orthodox Church, centered in Byzantium, whose art had long been admired by its Venetian neighbors. The multiplicity of such distinct cultural influences—inspired by the city's diverse population of Muslims, Jews, Slavs, and Germans, as well as other Italians—set Venice apart from more homogeneous places like Florence. Its art, in contrast to that of the Florentines, tended to be less idealized, more earthy and varied, softer, and certainly (as befitted a tourist mecca, famous for its courtesans and night life) more exuberant and sensual. In Florence the sky is always blue, the beauty perfect and untouchable. In Venice the settings are recognizable, there are clouds, and the bodies are fleshy and tangible. Nobody was to display these qualities more vividly or profusely than Titian.

After his training in mosaics the young man, now in his teens, was accepted into the studio of Venice's official state painter, Gentile Bellini, where he learned such mundane skills as grinding colors and preparing panels and canvas. But the teenager apparently did not get on with the old master. His fondness for drawing at speed distressed Gentile, who is said to have commented: "This boy will never succeed as a painter." Impatient to move on, Titian went to study for a while with Gentile's brother, Giovanni Bellini, and then with another famous and original artist, Giorgione. But by the time he was in his mid-twenties, he was on his own, receiving commissions for religious pictures and helping his former master, Giorgione, to decorate the huge warehouse for German traders on the Grand Canal, the Fondaco dei Tedeschi. In 1513, when he was around twenty-five, he won the most important commission of the time, for a large painting in the palace of the Doge, and soon thereafter he was appointed the chief painter to the government of Venice.

Titian was now at the heart of Venetian society, and the local and international fame he soon acquired gave him virtually the status of a patrician. Such standing, which became official when the Holy Roman emperor, Charles V, conferred a knighthood on him, was unprecedented for an artist. Previously, painters or mosaicists had not been essentially different from other craftsmen. Like clockmakers or jewelers, they were highly respected figures, performing a valuable service, and certainly admired for their esthetic skills. But they were still manual laborers, and although higher in the scale of tradesmen than butchers or bakers, they were obviously not the equivalent of professionals who worked with their minds, like doctors, scholars, or international merchants. The last were the true patricians, members of some 150 families that ruled Venice and commanded its armies and navies.

It was in Titian's lifetime, however, that a rather different view of art began to take hold. It was documented by a younger contemporary of his, the Florentine painter, architect, and biographer Giorgio Vasari. Like Titian, Vasari was welcomed into the highest social and political circles, and was made much of by his patrons, the Medici. But his enduring fame rests on his effort to chronicle the transformation of art during the previous century. The result was the first major work in a new discipline, the history of art: Vasari's *Lives of the Painters*. He concentrated especially on his compatriots, because, as he put it:

> The benign ruler of heaven saw that in the practice of painting, sculpture, and architecture, the Tuscan genius has always been preeminent, for the Tuscans have devoted to all the various branches of art more labor and study than all the other Italian peoples.

The origin of the new reverence for artists lay in a quality that Vasari called genius. This was a special spirit of creativity, derived from the Latin word for a divine influence on human affairs, that not only defined the character of a large group (like the Tuscans) but now also identified specially gifted individuals, whose genius set them apart from other people, and made them objects of wonder and admiration. Although, quite naturally, Michelangelo was Vasari's chief hero, Titian was given a high place in the pantheon of genius.

There is little doubt that around 1500 a fundamental shift in cultural perception did take place. A story circulated, for example, that while Titian was painting Charles V's portrait, his brush slipped, and the emperor himself bent down to return it to the artist. Intended to echo an episode in the life of Alexander the Great, when he was sitting for the painter Apelles, the anecdote not only gave distinction to Charles but confirmed the special honor due to art. And the analogy between the two artists and the two emperors was specifically mentioned in the patent of nobility by which Charles made Titian the first artist to be raised to the very highest level of European society.

Titian met such admiration at every turn. His great friend, the satirist Aretino, said that the colors and shapes in a Titian painting looked more real than the original. He felt that the very way he looked at the world had been formed by his friend. Sitting at his window overlooking the Grand Canal one day, he watched a stunning sunset, and at once wrote to Titian:

> I turned my eyes up to the sky; not since the day that God created it was it so embellished by such a rich painting of darks and lights. The buildings in the foreground, although of real stone, seemed made of some unreal substance. Oh, with what beautiful strokes did nature's brush push back the atmosphere, clearing it away from the palaces, just as Titian does in painting landscapes! With lights and darks she created the effects of distance and modelling, so that I, who know that your brush is filled with the very spirit of nature, cried out three or four times: "Oh, Titian, why are you not here?" For, on my honor, if you had painted what I have described to you, you would certainly have awakened in men the same amazement that I felt when I beheld that scene; and lasting longer, the marvel of such a painting would continue to nourish the soul.

That Titian also felt himself surrounded by beauty was clear, for he always resisted any attempt to draw him out of Venice for long. Sought by the greatest crowned heads of his time both for portraits and—especially in the case of the devout and austere king of Spain, Philip II—for lush nudes, he refused all requests for permanent appointments away from home. Treated like an aristocrat, he won an independence and an international social stature that no artist before him had achieved. Nor would anyone of his time have had reason to question Titian's decision to remain in Venice. The young Isabella d'Este, whom he later painted, wrote breathlessly of the gorgeous sight that was revealed by a climb up the campanile of San Marco. A French historian and diplomat called the Grand Canal "the most beautiful street on the face of the earth," in "the most splendid city I have ever seen."

And Titian really did live like a prince. A contemporary described a party at the artist's house as a memorable occasion:

> I was invited to celebrate in the manner of a bacchanal the feast of *ferragosto* in the delightful garden of the renowned painter Titian, a man most suited to hosting a fine banquet. There I found some of the most brilliant personalities of the day. Before seating ourselves at the table, we wandered through the house, admiring our host's magnificent paintings. As the sun was setting the lagoon became filled with gondolas, adorned with the most beautiful women, and sounding with the musical harmonies of various voices and instruments, which accompanied our happy dinner until midnight. The dinner itself was no less bountiful: in addition to the most delicate meats and precious wines, it included all the pleasures and entertainments befitting such a festive occasion.

This was certainly not the home or the life of a mere craftsman.

The patrician class in which Titian moved created what was regarded as the model government of the age. Venice's institutions and remarkable history of political stability were as much the focus of tourist interest as were its buildings and its brothels. For English parliamentarians, Dutch oligarchs, and theorists of the well-ordered state throughout Europe, great families like the Contarini and the Gritti seemed reincarnations of the senators of the Roman republic.

Titian, Self-Portrait. This self-portrait, with its broad brushstrokes and uncompleted details, is characteristic of Titian's late painting. The commanding figure creates an impressive presence that was commensurate with the patrician-artist's self-image.

They offered an ideal, observable at first hand, of how to rule firmly yet wisely.

Titian captured their assurance and their gravity in his portraits. Doge Gritti is the very embodiment of authority, with an enormous, sinewy hand that intimates the power he exercises. The Pesaro clan, at the feet of the Virgin, or the Vendramins, arranged in front of a relic of the true cross, display the essential unit of Venetian society, the family, in full splendor. As one of these patricians, the head of the Cornaro family, put it: "When I am surrounded by my children and grandchildren, I feel like God the Father" (PLATE IV).

The hierarchy of power, even among kin, is carefully displayed by the height and prominence of each figure—which makes the complete absence of half the family starkly revealing. Small boys are included, but not a single daughter, sister-in-law, or aunt. This is a male world, in which wife and courtesan occupy sharply defined roles on the edges of the social and intellectual life of the time. It is not surprising that we know almost nothing about Titian's own wife, a girl from Cadore to whom he was married in his forties for six years until she died, probably in childbirth. They had three children; the painter's favorite, his son Orazio, was to die in the same plague that probably killed the father.

That Titian delighted in depictions of the politically important, and the mythological and religious scenes they enjoyed, does not lessen his role as a propagandist. For Venice was not exactly the free and open republic it claimed to be. The stability was maintained by a small elite's shrewd exercise of power. And not only power, but the most lucrative trades, were stringently restricted to some 10 percent of the population. These patricians were astute rulers. They established a superb system of social welfare and poor relief, which Titian celebrated in a glowing portrayal of the officers of one of these institutions as they gave alms to the poor. The Venetians' university in nearby Padua was renowned throughout Europe, especially for its medical faculty. And Venice's huge arsenal, which was capable of building a ship in a single day, was the first major public works enterprise—employing thousands, and providing welfare for the families of all workers—in modern European history.

The patricians also gave freedom of worship and custom to all races and religions, most notably the Jews, for whom the first ghetto was built as a protected quarter. And they made certain not to isolate

Titian, Illustration for Vesalius: Musculature. Perhaps the happiest marriage of art and science in history was the work done by Titian's studio to illustrate the great work on anatomy published by Andreas Vesalius in 1543. Vesalius was at the nearby University of Padua, and the engravings of anatomical structures—with tiny letters as keys to the pictures—were essential records of his dissections. But the partnership with the renowned artist made these more than merely technical illustrations. Thus the musculature is posed in a dramatic gesture, and the landscape in the background shows a recognizable stretch of the countryside near Padua. (See also page 89.)

themselves. They mingled with the population—travelers were amazed to see patricians at the fish market—and their homes were located in every area of the city. With their storage facilities full of goods on the ground floor; the great reception halls above, on the so-called *piano nobile*, or grand floor; then the family bedrooms, then the servants' bedrooms, and finally, to top it off, that Venetian invention, the roof garden, these were houses to which many outside the patriciate had access. They may have been called palaces, but their interiors and their residents would have been familiar to all levels of the citizenry.

But their dispersal throughout every neighborhood had repressive purposes as well. Venice was a dangerous place, full of dark alleys and corners on the hundreds of islands that made up the city, each of which could cut itself off from its neighbors by blocking its bridges—as did the ghetto each night. The propaganda of the name Serenissima notwithstanding, street violence was common among its more than 100,000 inhabitants. The future cardinal Pietro Bembo, for example, lost a finger in a street brawl. By living throughout the city the patricians could keep an eye on each locality, and if that did not work, they had an elaborate system of informers to warn them of trouble. Grand processions served much the same purpose as Titian's family paintings: to demonstrate the serenity, unity, and harmony of the citizens. But the government had also built one of the most notorious prisons in Europe, adjacent to the aptly named Bridge of Sighs, and did not hesitate to punish wrongdoing—particularly the slightest hint of subversion—with merciless force. A traveler described the public treatment of a group of such miscreants (starting with their leader, a cleric) in the Piazza San Marco during Titian's lifetime:

> He was tied to a scaffold between the two columns [at the water's edge], wearing only a shirt and hose. They had pulled his tongue out. They cut off the hands and tongues of his four accomplices and dug out their eyes. Then they put him in an iron cage and hoisted it a hundred feet up the campanile. He was to stay there for three months on bread and water.

This other side of Venice neither Titian nor any of his contemporaries showed to the world. Instead, it was with lushness and fleshiness that he characterized his city, in paintings that have seduced us ever since (PLATE V). The richness suffuses his religious works as well, and at first his boldness disturbed Venice's clergy. In the year he became official painter to the government, for example, Titian unveiled a monumental panel on the altar of the Franciscans' church, the Frari. Nearly seven meters high, it depicted the Assumption of the Virgin (PLATE III). Its dazzling colors, huge figures, dramatic gestures, and cluster of adorable cherubs created a sensuous effect that initially made the timid Franciscans reluctant to accept the picture. They were also shocked by the unprecedented feeling of monumentality that Titian achieved. One account describes their reaction:

> He was disturbed by the frequent visits of the monks, and especially by Fra Germano, guardian of the work, who complained that the Apostles were much too large. Trying desperately to correct their ignorance, Titian explained to them that the figures had to be proportioned to the vast space in which they were to be viewed, and that from that distance they would appear in proper scale.

Eventually, as another account put it, "the truth slowly dawned on them, and people began to marvel at the new style established in Venice by Titian." A new style it certainly was, with a power that was to revolutionize the painting of altarpieces, and make both Titian and the Frari Church famous.

For all the influence of the Florentines, the originators of the new artistic styles of the Renaissance, and for all the impact of the esthetic of idealized beauty they forged, it was the Venetians (and primarily Titian) who were often the painters most extravagantly admired outside Italy. What patrons seemed to like was that pictures from Venice tended to show real, rather than perfect, people and places: their dogs wagged their tails, and one could usually tell what the weather was like. Over Florence and Rome the Raphaels and the Michelangelos held unchallenged sway, but in Germany or Spain the aristocrat of art was Titian.

Nor was the difference unremarked at the time. Perhaps the most fascinating moment in the history of Renaissance art was the brief encounter, in Rome in 1545, of Titian and Michelangelo. Between them, they had created an entirely new image and revered status for the artist, though their styles and interests—one soft, elegant, and urbane, the other tough, powerful, and almost forbidding—could hardly have been more different (as Michelangelo was to note with some satisfaction). It was at the invitation of the pope that Titian was in Rome, where he was given a studio for a few months in the Belvedere, a small palace in the Vatican. He was much feted, and Vasari himself showed the Venetian the sights of the city.

Titian's major commission was to depict his patron, and he created an extraordinarily powerful psychological portrait of the aging pontiff, Paul III, shrewd and watchful even while he was posing. Paul was a Farnese, a member of a family that was famous for its generals and diplomats, and he was one of the master politicians of the Church, a brilliant strategist who was the chief architect of the Counter-Reformation. Another portrait Titian undertook at the time, showing Paul with two of his grandsons, was so full of tension and hostility that, for reasons we can only guess at, it remained unfinished, though the effect of the painting is still devastating (see back cover).

It was during this stay in Rome that Michelangelo visited Titian. On his easel at the time was an alluring portrayal of the nude Danaë, languishing on a rumpled bed, a picture commissioned by one of the papal grandsons, Cardinal Alessandro Farnese. Michelangelo admired the coloring but was disturbed by the softness of the forms:

> It is a pity that these Venetians are not taught from the beginning to draw well, that they do not apply themselves better. For, if this man were aided by the true art of drawing, as he is by nature herself, and particularly in copying from life, he would be without equal, since he has great spirit and a lively manner.

There is no record of what Titian thought of Michelangelo's tougher and more sinewy art.

That he never had the problems with patrons for which the moody and defiant Michelangelo was notorious, however, was well known. It is true that he did complain about payments; that he was shameless enough to claim poverty in order to exact higher fees; and

Titian, Charles V on Horseback. The occasion for Titian's heroic portrait of the emperor was the victory his troops won over a Protestant army at Mühlberg. Following a celebrated ancient model, an equestrian statue of Emperor Marcus Aurelius, Renaissance sculptors had glorified their subjects as warriors in imposing array on horseback. Titian's is the first painting of this type; even though the scene is entirely artificial, it creates an image of magnificence and power that remained influential for decades.

that he even misled the authorities about his considerable wealth when hard times forced Venice to end the special tax exemption he had been granted. But these maneuvers had no adverse effect on Titian's reputation. In addition to the call to Rome, he was twice summoned by the Emperor Charles V to Augsburg, where he depicted the greatest monarch in Europe both as a lonely and grave figure, seated on a modest, unthronelike chair, and as the mythic victor, in armor and on horseback, of a battle at which he was not even present. Titian seemed entirely at home at Charles's court, an ease that only confirmed his image as a natural aristocrat. As Vasari remarked:

> Apart from his eminence as a painter, Titian is a gentleman of distinguished family and most courteous ways and manners. So he has easily surpassed his rivals through the excellence of his work and his ability to mix with, and win the friendship of, men of quality.

Typical of his time, Vasari assumed that only a distinguished family background could have produced so accomplished a courtier. That the assumption was wrong merely confirms how deeply people were affected by the new standing that artists had achieved.

Among the paintings the emperor commissioned from Titian was a *Gloria*, a glorification of the Trinity that showed Charles, in a posture of adoration, clothed in his shroud. Four years later he abdicated, and retired for the remainder of his life to a remote monastery in Spain. The *Gloria* accompanied him, and was hung in the bedroom where he died. His son and successor, Philip II, is shown in the *Gloria*, and he inherited his father's fondness for Titian. If his taste was more for the artist's sensual and celebratory skills—including a portrait that commemorated the famous victory by an alliance of Spaniards and Venetians over the Turks at Lepanto—he himself was no less pious or devout than the old emperor, and these qualities also became increasingly apparent in Titian's work.

The depiction of the victor at Lepanto, which promised a great future to Philip's infant son, was one of Titian's last paintings. In most of these late works the mood darkens. The terrible moment of *Christ Crowned with Thorns*, for example, is presented in muted colors. It is night, the pain of the suffering Christ is inward, and the whole is painted, as Vasari remarked, "with broad strokes, dashed off in a rough manner and in patches, so that it cannot be enjoyed at close range and appears perfect only from afar." The old master, whose surfaces had once been perfectly finished, now relished a sense of incompleteness. It was reported that he applied paint with his fingers—"like God when he created man," he himself supposedly said—or with brushes "big as broomsticks."

Titian, The Flaying of Marsyas. This late masterpiece, with its somber tones, brooding atmosphere, and ghastly subject, offers a sharp contrast to the exuberant lushness of Titian's earlier work (PLATE V).

That Titian was still active into his nineties may explain the interest in extreme emotion and in representations of old age that appeared in the late works. For more than twenty years before his death, he never left Venice, and he felt free to explore new areas of feeling and style that were to leave an indelible mark on European

Titian, Pietà. The classical architecture and sculpture that frame Titian's last painting testify to the continuing influence of antiquity in Renaissance art.

art. His *Flaying of Marsyas* epitomizes the philosophic concerns that now occupied his attention. The gruesome scene depicts the punishment the god Apollo meted out to a satyr, Marsyas, who had dared to challenge him to a musical competition. Hung by his feet, the satyr has his skin flayed off and dies an agonizing death. For all the anguish, even Marsyas seems calm. The flayers concentrate on their work, while a dog licks up the blood dripping from the body. Everything is dark, and the colors are subdued.

In some ways, however, the most disturbing figure is the seated King Midas on the right. He had been the judge of the musical contest, and now, faced by this horrible punishment, he drifts off into reverie, his thoughts far away. It has been suggested that he is pondering the dilemma of creativity—whether it is divine or earthly—and the meanings of death and immortality. Since the king has Titian's own aged features, one can imagine that the latter was indeed much on the artist's mind at the time.

His very last painting, an enormous *Pietà*, again includes a self-portrait, this time as a venerable St. Jerome, Joseph of Arimathea, or perhaps Job, on his knees before the dead Christ. This picture was intended for Titian's own tomb, but the friars of the Frari Church, where he was buried—hastily, because the plague was raging—decided otherwise, and it ended up with one of his pupils. Here the purposes are openly spiritual, though the figure of a screaming Mary Magdalene, with her arm raised, suggests that calm resignation is by no means the only response to death.

Although few at the time realized it, the golden age of Venice was already fading by 1576, when Titian died. A combined attack by a league of her enemies early in the century had conquered nearly all of her possessions on the Italian mainland, the Terrafirma, and only a succession of strokes of luck had enabled her to regain them. Perhaps in relief, but perhaps also in emulation of the elegant country lifestyles being adopted by aristocrats elsewhere in Europe, the Venetian patricians began to devote themselves increasingly to their estates on the Terrafirma. In this, as in so much else, they set the style that the whole continent sought to imitate. For what they created was the world of the great country villas, made famous by the architecture of Palladio and the decorations of Paolo Veronese. But the effects on Venice itself were less benign. The shift from trade to agriculture of its leading citizens clearly hurt the empire's economy, and well before 1576 its long decline had begun.

That the city remained the envy of Europe for centuries, and that its greatest artist, Titian (unlike Raphael and even Michelangelo), was never to be out of fashion or disparaged by the taste of any subsequent generation, demonstrates the extraordinary hold that the art and life of Renaissance Venice has exercised over the imagination of modern times. Perhaps because the place itself is so beautiful, its citizens have been able to relish ordinary life, and revel in the physical presence of nature, to a degree that still astonishes. It may be, in other words, that the praise that Titian has always inspired is also indirect testimony to our affection for the city he epitomized.

Albrecht Dürer

THE cultural and economic life of the German-speaking areas of Renaissance Europe was dominated by a remarkable cluster of thriving and cosmopolitan cities. Some, like Cologne, were controlled by bishops; others, like Leipzig, were under the thumb of powerful territorial princes. But a few—notably Augsburg and Nuremberg in the south, and Hamburg and Lübeck in the north—were entirely independent. Ruled by their own rich merchant families, they had European-wide connections. Although they never achieved the wealth or the prominence of a Florence or a Venice, they were nonetheless vital international centers of commerce, learning, and the arts.

Among these great German cities, one of the most prominent was Nuremberg. Standing at the intersection of major trade routes, and with a population of some 20,000, it was an affluent place, widely admired for its stable government. Its laws were often copied, and visitors marveled at the orderliness of its citizenry, maintained by a ruling forty-two-man council that oversaw all aspects of life:

> No more than 24 guests shall be invited to a wedding feast, 12 from the bride's side and 12 from the groom's. Partridge, peacock, capons, and venison may not be served at wedding meals. No table shall be set with more than one roast or, on meatless days, two fish of moderate size.

The regulations issued by the council created a carefully structured society, which took comfort from its own predictability and coherence, rarely questioned the need for conformity, and tried to ensure (as in the wedding regulations) that public modesty was maintained and conspicuous expenditure avoided. For most, the assumption was that the city's rulers were beyond challenge:

> The government of our city rests in the hands of ancient families, men whose ancestors also ruled. Latecomers and the common people have nothing to say, nor should they.

Equally important, the patricians never doubted themselves. As one of them put it, the secret of keeping order was "kind words and heavy penalties." The result was a cohesion that was summed up by the famous cobbler-poet, Hans Sachs, whose light verses were memorized by generations of his countrymen, and who helped give the city its reputation as the quintessence of the German spirit for centuries to come:

> The source of all our joy and pride
> Is that our town is unified.
> Subjects and rulers, all estates,
> Exist in peace within our gates.

Perhaps the chief glory of Nuremberg was its craftsmen. They were celebrated for creating some of Europe's most beautiful tools,

Gilt Silver Apple Cup. This presentation cup, made to Dürer's design, lacks the serpent he included to recall the Garden of Eden. But the delicate workmanship in every blossom and even the bark of the tree exemplifies the craftsmanship for which Nuremberg was famous. It was the kind of object Dürer's father could have made, and the price such treasures commanded was one reason he was unhappy that Albrecht left the goldsmith's trade for the less well rewarded craft of painting.

scientific instruments, armor, guns, silver, bells, toys, locks, cabinets, and musical instruments—objects that united elegance and practicality. They also designed the most profusely illustrated of the Renaissance's incunabula (books printed before 1500), *The Nuremberg Chronicle* (see page 9). This huge volume, a chronicle of world history, was perhaps the most prized publication of its day, regarded throughout Europe as a model of beautiful book production. Among the city's many tradesmen, however, none had higher standards or a finer reputation than the goldsmiths. The goldsmiths were not in the ruling elite—which consisted mainly of leading merchants—but they did pursue one of the city's most lucrative occupations. And they were immersed in esthetic concerns and values that made their craft one of the principal training grounds for the artists of the Renaissance.

Among the Nuremberg goldsmiths was the prosperous family of Dürers, who, like many of their trade, lived in a comfortable house whose entire ground floor was given over to a workshop. Not un-expectedly in such a family, they assumed that the privileges and income that went with their particular skill would be passed on to the next generation. Accordingly, the young Albrecht was apprenticed to his father, and the mastery of the cutting instrument, the burin, that he now acquired gave him a facility as an engraver that later was to help make him famous.

The trouble was that there were lots of other craftsmen in the neighborhood, and Nuremberg had none of the strictly regulated guilds that in other cities made entry into a trade difficult. Down the street from the Dürers lived Michael Wolgemut, Nuremberg's leading painter, whose skills the young Albrecht found more interesting than his own. Despite his father's opposition, he was determined to switch crafts, and in 1486, at the age of fifteen, he started a new apprenticeship with Wolgemut. It was a large workshop, with lots of tedious work for trainees: grinding and mixing paints, preparing wood panels for the paintings that would go to churches and private homes, copying, and applying goldleaf to the backgrounds of the pictures. The other boys teased him, and Dürer did not look back fondly on the experience: "I learned well," he later wrote, "but I had to endure much from the apprentices." His affection for Wolgemut, however, never flagged, nor his delight in one specific skill that he learned.

While he was an apprentice, the Wolgemut workshop produced over a thousand illustrations for *The Nuremberg Chronicle*. They were made by cutting the outline of a picture into a block of wood, and chipping away around the outline until only the lines of the picture were raised. This woodcut, placed within a page of type, inked, and pressed on to paper, could be reproduced in multiple copies until it wore out or cracked. Improvements in manufacture had also made paper more easily available, and thus hundreds of impressions could be printed from a single block, though the results were still primitive, for the technique was as young as the practice of printing with movable type. The latter, which was itself something of a local specialty, had been invented by another goldsmith, Johann Gutenberg, in another German city, Mainz, only a few years before Dürer entered Wolgemut's workshop.

Dürer, The Four Horsemen. The most famous page in Dürer's *Apocalypse* shows the mysterious horsemen who, according to the book of Revelations, bring vengeance upon the damned on the Day of Judgment: Conquest holding a bow, War holding a sword, an enigmatic figure holding scales who may represent Famine or Justice, and Death or Pestilence riding a pale horse.

Because of the huge amount of work *The Nuremberg Chronicle* required, Dürer became adept in these arts as an apprentice, and it was his early expertise that made it possible for him to transform both the woodcut and the form of the printed book while he was still in his twenties. That remarkable achievement was the fruit of his first major project after he set up his own independent workshop: the publication in 1498 of *The Apocalypse*, the first printed work designed and published entirely by an artist. It told the story of the biblical book of Revelations in an unprecedented format—fourteen full-page woodcuts on the right, and the corresponding text (in separate Latin and German editions) on the left. Because it could be enjoyed even by the illiterate, and because its woodcuts displayed a freedom and power never seen in prints, *The Apocalypse* sold out rapidly, and spread Dürer's fame far beyond Nuremberg.

The book's depiction of the Day of Judgment captures vividly the Bible's terrifying evocation of the majesty of God and the punishment for sin, and one can readily understand its appeal to the deep religious piety of the time. But that was only one side of Dürer—of major importance, without a doubt, especially during the upheavals of the Reformation—and it was often overshadowed by another love: Italy.

For a young man of high intelligence like Dürer in the 1490s, open to new ideas and eager to sample the latest ventures of the age, Italy must have seemed irresistible. It certainly was to the leading intellectual figures of Nuremberg, who were proud to have absorbed and to have emulated the latest teachings of Italian humanism. Nuremberg scholars built libraries of classical authors, collected coins and engravings of ancient monuments, wrote letters in the style of Cicero, and proclaimed Roman ideals of virtue as the model for all behavior.

The most brilliant of these humanists was a member of one of Nuremberg's finest families, Willibald Pirckheimer. He had studied law in Italy, and served as a councillor, diplomat, and military commander for his native city. But he also observed the humanist injunction to combine the active life and the contemplative life, and he achieved fame as a scholar, editor, translator, and historian. That this

Dürer, Willibald Pirckheimer. To this 1524 etching of Pirckheimer at the age of fifty-three, Dürer adds an inscription like that on a Roman tombstone, prophesying the immortality of his friend's spirit.

lofty patrician, with his international contacts, could befriend the more humble Dürer was an indication both of the homogeneity of Nuremberg society and of the bonds that could be forged by the new intellectual interests of the day.

That there was real affection between the two men, who were almost exactly the same age, is apparent from the letters they exchanged, as in this passage by Dürer:

> I must write of the great pleasure I take in the honor and fame you have earned through your manly wisdom, learning and skill. But these things come to us by the special grace of God. How happy we may be, you and I, in our accomplishments, I with my paintings and you with your learning. If the world wants to glorify us, let us raise our eyebrows and believe it.

It may have been partly at Pirckheimer's urging, and partly under the inspiration of the Florentine and Venetian art that was reaching Germany, but most of all it must have been because of the excitement

Dürer's drawing of Agnes in 1521 shows her as solid and alert, with perhaps a hint of a smile. The portrait pays tribute to their relationship, for she is wearing a Netherlandish hat Dürer had just bought for her, and he noted that he drew her on their twenty-sixth wedding anniversary, during a trip to the Netherlands.

that Italy embodied, that Dürer decided in 1494 to go south to see for himself. The journey was to have a decisive influence on his career, but its timing has always seemed slightly odd.

Dürer had just returned from a four-year "bachelor" trip to cities along the Rhine, studying art and honing his skills; when he got home, he discovered that his parents had arranged for him to marry the wealthy daughter of a master brassworker. Within two months, however, he had dipped into the dowry to get money for his Italian trip and had headed south, leaving his new bride to live with her parents and to face a nasty outbreak of plague. It may all seem decidedly unromantic, and even callous, but in an era of arranged marriages it would have aroused no comment. Dürer's drawings of his wife—except for the first, which was done around the time of the wedding and inscribed "my Agnes"—were unsentimental portraits of a pleasant but stolid hausfrau. There is no reason to believe the couple was unhappy, but the union, like so many at the time, seems often to have functioned as a business relationship.

Agnes was apparently an excellent saleswoman: she managed the family shop, and sold her husband's work with great effectiveness. It was something she clearly enjoyed. On one occasion, for example, while Albrecht was being entertained by the city fathers of Bruges, and being shown the sights of the city, Agnes remained at her stall in the main square selling his prints. One does not get a sense of his wife playing a large emotional role in Dürer's life. Pirckheimer, for instance, dismissed her as a greedy housewife, and clearly disliked her—an opinion she reciprocated. But she may well have had good reasons for her feelings.

If either of the Dürer couple might have felt disappointed by the marriage, it was Agnes. She had doubtless anticipated the relatively uneventful life of the craftsman. Instead, she got someone with high intellectual interests, far-flung European contacts, and patrician friends. Even on trips she would have supper at the inn with their maid while Albrecht dined with local leaders. It has also been suggested (and Agnes shared the suspicion) that Pirckheimer and Dürer contracted what in Florence was called "the humanists' disease," a homosexual relationship, which would have been anathema in conservative Nuremberg.

Regardless of such worries, exacerbated though they were by a lack of children, Agnes undertook her family financial responsibilities with great skill, making a major contribution to her husband's extraordinary financial success. Indeed, it is difficult to decide which member of the couple, both of whom had been raised with shrewd trading instincts, was more responsible for the startlingly new relationship between artist and market that, as we shall see, was to be one of the principal ways Dürer transformed the status of his chosen calling.

For the time being, however, it was the journey to Italy that shaped his art. His sketches en route were among the first pure landscapes—early examples of a fascination with nature that was also to produce marvelous drawings of animals and even blades of grass (PLATE VI). But his destination, Venice, affected his very image of himself as an artist. The myriad new impressions created by this bustling port, with its polyglot population, its sunnier climate and

Dürer, Venetian Lady and Nuremberg Lady. The Venetian lady, with her jewelry, loose clothing, and decolletage, contrasts sharply with her tightly encased Nuremberg counterpart.

disposition, and its relaxed mores, cast his beloved Nuremberg in a new light. The direct, and rather sly, comparison we see in a picture of a Venetian beauty standing next to a Nuremberg housewife hardly flatters the German. In the long run, Dürer found the most enduring values in his native city, but for a few months—and on a return trip ten years later—he was absolutely dazzled.

Dürer said he went south to "study the nude pictures of the Italian artists," and that was exactly what he encountered in the studio of the leading painter of Venice, Giovanni Bellini, who became a good friend. This was an art that, like the subjects of ancient mythology, he felt had been "lost and hidden for a thousand years," to be rediscovered by the Italians. He also learned that there was a geometric basis not only for depictions of the body but for beauty itself, and he was to experiment with systems of perspective and proportion for the rest of his life.

The lively pleasures of Venetian society soon seduced the young German, but he never lost the ability to see both sides of the glitter:

> There are so many nice fellows among the Italians who seek my company more and more every day that it warms one's heart: wise scholars, good lute players, connoisseurs of painting, and many noble minds, true models of virtue. On the other hand, there are also among them some of the most false, lying, thievish rascals, the like of which I should not have believed lived on earth. If one did not know them, one would think them the nicest men the world could show. I cannot help laughing at them, for they know their knavery is no secret but they don't care. I have many good friends who warn me not to eat and drink with the painters. Many are my enemies, who copy my work and then revile it and say it is not in the "antique" manner and therefore not good. But Bellini has praised me highly before many nobles.

As he prepared to return home, Dürer lamented: "Oh, how I shall long for the sun! Here I am a gentleman, at home only a parasite."

The contrast in status was indeed startling; and yet, though he was taken with the notion of the artist as gentleman—in a self-portrait, he showed himself as an intellectual outfitted like a nobleman, in a fine Italian setting, and without any of the tools of his trade—he resisted the temptations of the elegant life (see page 34). Preferring his role as a craftsman who fashioned objects with his hands, he refused splendid offers to settle in Venice, in Antwerp, or at the court of the Holy Roman emperor. He certainly enjoyed the acclaim; on one occasion in the Netherlands, he noted proudly that when he came to the dinner table "the people stood, on both sides, as if they were introducing a great lord, and many persons of excellence bowed their heads to me." It was clear that he felt entirely at ease in the company of the great and famous—the scholar Erasmus, the banker Jakob Fugger, the reformer Philipp Melanchthon, and even the Emperor

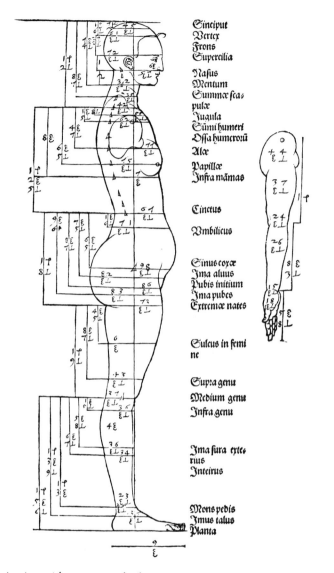

Sinciput
Vertex
Frons
Supercilia

Nasus
Mentum
Summæ sca=
pulæ
Juqula
Sūmi humeri
Ossa humeroū
Alæ

Papillæ
Infra mamas

Cinctus

Umbilicus

Sinus coxæ
Ima aluus
Pubis initium
Ima pubes
Extremæ nates

Sulcus in femi
ne

Supra genu
Medium genu
Infra genu

Ima sura exte=
rius
Interius

Mons pedis
Imus talus
Planta

Dürer's fascination with geometry, both in perception and in nature, culminated in his *Treatise on Human Proportions*, published posthumously in 1528 as a result of Agnes's efforts. Here he lists the parts of a woman's body, and indicates in a complex set of symbols the proportion each part makes up of the whole. Thus, from the bottom of the kneecap (*Medium genu*) to the sole of the foot is just over a quarter of the body, and this is in turn divided into other fractions; and from the shoulder to the elbow is one sixth of the body.

63

Maximilian—but his enduring commitment was to the habits and outlook of his "fatherland," Nuremberg.

Essential to that outlook was a hard business sense and the determination to live the comfortable life of the well-to-do burgher. It was this ambition that drove Dürer to devise the means of earning a good income, which in turn gave him the potential to become the first truly independent artist in European history. He never rejected the patronage of the powerful; indeed, the annual retainer of 100 gulden that he received from the emperor was enough, on its own, to put him high in the middle class. But he wanted to be able to provide for his family without relying on the uncertain demands of patronage. The lack of a painter's guild in Nuremberg had enabled him to experiment in his art, and the absence of its restrictions also allowed him to fashion a new way of making a livelihood.

The success of *The Apocalypse* gave Dürer his start. What he (or maybe Agnes) realized was that different techniques could command different prices and thus quite distinct markets. The woodcut, cheap to produce, and capable of bold and relatively simple effects, was a natural for a popular audience. Affordable and accessible, it could be sold in significant quantities at fairs and markets, especially if it focused on the traditional devotional themes that the ordinary buyer expected from art.

Considerably more expensive was the engraving. This could also be reproduced many times, but it required much more delicate skills. The picture was cut into a piece of copper, inked, wiped clean, and then pressed with great force against dampened paper, which drew the ink out of the incised lines. Not only was the preparation more laborious, but the frequent failures in the printing process made the results far more expensive. Since the technique permitted much subtler shadings and effects, however, he could direct his engravings at a wealthier, more sophisticated clientele, which could afford higher prices. The fact that the subject matter could be adapted to more refined tastes made this a favorite medium for Dürer, and he used it for some of his most profound psychological studies, such as the depictions of *Melencolia* and *Knight, Death, and the Devil*. There is no

Dürer, Melencolia. This elaborate etching, produced for highly refined and literate clients, depicts what the Renaissance considered one of the four basic human temperaments—phlegmatic, choleric, sanguine, and melancholic. The last, associated with pensiveness and ultimately inaction, inspired Dürer to create a figure of profound contemplation. There are so many arcane details, however —tools of geometry and construction, symbols of time and mathematics (the magic square that adds up to 34 in all directions), keys, millstone, cherub, dog, comet, bat—that the full meaning of the print remains unknown. For some, it contrasts the active and the contemplative life; for others, it shows the artist's mastery of geometry as well as practical skills; and it has even been suggested that it is ultimately a portrait of creativity and perhaps of Dürer himself.

other figure in European art of his stature whose reputation is so closely identified with engravings.

At the top of the economic scale was painting. This could command the highest prices, but Dürer realized that, in relative terms, it was simply not cost-effective. If the emperor wanted a portrait, one could hardly refuse; but otherwise even a fat fee might not be the best way of earning the maximum return. As he informed one wealthy patron:

> Only from quickly painted mediocre works can I really make a profit; but my painstaking care in producing excellent paintings for you, sir, is far too time-consuming. Therefore I will take up engraving again. Had I done this in the past, I would be a thousand florins richer today.

Not that Dürer failed to make a great deal of money. For all the complaints, he and Agnes had a unique ability to gauge their markets: they demonstrated for the first time that an artist could achieve financial independence without patrons, relying solely on the public. When Albrecht died he was worth 7,000 gulden, a small fortune in an age when a poor family of four could survive on 15 gulden a year.

The great crisis of Dürer's life was the Reformation. The depth of his spiritual commitments are apparent not only in his many religious subjects, but in a stunning self-portrait. Bringing to life his belief that creative power comes from God, he presented his own features in a way that suggests the image of Christ (PLATE VI). In his view, the artist reflects God, because "God is honored when it appears that he has given such intelligence to a creature in whom such art resides." Profoundly attuned to the sacred, Dürer was quick to respond, as were most of his contemporaries, to any intimation of the divine. When he heard, for example, that "blood rain" had fallen on a girl's dress in the shape of a cross, he went to see the portent and make a drawing of it. He also drew a dreadful nightmare he had had, in which waters falling from heaven "drowned the whole land."

In such an atmosphere Luther's teachings had a powerful impact, especially since he offered a direct remedy for the inherent sinfulness of mankind. Just as "flesh imbues us with the wish to commit wicked acts," he wrote, so "faith alone justifies and gives us the spirit and the desire to do good works." Dürer was deeply moved by what he heard, and sent a message to Frederick of Saxony, Luther's prince, whose portrait he had painted:

> I beg you to convey to Elector Frederick my most humble thanks for his kindness in sending me some writings of Martin Luther. God grant that I may soon see this good Doctor Luther, for I would dearly love to draw his portrait and engrave it in copper in order to preserve the memory of this Christian man who has shown me the way out of my soul's deep anguish.

When he heard that Luther had disappeared after defying the emperor at the Diet of Worms in 1521—it turned out that he had been kidnapped by supporters for safekeeping—Dürer's distress was palpable:

> Is he still alive, or have they murdered him? If we have lost this man, who has written more clearly than anyone else, send us another who will show us how to live a Christian life. O God, if Luther is dead, who will explain the Gospel to us?

The city of Nuremberg, as could have been predicted, decided to address the issue of religious reform in orderly fashion. Many in the elite accepted the new teachings, but the proper course, they felt, was to have the two sides, Roman and Lutheran, debate their doctrines in front of the council. The conclusion may have been foregone, but the city felt it could switch its allegiance only through this formal, officially sanctioned procedure. Pirckheimer (in whose house Luther once stayed) opposed the change, and Dürer never left the Roman Church, but neither man objected as monasteries were closed, traditional practices were banned, and the Reformation was put into effect in Nuremberg.

Until the mid-1520s, such temperate policies seemed entirely appropriate. But then it became clear that the Reformation also threatened social upheaval. Fiery preachers denounced Luther as too moderate, peasants erupted into revolt against their overlords, and the effects were felt even in Nuremberg. The patricians had always been

Dürer, The Four Apostles. Dürer expressed his concern over the religious disputes that arose during the Reformation by showing saints John, Peter (with his key), Mark, and a glowering Paul as heroic figures. With quotations from their writings—in Luther's translation—at their feet, they represent true Christian teaching and a warning to false prophets.

paranoid about the danger of subversion, but now they had good cause for their anxiety as radical ideas swept into the city. Among those investigated and imprisoned in 1525 were three pupils of Dürer, one of whom rejected baptism, Scripture, and the authority of the Nuremberg council. The master was distraught at this turn of events, and until his death, three years later, he remained unable to come to terms with the religious upheavals that surrounded him.

In the early days of the Reformation, Dürer had been troubled by attacks on images, and by the suggestion that devotional pictures were idols. Luther did not approve openly of art as a means of spreading God's word until 1525, and that may explain why the relieved artist put the date 1526 on an engraving he had held back three years earlier. But now the violence disturbed him anew. It was in 1525, at the height of the peasants' revolt, that he had his nightmare of the waters drowning the earth, and the following year he presented to the Nuremberg council a large painting of four apostles with a pointed caption:

> In these dangerous times, let all rulers beware of mistaking the deceptive teachings of men for God's word. Peter writes in his second epistle: "False prophets also arose among the people, just as there will be false teachers among you, who will secretly bring in destructive heresies."

Eventually, urged on by a Luther who feared for the survival of his reforms, the princes and cities of the empire crushed the peasants and the radicals. But Dürer was more ambivalent. A sympathy for the individual was essential to his art, as was an openness that enabled him not only to mediate between Italian and German styles but also to remain uncommitted in an age of competing faiths. His design for a column to commemorate the defeat of the peasants is therefore an ambiguous comment on the violence he witnessed. It is crowned with a peasant, stabbed in the back, who may be as much the victim as the perpetrator of the disorder.

In his combination of brilliant innovation with a yearning for stability Dürer reflected the instinct for change, even amid the re-

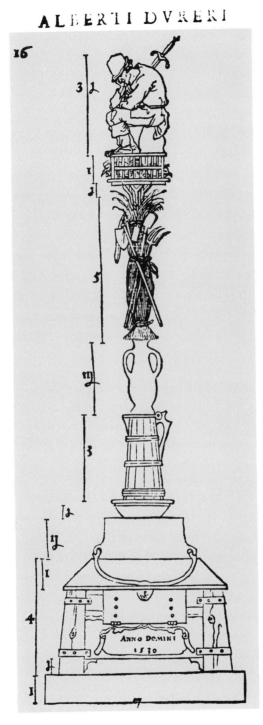

Dürer, Design for a Monument for the Peasants' Revolt. The column commemorating the peasants' uprising of 1525 shows the tools and fruits of their labor, but commentators have disagreed about the meaning of the figure Dürer placed at the summit. Is it a reproach to peasants who neglected their lands, or to the authorities who suppressed the revolt?

verence for the past, that characterized much of Renaissance culture. But his conservatism must not be minimized. Notwithstanding the revolution he wrought, both in the techniques and esthetics of engraving and the graphic arts, and in the economic position of the artist, Dürer, like many of his contemporaries, had a sense of rootedness that was a shield in difficult times. He could find comfort in the familiar patterns of the burgher world, despite the religious conflicts of his last years, because of the credo he had adopted long before, in response to the invitations to leave his cherished native city:

> I would rather live a modest life here, in Nuremberg, where I was born, than achieve fame and riches in other places.

PART III

The Enthusiasm for Change

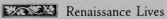

Thomas Platter. This engraving of Platter shows the respectable printer-educator in his dignified old age.

A Student

B Y THE EARLY SIXTEENTH CENTURY, humanism was beginning to transform intellectual life at its most fundamental level: in the methods and aims of many European
schools and universities, which were creating a new curriculum with a major emphasis on classical studies. At the same time,
the religious dissenters who were creating the Reformation were trying
to ensure a more central place in the schools for the advancement of
the godly life that they felt education was supposed to instill. Both
movements, moreover, had received a powerful boost from one of
the most consequential inventions of the Renaissance, the printing
press. ⟨Few people who lived through the turmoil of the years
following 1500 were touched by so many of its elements, or threw
themselves into its excitements with as much passion, as a relatively
obscure Swiss schoolmaster, eternal student, and jack-of-all-trades
named Thomas Platter. Thanks to the autobiography he wrote in his
last years, we can perceive how the vast upheavals of more than half
a century were experienced; and, because of his versatility, we can
come to realize that even a single figure can encapsulate an age of
extraordinary and rapid change.

Thomas Platter

SWITZERLAND contains some of the most forbidding landscape in Europe. What today would be considered picturesque, or splendid skiing territory, was long regarded as merely fearsome and dangerous. And those who chose to live in the mountains were thought of as fierce, incomprehensible, and primitive. That the Vatican is still defended by a detachment of Swiss Guards is testimony to the reputation of the Swiss people throughout the late Middle Ages, and well into the 1500s, as the most formidable soldiers of the time. Yet they were by no means isolated from the new ideas of the day. Indeed, it was in one of Switzerland's most remote and impenetrable areas, the Valais, to a typical life of hardship and abject poverty, that one of the most dogged and versatile men of the age was born.

His name was Thomas Platter. He never knew his father, who died soon after his birth in 1499, and he knew his mother, who remarried almost at once and farmed him out to relatives, little better. From the start things did not go well for him:

> When my mother recovered from my birth, she could not nurse me, and I never once had any mother's milk, as she herself told me. That was the beginning of my misery. I was obliged to drink cow's milk through a little horn, as is the custom in that land. When they wean children, they give them nothing to eat, but only cow's milk, until they are four or five years old.

Of the five siblings he knew, two sisters died young, one of them of the plague, and two of three brothers were killed in battle. Only his grandfather seems, in his mind, to have been an unusual figure—reputedly having survived to the age of 126 and having had a son, at 100, with a woman of 30.

Endurance was an essential virtue. As a toddler, Thomas wandered off into the snow, was found half frozen, and was placed between two men, who lay down and thawed him out with their bodies. At the age of six he was sent off to be a goatherd:

I was so small, that when I opened the stable door and did not jump aside quickly, the goats knocked me down. I once drove my goats up to a ledge, which was one step wide, with nothing but rock below it for over a thousand fathoms. From the ledge, they climbed a rock face covered in tufts of grass. But when I had gone up the grass a small step, I could go no further, and I dared not jump back to the narrow ledge in case I jumped too far and fell over the terrible precipice. I stayed there for a good while, holding on to tufts of grass with both hands, and supported by my big toe on another tuft. I feared that the great vultures who flew below me would carry me away, as sometimes happens in the Alps. When my friend Thomas saw me from afar, he saw my little coat fluttering, and at first thought I was a bird.

Rescued by Thomas on this occasion, trapped in the mountains overnight on others, narrowly missed by falling boulders, the child lived in almost constant terror. After three years, however, he moved on to a new career.

Concluding that the boy, now nine years old, was not cut out for the life of a goatherd, the aunts who looked after him decided that the obviously intelligent youngster might benefit, instead, from an education.

Things now really went evilly with me. It was now that hard times really began. The schoolmaster, my cousin Anthony Platter, was short-tempered, and I was but an awkward peasant boy. He beat me very severely, and often took me by the ears and dragged me on the ground, so that I screamed so much that the neighbors cried out, asking whether he wanted to kill me.

Little Thomas learned virtually nothing from Anthony, but he did acquire one skill: the ability to sing for his supper, a valuable talent (as Hus had discovered) for the Renaissance beggar. It was to stand Platter in good stead when he was rescued from Anthony by a cousin, Paul, who introduced him to the world of the *bacchant*, the wandering student of Germany.

There were thousands of these roving young men, who moved from town to town, attending schools of various kinds, giving lessons,

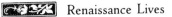

Peter Brueghel the Elder, Carnival and Lent. This detail from Brueghel's evocation of the season of Lent reflects the tradition that this was a time to give alms to beggars. The group shown here, near a church door, evokes a scene that must have been familiar to Platter in his early days.

and almost always making nuisances of themselves. According to Platter, there were over a thousand of them in the city of Breslau alone. Special dormitories were often set aside for them, and for food they relied either on the charity of religious institutions or on begging. This last gave little Thomas his opportunity, because the *bacchants* often took along with them young boys, known as shooters, who were ostensibly pupils, but in fact served their scholars as foragers and beggars.

> For me, not accustomed to travel, our journeys were very long. Besides, I had to obtain food on the way. Eight or nine of us travelled together—three little shooters, the others great *bacchants*, and I was the smallest and youngest of the shooters. When I did not move fast, my cousin Paul walked behind me with a rod, and beat me on my bare legs, for I had no trousers and only poor shoes.

In addition to singing and begging, the shooters were encouraged to steal food. They may in fact have received their name from the practice of throwing stones at small animals, especially geese, and killing them. Thomas was particularly skilled at this activity, and many of his stories recount his being chased by enraged farmers. He also recalled encountering murderers and robbers, joining in fights with city authorities, and taking on rival shooters. Roaming across central Europe, Poland, and Hungary, he slept amid vermin, was often frostbitten or ill (though he did receive treatment from the students' own physician), and was almost always hungry, unlike the *bacchants* he supplied.

There were few acts of kindness, though people did apparently take to the teenaged Thomas, who was still quite small, with a fine voice, and an appealing look—he called himself "more pert than the other" shooters. He mentions an offer from a rich merchant to adopt him, which Paul refused, and describes the scene one night in Munich, as he was trudging toward the corn market to find some sacks of corn on which to sleep, when a butcher's widow whom the Swiss had once treated well took him in. She protected him when Paul came to claim him, full of threats, but then he decided to fend for himself. Nearly nine years of exploitation and hardship at Paul's hands made him determined to run away, and so he fled through the wintry countryside, without shoes, "only torn stockings, no cap, and a little jacket without folds."

For months Paul pursued him through what is today southern Germany, Austria, and Switzerland; after all, as the little shooter later noted, Thomas had provided him with a good living. But he had not allowed the boy to study, and that was above all what Thomas now wanted to do. He realized that the *bacchants* themselves often led dull and difficult lives—there were no books, so they had to take endless dictation: "What they read first had to be dictated, then defined and construed, and only then could the teacher explain it; so that the *bacchants* had to carry home with them huge, miserable books." But the content of those books intrigued him, and he even offered his services to some *bacchants* he met in Zurich, if only they would let him learn, too. When they rejected him, he joined a countryman who was headed for a well-known school in Schlettstadt, near Strassburg.

Here, a young adult sitting among schoolchildren, he began the education he was to pursue all his life. The basic introductory text in the sixteenth century was the massive Latin grammar of Donatus, which the eighteen-year-old now learned by heart. What followed was endless conjugation and parsing and memorizing of classical authors. The new learning of the Renaissance took its inspiration from the notion that true virtue had been achieved by the ancient Greeks and Romans, and that by studying their writings one could emulate their high moral standards. But this freeing or "liberalization" of traditional education, for all its opening up of such neglected subjects as the Roman poets and music, and its encouragement of sports as well as classroom work, very quickly became rigidified into rote learning of the new texts, accompanied by monotonously predictable beatings. That was the system Platter encountered. He never complained of its tedium; instead, persistent as ever, he thrived.

He returned to Zurich in the early 1520s, and attached himself to the cathedral school, where a noted Swiss educator and reformer, Oswald Myconius, had just become the master. Here Thomas's command of Donatus proved fortunate:

Titian, Venus with a Mirror. Cupid, with his arrows at his feet, holds up a mirror to Venus as she is fitted for a floral wreath. The lushness of the picture, with its gold and velvet surrounding soft flesh, is Titian's tribute to the beauty and sensuality for which Venice was famous.

PLATE V

Dürer, Self-Portrait. Dürer in 1500 is the Nuremberg citizen—well off, to judge by his cloak, but in a sober and straightforward setting unlike his "Venetian" self-portrait (see page 34). He gazes directly at us, and he now rises above mere artisan status, not by appearing as a figure of fashion, but by echoing the image of Christ and by drawing our attention to his pale eyes and long, slim hand—the instruments of his creativity.

Dürer, Castle of Trent. Only a single tiny figure appears in this portrayal of a major landmark on the route between Nuremberg and Venice—one of the first landscape scenes in Renaissance art.

PLATE VI

fellen frouwen und junchfrouwen wer fin bedarff der kum har jn·dr
wirt drüwlich glert vm em zimlichen lon· Aber die junge knabe
und meitliu noch den konualten wie gewonheit ist · 1 5 1 6 ·

Ambrosius Holbein, The Schoolmaster. Painted as an advertising signboard for Platter's patron Myconius in Basel, this scene of a schoolroom, with schoolmaster, schoolmistress, and pupils, promised all who enrolled that they would learn to read and write.

Peter Brueghel the Elder, Parable of the Blind. The only contemporary of Montaigne who matched his ability to expose the absurdities and cruelties of his times was the Flemish painter Peter Brueghel. Ordinary people and the downtrodden populate his canvases, but always there is a deeper message. The scene he depicts here, grim as it is, illustrates a verse from Matthew: "If the blind lead the blind, both shall fall into the ditch." The Montaignean point Christ (and Brueghel) were making was that only God sees the truth, and therefore the religious persecutions of the age were futile.

PLATE VII

El Greco, Resurrection of Christ. El Greco, who settled in St. Teresa's ancestral home, Toledo, in the late sixteenth century, was the artist of Spanish mysticism. The eerie light, the muted colors, and the elongated and contorted figures in his paintings give us a glimpse of the otherworldly visions that inspired a Teresa and a John of the Cross.

PLATE VIII

Hans Leu the Elder, The Zurich Martyrs. This detail from a series of panels painted around 1500 shows Zurich as it was in Platter's time. The church with twin towers remains a landmark to this day, but the paintings themselves barely survived the Reformation. Because their main subject is a group of saints—the martyr St. Felix is in the foreground—they were defaced during the early days of Zwingli's assault on images and Church practices, when Platter was burning the statue of St. John.

> For when he began, he read Terence with us, and we were forced to decline and conjugate every word of the entire comedy. He often worked so hard with me that my clothes were soaked with perspiration, and even my eyes began to dim. Yet he never beat me—only once, with the back of his hand, on my cheek. When he was rough with me, however, he took me to his house and fed me, for he liked to have me recount how I had traveled through all the lands of Germany.

And it was Myconius who introduced Platter to the new religious ideas of the day.

These were times of fierce intellectual debate in Zurich. A

learned and magnetic preacher, Ulrich Zwingli, who had reached many of the same conclusions about the emptiness of traditional Church teachings, and at the same time, as Luther, was beginning his own protest, and was attracting an ever-growing number of followers. Zwingli was the most thoroughly committed humanist of the Protestant reformers, a disciple of the greatest scholar of the day, Erasmus, and a believer, like him, that truth was to be found only in the words of the Bible. He thought of theology as a form of moral philosophy, rather than as an ideology, and education as central to belief. Soon the city as a whole was to adopt his views, which went even further than Luther's. It was Zwingli, more than any other of the reformers of this era, who made austerity and discipline central to the Protestant faith. The Christian had to struggle to salvation with no outside help. There was not even a miraculous moment in the mass—the service was merely a symbolic reminder of Christ's sacrifice. Instead, there were three- and four-hour sermons that harangued the congregation, sitting on hard benches within bare walls, for its depravity and sin. There were public confessions, and support for those who reported the moral lapses of neighbors or family members. It was Zwingli's tremendous stress on the importance of education, however, that probably first attracted both Myconius and Platter.

Many in Thomas's family, including the boy himself, had long assumed that he would become a priest. But a sermon by Zwingli, "expounded so powerfully that I felt as if someone was pulling me up by my hair," convinced him otherwise. Zwingli said priests were like shepherds, responsible to God for every drop of blood—or sin —shed by their sheep. By then, however, Thomas, who had been appointed by Myconius custodian for the cathedral choir, could see for himself how poorly qualified many priests were, and his contempt extended to their symbols.

When I was custodian I often had no wood for heating. One morning I had no wood, and Zwingli was to preach before dawn. As the bells rang for the service, I thought: "You have no wood, yet there are so many idols in this church." So I went to the nearest altar, seized a statue of St. John, and put it in the stove. "Johnny," I said to him, "bend yourself, because you have to go into the stove even though you may be St. John." During the sermon, Myconius said, "You surely had wood today," and I thought: "St. John has done his best."

During this early period of religious reform, it was far from clear where hard lines would be drawn. Even at the service warmed by St. John, at which Zwingli preached, a traditional mass was sung. But whenever there was a choice, Platter took the side of the reformers. On a visit to his home village he was attacked by a local priest for consorting with the heretics of Zurich. "Why are they heretics?" asked Platter. "Because they do not consider the Pope head of the Christian Church." "Why," continued Platter, "is the Pope head of the Christian Church?" "Because St. Peter was the Pope at Rome." Whereupon, in Platter's account, "I drew my Testament out of my little sack" and proved to the priest that "St. Peter had never once been in Rome."

Most of Platter's time was now spent on his studies. He was still desperately poor, but his knowledge of the countryside enabled him to make something of a living as a carrier of messages, notably for Zwingli himself and his allies in other cities. In his mid-twenties he lived for a while with Myconius, and he landed a job as tutor for two boys. Already a master of Latin and Greek, he now learned Hebrew from an erudite grammarian who was staying with Myconius, secretly made a copy of his grammar, and then obtained a copy of one of the first printed Hebrew Bibles from Venice. It was this knowledge of Hebrew that gave him real standing in the intellectual circles in which he was beginning to move, and it landed him an even better tutoring position. But the studying did not stop. He mastered a new Hebrew grammar produced by Sebastian Münster, one of the leading scholars of the age and the creator of the first great modern atlas. And he spent every spare moment on detailed annotations of Homer and Euripides.

The opportunities for self-education that Platter enjoyed had not existed a mere half century before. For it was only printing that made the books he devoured available. Previously, education had depended largely on the dictation and explanation provided by the schoolmaster from a hard-to-obtain manuscript. Pupils spent their time copying and reciting. Now, in an age when the texts could be obtained in standardized editions, and when some of them, like the Bible, were even cheap to buy, the world of learning became accessible to an avid reader like Platter.

His problem was to find steady employment while pursuing his reading. He was getting too large and old, he felt, to continue his old ways and sing and beg for food. When he heard, therefore, that a fellow scholar—advised by Zwingli and Myconius to take up rope making as a solid source of income—had set up shop, Thomas asked to be apprenticed to him. And so he acquired yet another skill, though not one that he seems to have taken seriously or performed particularly well. What it did give him, though, was the opportunity to move to the city that was the most important center in Switzerland of the intellectual ferment of the time, Basel.

For a young Swiss like Platter, who was more serious about the new learning than passionate about the new religious ideas with which Zurich and, later, Geneva were identified, Basel was the place to be. Its university and its publishers were famous throughout Europe, and attracted the leading humanists and scholars of the day. Indeed, it was here, working with the famous publisher Froben, that Erasmus settled for the last years of his peripatetic life. Equally important, the city tolerated a wide variety of religious beliefs, and was as well-connected to the French-speaking as to the German-speaking world—a breadth of contacts that enhanced its importance as a center of scholarship and printing.

To finance his move Platter offered himself as a journeyman to a rope maker, who admired the young man's learning but soon grew irritated at his neglect of the trade. On one occasion he caught Thomas with the pages of an unbound copy of the plays of Plautus, fixed in such a way that he could read them as he turned the hemp. "Damn it!" he said. "Villain that you are. If you want to study, go ahead; if not, work at your trade. Is it not enough that I allow you to study at night and on holidays. Must you also read during the turning?"

It was exactly the same complaint he had heard from his master in Zurich.

Again, it was his knowledge of Hebrew that gave Platter new opportunities. He was making friends with some of the humanists in the city, and through them even Erasmus himself offered to help find the young scholar an appropriate position. But he was still diffident about the learning he had acquired on his own; fearful that he would let his patrons down, he declined their help. After much cajoling he was persuaded to offer Hebrew lessons, though he was ashamed to do so in his rope maker's apron. But even the attention he now received left him uneasy. Among his pupils was an emissary of the queen of Navarre, one of the leading patrons of learning and reform of the time; he promised Platter the queen's patronage, yet this offer, too, the young man refused, certain that he was not worthy of such support. Well into his late twenties, Thomas still had no stable future.

But now outside events intervened. Between 1529 and 1531 the growing hostility of the supporters and opponents of Zwingli finally erupted into civil war. When it ended, Zwingli had been killed in battle, but his followers in Zurich and other cities were able to resist sufficiently to keep his reform alive. What the war did was to close the rope maker's shop and send Platter back to Zurich, first to accompany the rope master to war and then in his old role as a messenger for the Zwinglians. He was present at a number of episodes in the conflict, including the dramatic moment when a prowar group tore up a potential peace treaty, but the chief effect of these years resulted from his renewed friendship with Myconius. For his old teacher persuaded Platter to marry his maid, Anna (the main argument apparently being that she shared Thomas's Zwinglian views), and to stop wandering.

What this meant initially was one more brutal journey, over the mountains to his home town in the Valais. It was terribly cold; they had to sleep on straw; and Anna's clothing froze to her body. But she proved as hardy as Thomas, and equally impervious to the scorn with which the locals greeted their religious ideas. However difficult the situation, though—and it troubled Platter to be back in traditional Church territory—he was determined to settle down. For his region, the skills he had acquired required no apology, and he established himself as both rope maker and schoolmaster. Between the two professions, he could make a comfortable living, although one has to wonder how he found the time, as he later claimed, to look after more than thirty students, make rope, and still travel around the mountains through further hair-raising adventures.

Eventually, the hostility of those who did not share the couple's religious views became too much for him, and he decided to try to return to Basel. By then he had become the father of a baby girl, and his kinfolk assumed that it was Anna who convinced him to leave. "They did her an injustice," he later said, "for she would have lived in that region willingly enough. It was the priests who were anxious for me to leave." And so, with his baby on his back, and his wife "following along behind like a cow with a little calf," he set out again. Myconius and his Basel friends had secured for Platter a position as the assistant to the leading schoolmaster of the city, and thus he had at last the steady income and comfortable household that had been so elusive during his first thirty years. Yet his troubles were not over:

> However poor we were at first, once we began to keep house I cannot remember that we ever ate without bread and wine. So I could study industriously, and could rise early and go to bed late. The result was that I often got headaches, and such terrible dizziness that I had to hold myself up by the bench. The physicians gladly helped me with blood-letting and drugs, but it was all in vain.

Until then Thomas had been able to escape almost miraculously from the ailments of his day. People had died of the plague around him, but he had survived. Now, however, the family's luck changed. A famous Italian doctor in Basel did cure Platter's headaches by recommending more sensible sleeping and eating habits, but he then persuaded the restless young man to give up his teaching job, leave Basel, and become his servant. Soon after this move our little child, on the evening she had learned to walk five little steps, was attacked by the plague, and died on the third day. Since the spasms also attacked her, so that we saw her in the greatest pain, we wept, when she died, not only from sorrow, but also from joy at her escape from the suffering.

Within a few weeks the doctor, too, succumbed to the disease, and Thomas, true to his scholarly instincts, immediately copied his master's medical handbook for his own collection. He and Anna were to lose two more children to the plague; only a son, Felix, was to outlive them.

When Platter returned to Basel in the early 1530s, to settle down for good after his stint with the doctor, he could not have foreseen that he would live another fifty years and become one of the city's most respected citizens. But the death of his daughter in the course of his wanderings, the death of Zwingli, which had driven Myconius to leave Zurich and take a post at the University of Basel, and the opportunities offered by yet another new profession, may finally have persuaded him to repress his nomadic instincts. The new profession in particular, though short-lived and financially volatile, gave him important connections and also his chief claim to fame.

For a man so enamored with books, and with so many contacts in Basel's intellectual world, the attractions of the city's great publishing industry must have been irresistible. During his earlier stays Thomas had helped a number of printers, and now, in the 1530s, he took up the occupation himself. Compared to his earlier ventures, he found this an easy trade to learn, and he soon ran a workshop with fifteen employees. Except for difficulties with business partners, and a failed attempt to become a bookseller, he found both comfort and contentment as a printer.

Indeed, it is as a printer that Platter earned his small place in history. He was by no means the most notable of that distinguished company in Basel—one of his early partners, for instance, went on to produce what is arguably the most beautiful illustrated book of the sixteenth century, Vesalius's study of the human body—but it was an impressive career nonetheless. During the seven years it lasted,

Der Buchdrücker.

Ich bin geschicket mit der preß
So ich aufftrag den Firniß reß/
So bald mein dienr den bengel zuckt/
So ist ein bogn papyrs gedruckt.
Da durch kombt manche Kunst an tag/
Die man leichtlich bekommen mag.
Vor zeiten hat man die bücher gschribn/
Zu Meintz die Kunst ward erstlich triebn.

Jost Amman, The Printer. The most famous sixteenth-century depiction of a printer's shop is this page from the 1568 *Das Ständebuch*, a book of trades illustrated by Jost Amman, with verses by Hans Sachs. Each page is printed on only one side, so that it could be obtained on its own and stuck on a wall, like cartoons in offices today. The verse explains the elements of the craft, and notes that it was invented in the German city of Mainz. (See also page 216.)

he produced thirty-seven books, mainly on philology, philosophy, and medicine. And he printed one which—as Thomas, the dedicated adherent of reform, would have been pleased to know—has remained famous ever since: the first edition of John Calvin's *Institutes of the Christian Religion*.

Eventually, however, Platter once again had to choose between careers. By 1541, in his early forties, he had achieved considerable

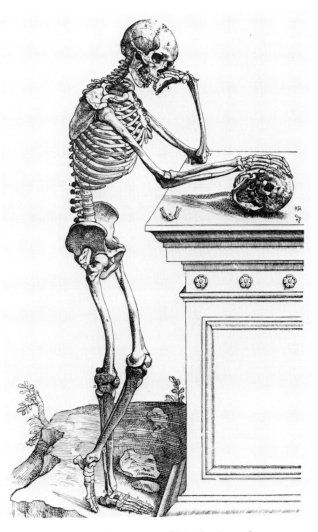

The most famous of Titian's illustrations of Vesalius's work on anatomy (see also page 43), published in Basel by Platter's former partner, shows a skeleton contemplating a skull, the symbol of death.

prosperity. He was the owner of a row of townhouses, he had been made a citizen (that is, with full political rights) of Basel, and he moved easily in its leading intellectual circles. When, therefore, the headmastership of the city's main school, the Castle School, fell vacant, the mayor and the council urged him to take over.

They got Dr. Myconius involved, too, for they thought I could not refuse him. He told me how they had consulted with him about me. I asked him what he advised. He said: "I would prefer you to anyone else in the city. But I will not advise you. You will not be able to get on with the people at the University. I know you: you will want to follow your own ideas, and they will not allow that."

It was a shrewd prediction. Platter did accept the offer, tempted by the opportunity to create his own curriculum, and two years later gave up the printshop. But a major function of the school was to supply students for the university, and throughout his years at the Castle School he was in a running battle with that august institution. He was not always able to resist the faculty's interference—it wanted more of his pupils, it tried to stop him teaching subjects that were not supposed to be introduced before university, and it sought to supervise his examinations. Yet he persisted for over thirty years, and created a pioneering school that combined the latest ideas of humanism and religious reform (PLATE VII).

Such schools had already been established elsewhere. In particular, German reformers had added detailed study of the Bible to the Italians' emphasis on the classical authors, and Platter was well aware of these developments. Still, conscientious as ever, he traveled to the nearby city of Strassburg to look more closely at the new curriculum before creating his own version in Basel. The result was a carefully structured progression, from mastery of the Donatus Latin grammar, through Cicero, Vergil, other Roman authors, and the contemporary writings of Erasmus, to Greek, the fables of Aesop, the catechism, and the New Testament. It was a humanist and religious program —grounded in the belief that virtue could be attained from reading the right books—which was to dominate western education for nearly four hundred years.

As he looked back over his life, in order to write for his son Felix an account of the struggles that had led to his final good fortune, the three decades as schoolmaster occupied little of Thomas's attention. Perhaps these later years were more familiar; perhaps his life now slipped into a routine that seemed unremarkable. Nevertheless,

Platter's autobiography evokes rich images of levels of Renaissance society—the wandering student, the beggar, the artisan—of which we have few firsthand descriptions, and which otherwise we can glimpse but dimly. It is a unique, literate account of the poverty that would have been far more familiar to most Europeans than the lives of artists, courtiers, and clergy that we, dependent as we are on sources produced by the elite, tend to see as typifying the age. Yet even as he completed his manuscript in February 1572, in his seventy-third year, Platter still had surprises in store for us.

Eight days after the work was done, Anna died, and just two months later Thomas remarried. His young bride, Hester, the daughter of a preacher, promptly started a second family for him. As if determined to outdo his vigorous grandfather, he sired six more children between 1575 and his death in 1582. The redoubtable old survivor was going strong to the very end, and by now he could take enormous pleasure from the distinguished career of his son. Felix had become a learned scholar, trained in medicine at the renowned French university at Montpellier. As a celebrated doctor, consulted by nobles and princes, he was appointed official physician to the city of Basel, and soon was to become rector of Basel's university. Interestingly enough, like their father, both Felix and his half brother Thomas were to write autobiographical sketches.

The honor and position of his progeny gave Thomas enormous pleasure, for all his insistence that thanks be given only to God. What amazed him the most, though, was how all this had arisen from such an unpromising beginning:

> So much have I suffered that I have often wondered how it is possible that I am still alive, and can stand or walk for such a long time. And yet you can see that, however poor my beginning, and however perilous my life, I have nevertheless come into considerable fortune and honor, though I received almost nothing from my parents, nor my wife anything at all from hers. Yet we have come to own houses in the lovely city of Basel, and a farm besides, through the enormous labor of myself and my wife, even though at the outset I could not even call a little hut in Basel my own. However humble my origin, God

has granted me that, in so widely famous a city as Basel, I have taught for thirty-one years in the school next highest to the University, teaching many noblemen's sons and many doctors and learned men. Zurich, Bern, and Strassburg have given me their toast of honor, and when the city of Sitten [from his home province of Valais] sent me its wine the lord said: "This wine of honor Sitten gives our dear fellow countryman Thomas Platter, as the father of the children of our common land of Valais."

It was a heartwarming end to a life which, for all its shifts of scene and fortune, had always been shadowed by the memory of the great mountains of the Valais.

PART IV

The
Response
to Change

Left: Teresa of Avila. This portrait, painted in 1576 when she was sixty-one years old, gives a better sense of the image of Teresa in her own times than the idealized Bernini sculpture (page 104). The devout saint, with the dove of the Holy Spirit descending toward her, promises in the scroll that she will seek the mercy of God for eternity.   *Right:* Michel de Montaigne. This simple portrait conveys the austerity of Montaigne, relieved only by the magnificent ruff that suggests (as he would have wished) his high social status.

A Believer
and a Dissenter

HE RAPID CHANGES of the early sixteenth century, as the Reformation took hold, provoked reappraisal as well as violence. The Roman Church, for example, found new vigor in response to the challenge posed by Luther and his followers. To its leaders the proper road to the future was a strengthening of belief, not dissent. And none of its models of appropriate faith and behavior became more beloved than the devout Spanish nun who was soon to be sanctified as St. Teresa. For her, and for the Church at large, the essential response to change was to believe more strongly, not to doubt. ⟨To her younger contemporary, the French lawyer and philosopher Montaigne, such a response was impossible. Seeing change and the violence inspired by religious conflict everywhere around him, he turned away from all claims of certainty. The heritage of Petrarch's humanism and his profound effort of self-analysis remained a powerful influence, but in the end Montaigne, like his Italian predecessor, could express his dismay at the failings of his age only by taking on the mantle of the dissenter. Yet it was not change itself that he rejected, as Teresa did. Rather, it was the struggle over change that earned his contempt and drove him to add a skeptical and ethical dimension to the culture of the Renaissance.

Teresa of Avila

THERE could hardly have been two more different places in Renaissance Spain than Toledo and Avila. Toledo was one of the great cities of Europe, a cosmopolitan center of intellectual life, famous for its crafts and its metalwork, and the cultural heart as well as the capital of the ancient kingdom of Castile. It was located on a magnificent site, rising steeply from the river Tagus, and, to a degree that not even Venice could match, its life had been dominated, since the twelfth century, by the interaction of three entirely distinct cultural traditions: Christian, Muslim, and Jewish. Each of these communities had its own international connections, and yet each made a vital contribution to Toledo's history, symbolized by its great Gothic cathedral, its splendid mosque in the Cordoban style, and its imposing yet delicate synagogues. The first assault on this mixture of faiths and outlooks began in the 1390s, with persecutions that mounted steadily until the 1490s, when, in a fateful climax, all Muslims and Jews were forced either to convert to Christianity or to leave Spain. Toledo was never to be the same again, though it was to enjoy a final flowering a century later, in the age of El Greco.

Avila was entirely unlike the great city that lay some sixty miles to its south. Situated on the rocky and difficult terrain of the Castilian plateau, it did not offer its inhabitants easy ways of making a living. Liberated from the Moors earlier than Toledo, and at most a third the size, Avila was no cultural center, either. It did boast a fine Gothic cathedral, but its main Moorish relics were its walls, which to this day remain one of the architectural glories of Spain. The daunting towers and ramparts, however, merely emphasize the inward-looking atmosphere of the city—closed, cold, and tough where Toledo seems open, warm, and soft.

It was a dramatic change of scene, then, for Juan Sánchez, a rich merchant with governmental contacts who was a well-known figure in Toledo until 1485, when the Inquisition accused him of practicing

Judaism in secret. Juan was in fact a *converso*, one of a large number of Jews who had converted to Christianity in order not merely to remain in Spain but to continue in their professions. They were always suspect in a country which, largely because of its mixed heritage and its crusading traditions, set great store by *limpieza de sangre*, purity of blood. Proceedings against prominent *converso* merchants were a common occurrence, and Juan was far from unique in being ordered to march in penitential processions, together with his children, so as to demonstrate his repentance and true conversion.

But the public display only shamed the family, and soon thereafter they left Toledo for the quieter and less visible city of Avila. This was a more close-knit society, yet here, too, the commercial district, where they settled, was known as the *converso* area. Taking up the wool and silk trade, Juan soon displayed his old commercial prowess, resumed his old contacts, and restored his fortune. By 1500 he was recognized as a *hidalgo*, a minor nobleman. And the career of the grandchild who was born fifteen years later to his daughter-in-law, a local woman of impeccable Christian ancestry, was to give an air of orthodoxy, and ultimately of sanctity, to this family of classically Spanish mixed faiths.

The grandchild, Teresa, grew up in a prosperous household, surrounded by well-fed and (as she later noted) socially sophisticated playmates. She was one of twelve children, though her particular attachment was to an older brother, Rodrigo. His passion was for the tales of chivalry and the heroic lives of saints that were the favorite reading of many Spaniards in this age. But for him, and soon for his sister, these were more than stories: they were models for action.

> It was [Rodrigo] whom I most loved. We used to read the lives of saints together, and when I read of the martyrdoms suffered by saintly women for God's sake, I thought they had purchased grace very cheaply. I had a keen desire to die as they had done, in order to attain as quickly as possible the great blessings which, as I read, were laid up in Heaven. I used to discuss with my brother how we could become martyrs. We agreed to go off to the country of the Moors, begging our bread, so that they might behead us there.

The two children apparently set out on this venture, but soon encountered an uncle who brought them home.

This sense of driving purpose stayed with Teresa throughout her life. What was not clear to her for a long time, however, was what form it should take. Her mother's death certainly seemed to send her in a very different direction. Teresa was thirteen at the time, and the marriage of her oldest sister soon thereafter left her increasingly to her own devices. Her not unexpected response to her double loss was to give herself up to things of this world, rather than the next:

> I began to deck myself out and to try to attract others by my appearance, taking great trouble with my hands and hair, using perfumes and all the vanities I could get—and there were a good many of them, for I was quite meticulous. This excessive concern for my personal appearance lasted for many years.

She joined a fast crowd, and found herself drifting into what later she would condemn as abject sinfulness. Eventually, though, her father, worried by what was happening, placed the teenager in a nearby convent that was known for its strict regimen, and instructed its Augustinian nuns to give her a solid and more disciplined religious education.

For a while, Teresa did not much like her encounter with a cloistered world:

> For the first week I suffered a great deal, though not so much from being in a convent as from the suspicion that everyone knew about my vanity. At first I was very restless; but within a week, I was much happier than I had been in my father's house. Although at the time I had the greatest possible aversion from being a nun, I was very pleased to see nuns who were so good.

It was that example of goodness, and the wish to emulate it, that was to transform the young woman into a symbol, for her age, of the power of piety and virtue.

Teresa remained in the Augustinian convent for a year and a half. She became used to its relentless routine—the early rising, the prayers at the same time each day, the periods of reading and work, the regular rituals—and she soon absorbed the liturgical, spiritual, and scriptural teachings that occupied the nuns. She also had to grapple, as had Luther a few years earlier at his own Augustinian monastery over a thousand miles away, with the message of St. Augustine, the inspiration of the monastic order that bore his name. This Father of the Church had never actually laid down a rule, as had St. Benedict, the founder of the Benedictines; but in the eleventh century, more than six hundred years after he died, a group of reformers had drawn from his writings about the nature of the Christian community the guiding principles for a community of monks. What they taught, above all, was the overpowering majesty of God. A belief in the dominance, mystery, and unapproachability of God was central to Augustine's thought, and that doctrine had a variety of consequences for his adherents. For Luther, the response at first was terror, and then trust; for Teresa it was to be obedience, faith, and love.

At the end of her stay with the Augustinians, Teresa was still doubtful about becoming a nun. She had been with them only as a student-boarder, and she left largely because of a serious illness, which included the onset of the bouts of fainting that were to plague her all her life. But as she was recovering, she grew increasingly resolved to take up the religious vocation, despite opposition from her father. Her main encouragement came from an uncle, Don Pedro, a pious widower who later retired to a monastery, and who now gave her inspiring books to read, notably a copy of St. Jerome's letters, full of exhortations to piety. Perhaps most surprising to her, she discovered that her comments about "the vanity of the world" had persuaded her younger brother to become a friar. Soon thereafter, in the mid-1530s, when she herself was in her early twenties, Teresa decided to enter Avila's convent of La Encarnación. She completed her period as a novice a year later, in 1536, and remained at La Encarnación for another twenty-six years.

Teresa chose an order much less demanding than the Augustinian for her new home, and this may indicate how gradually she moved from worldliness to the austerity for which she would eventually be known. The Carmelites whom she now joined had once been an almost hermitlike order. They had been founded on Mount Carmel during the Crusades, in the belief that a succession of hermits had occupied the spot from the time of the prophet Elijah until Christ's coming; they had then converted to Christianity, and had been able to maintain a continuous presence of holy men thereafter. When the Muslims overran the Holy Land, the Carmelite order moved to Europe, but soon became known as a lax and privileged retreat for the children of the rich. Its members kept their family names, and did not even have to give up their lands or other material possessions.

La Encarnación, like other Carmelite houses, distinguished between wealthy and poor sisters, between aristocrats and nonaristocrats. As one of the more fortunate, Teresa had the title of Doña, a lovely suite of rooms on two floors, with fine furniture and its own kitchen, and friends and relatives both inside and outside the convent. She was certainly not cut off from the world. She went home when she was ill, which was often; she undertook a pilgrimage; she did work for the convent; and she stayed with her father during his final illness. It was a life that had been available for centuries to women of good families who either had a religious vocation or, more frequently, sought an alternative to the subjection that often awaited them in marriage. In a convent their status and independence were unchallenged, and they could lead an existence similar in its privileges to that of an aristocrat. At poorer houses there might be more work and less comfort—though the main burden was usually carried by the few women of relatively humble background who were admitted to an order—but in general it was the only career that enabled women to establish a distinct and respected place in society.

If the social standing of the convent may at one time have been important to Teresa, other concerns increasingly occupied her at La Encarnación. One of the people whom she went to visit was her uncle Don Pedro, and the books he now recommended had a profound effect on her. Most notable was a work by a Franciscan friar, Francisco de Osuna, called *The Third Spiritual Alphabet*, which emphasized quiet prayer, meditation, self-effacement, and solitude. The qualities it demanded posed a direct challenge to her life at La Encarnación, and the internal conflict that ensued took her one more step toward her life's mission.

Between the mid-1540s and the mid-1550s—that is, throughout her thirties—Teresa had visions that she interpreted as reprimands for her many failings, especially her comfortable and materialist existence at La Encarnación. Christ himself appeared to her, as she recalled in 1576:

> I saw Him with the eyes of the soul more clearly than I could ever
> have seen Him with those of the body; and it made such an impression
> upon me that, although it is now more than twenty-six years ago, I
> seem to have Him present with me still.

The experience was deeply distressing, for Christ rebuked both her and her frivolous friends. On another occasion she collapsed in tears at the sight of Christ "sorely wounded" by the punishments of his last days, and she spoke about "the torture caused me by my thoughts." She had no doubt who her visitor was, because he identified himself, but she hoped desperately that the visions, which were so troubling, would not continue. Yet they did. And she knew the cause of the struggle they represented: "All the things of God gave me great pleasure, yet I was tied and bound to those of the world." In her own, highly personal way, she was echoing St. Augustine's famous distinction between the heavenly and the earthly city: "Love of God maketh Jerusalem, love of the world maketh Babylon."

Steadily, insistently, Christ gained the upper hand. Finally, in the mid-1550s, as Teresa entered her forties, she made a decisive break with her past. She abandoned, once and for all, the worldly goods and practices that had caused her such grief, and decided to return to the austerity that had marked the early days of the Carmelite order. She renounced her secular name, Teresa de Cepeda y Ahumada, and took up a name inspired by her visions, Teresa de Jesus. But she was deeply concerned that these visions might be the work of the devil, and so, "after much inward strife and many fears," she turned to the local Church establishment to reassure her before she acted further on her convictions.

She could not have chosen a more difficult moment. The Church was just beginning to mount a major offensive to recover the ground lost to the Protestants over the previous thirty years. In 1540 another devout Spaniard guided by visions, Ignatius Loyola, had founded a new society of priests whose central aim had been to roll back the tide of dissent. He himself had seemed a dissenter for a while. He wanted his order to owe allegiance only to the pope, and that aroused the resentment of the ecclesiastical hierarchy, which feared that it would lose control over the faithful and be unable to suppress idiosyncratic ideas. Loyola, too, had looked to Christ for inspiration; where Teresa put Jesus in her name, he put it on his order, the Society of Jesus. That the Church was uneasy about his work— despite the loyalty, observance of form, and endorsement of ritual that were among the Jesuits' main weapons in their quest for souls —suggests how natural it was, in this time of confessional struggle, to resist any hint of unorthodoxy. The emphasis on tradition and ceremony was also essential to the conclusions that were being reached by the Council of Trent, a body whose deliberations, starting in 1540, had begun to lay out for the Church a program of reform that relied heavily on public rites. Where, in this structure of formal procedures as means of salvation, of dependence on priests and ceremonial, was there room for a person whose visions gave her direct contact with God? How could she justify a piety that required no intermediary, no Church that interceded with Christ on her behalf?

The problem was made worse by a notorious case that had arisen just ten years before, when the visions of an abbess in southern Spain had proved to be a fraud. Teresa thus had good cause for concern; and indeed, the problems she encountered, from the time of her conversion to an austere life around 1555 until her death in 1582, demonstrated the resistance a highly personal religion could provoke in an age of growing conformity.

Her first difficulties arose with the preachers in Avila to whom she turned for advice about her visions. Their initial conclusion, cautious and defensive, was that Teresa had to be under the influence of demons. How else was one to explain the reliance on private prayer, the raptures, the self-doubts, and in general the lack of application to the normal rituals and procedures of the Church? Fortunately for Teresa, they decided to turn her inquiries over to a local college that had recently been founded by the Jesuits. Here she came into contact with some of the leaders of the reform movement within the Spanish Church and gained a much more sympathetic hearing.

The concern of these reformers was to revive what they regarded as declining standards. In particular, they, like many Spaniards, were shocked by the discovery in the late 1550s of two cells of supposed Lutherans in the cities of Seville and Valladolid. It quickly became apparent that Teresa shared both the reformers' goals and their anxieties, and her Jesuit confessors soon reversed the initial reaction to her visions, declaring them to be holy and divinely inspired. They urged upon her a more strict self-mortification, and in the years that followed, the episodes of mystic union with God became more frequent and more intense. She now wrote of "a transport so sudden that it almost carried me away," and of ecstasies so powerful that they brought terror as well as comfort. At the same time, she felt that at last her soul was gaining the strength and security "to pulverize the devils" who were so persistent in their efforts to tempt the faithful. She became convinced that her inspiration was indeed divine, although she never ceased to suffer from the fear and distress that her demons caused.

The most famous of her raptures occurred in these years, around 1560, when an angel appeared to her:

> In his hands I saw a long golden spear and at the end of the iron tip I seemed to see a point of fire. With this he seemed to pierce my heart several times so that it reached to my entrails. When he drew it out I thought he was drawing them out with it, and he left me completely afire with a great love of God.

The vision caused her to go about in a stupor for days, and inspired one of the Catholic Church's most celebrated images, Bernini's *Ecstasy of St. Teresa*. But her description of the appearance of Christ himself is in some respects even more vivid:

Bernini, Ecstasy of St. Teresa. Bernini's celebrated image of Teresa idealizes the rather matronly saint at the moment of mystical transport—as an angel pierces her heart—that she describes in her autobiography. This stirring tableau transforms its setting, a small chapel, into a theater, where we are moved by the drama we are witnessing to appreciate the mysteries of faith.

One day, the Lord was pleased to reveal to me nothing but His hands, whose beauty was so great as to be indescribable. I also saw the Divine face. On St. Paul's Day, I saw a complete representation of his sacred Humanity. If there were nothing else in Heaven to delight the eyes but the extreme beauty of the glorified bodies there, that alone would be the greatest bliss. If I were to spend years and years imagining how to invent anything so beautiful, I could not do it. Even in its whiteness and radiance, it exceeds all we can imagine. It is a soft whiteness and radiance, which causes the eyes the greatest delight. By comparison with it, the brightness of our sun seems quite dim. Though I sometimes see Him looking at me compassionately, His gaze has such power that my soul cannot endure it.

Gradually, Teresa was being fortified to undertake a new role in the world, though once again it was to be in the face of conservative opposition.

The crucial step was Teresa's departure from La Encarnación in 1562. A year earlier, she had had a vision so terrifying that, even when describing it much later, she felt "fear depriving my body of its natural warmth." What was laid before her was hell itself—filthy, full of reptiles, evil-smelling, and stifling. That, she believed, was what God had saved her from, but he had shown it to her in order to remind her "of the great number of souls who are bringing damnation upon themselves, especially Lutherans." Distressed by her self-absorption, Teresa determined now to help others.

She had never cut herself off from public duties. The motherly figure, with the quick wit, had long been a favorite confidante for the women of Avila. Aristocrats had always felt at home with her, but increasingly her devoutness and comforting advice had attracted a wide following. Her standing outside of the formal hierarchy caused some uneasiness in the local Church, especially because, according to official doctrine, women could not administer a sacrament, and thus could not hear confession, which was what some of her visitors thought was happening. The uneasiness intensified when Teresa announced the decision that was the consequence of her vision of hell. Together with four companions who had been won over by her example, she wished to found a new convent, true to the original austerity of the Carmelites. God himself had spoken to her, had given her this mission, and had urged her to call the new establishment San José, after Christ's earthly father, who had interceded for her during her earliest mystic struggles. The convent was to be the heart of a reform that would transform the Carmelite order and make it a much more disciplined means of redeeming souls.

In order to restore proper monastic standards, Teresa laid down four basic principles for her nuns. First, they had to take a vow of poverty. They were to be discalced—that is, barefoot (though in fact they wore sandals as a sign of humility)—Carmelites. All worldly possessions, dowries, and family connections were renounced; ordinary charity and their own work had to sustain them. Second, all class distinctions were dissolved. Never an advocate of *limpieza de sangre*, Teresa accepted piety wherever she found it and demanded equal humbleness for everyone. Third, she revived the notion of enclosure: of a convent cut off from the outside world, with interchange permitted only for strict necessities and for specific missions. Discipline and prayer could not flourish without this separate existence, free from temptation. To minimize even the internal conflicts and factions that could arise, Teresa also limited the size of her convents: San José was restricted to thirteen nuns. Finally, like Ignatius Loyola, she made obedience (especially to one's confessor) the heart of her order:

> I have seen through experience the great good that comes to a soul when it does not turn aside from obedience. Through this practice one advances in virtue and gains humility. In obedience lies security from the dread of straying from the path to heaven. If souls truly resign themselves, by practicing holy obedience and surrendering the intellect to it, the devil will cease attacking. Those who practice obedience have resolutely surrendered their will to God's will.

Following these principles, the Discalced Carmelites developed a vigor, and qualities of determination and devoutness, that soon set them apart from the unreformed members of the order.

But the initial response of the authorities was suspicion and resistance. "There descended upon us," Teresa later wrote, "a persecution so severe that it is impossible in a few words to describe it." The vow of poverty, the dissolution of social distinctions, and the insistence on enclosure aroused the hostility of the rich and powerful, who feared that their daughters would become destitute and inaccessible. Local municipal officials were concerned that the convent would become a public burden. And many in the ecclesiastical hierarchy were still uneasy about the internalized habits of prayer—what they regarded as uncontrolled forms of devotion—that Teresa promoted. Her more spiritual path to salvation, with its downgrading of ceremonial, smacked of Lutheranism. Even her emphasis on obedience did not seem reassuring. And they recalled, darkly, her *converso* background. At the very least, she did not fit easily into standard, orthodox structures, and thus doubt and opposition were unavoidable.

Eventually, however, Teresa's friends among local reform-minded churchmen convinced Avila's bishop, the crucial figure in the deliberations, that her inspiration was indeed divine and that he should endorse her new foundation. The Discalced Carmelites were at last established in 1562, and thereafter she was able to focus her attention on the tireless promotion of her new order. She journeyed throughout Spain during the remaining twenty years of her life, establishing convents, persuading Carmelites to reform, and ensuring that her ideas gained the largest possible audience. And she did not restrict herself to women. In her travels, she met a young Carmelite friar, Juan de San Matías, who felt drawn to the solitary life of the hermit. He became an instant disciple; when Teresa told him she would support his founding of the first Discalced Carmelite monastery only if he were patient, he replied: "On condition that I don't have to wait too long."

Juan, who took the name Juan de la Cruz (John of the Cross), became her most ardent follower, a tiny, dark, intense figure, for whom she developed great affection. "Although he is small," she said, "he is great in the eyes of God." Like his mentor, he embraced austerity and discipline, and he became a highly effective reformer. His special talent, however, was literary: he conveyed his vision of the soul's tribulations and redemption in works of both prose and poetry—notably *The Dark Night of the Soul* and *The Living Flame of Love*—that have become classics of Spanish literature. The bond between the two mystics, strengthened when Juan took on the role of confessor, both to Teresa and to the nuns of La Encarnación, was symbolized in a famous story told by one of the nuns. She apparently came into a room where they were discussing divine mysteries; as she watched, they became more deeply absorbed, and their chairs levitated to the ceiling. Although the spirituality they shared remains unfathomable, we can perhaps see it reflected in the unearthly scenes painted by their younger contemporary El Greco (PLATE VIII).

More common were the accounts that emphasized Teresa's simplicity and humanity, and her message of comfort to all believers. When her carriage got stuck in the mud one day, she was said to have looked heavenward and said: "God, if this is the way you treat your friends, no wonder you have so few of them!" That sense of a direct relationship with the deity, and of faith as a nurturing force, made her a legendary and redoubtable presence during her last years. But the opposition of the Church, which felt that she was circumventing its precepts and structures, never died away.

Some of Teresa's nuns were excommunicated, John of the Cross was imprisoned, and not until the last year of her life did her movement gain a sympathetic hearing from the stern and devout, but conventional, king of Spain, Philip II. Only then, in 1581, did the Discalced Carmelites finally gain the official acceptance and independence that ensured their survival. In the long run, their high standards won them a position in the Spanish Church far stronger than that of the traditional Carmelites. Yet it was a struggle, in which they succeeded largely because of the reputation and persistence of their founder.

Renaissance Spain, in other words, was not exactly welcoming to innovators. Although they may now be recognized as saints and stalwarts of the Church, in their own time Loyola, Teresa, and John of the Cross often seemed to be as compelled to play the role of the dissenter as had Hus, a hundred years before. Of the three, Teresa was perhaps the most remarkable, for she had the added burden of her gender in a fiercely male world. It was perhaps in recognition of her extraordinary achievement that Rome canonized her more rapidly than either of her famous contemporaries. In one of the fastest processes in its history, the Church made Teresa a saint in 1622, just forty years after her death. Yet the honor would have flabbergasted the anguished, ever-searching nun, who would have seen no glory for herself in the visions of goodness, light, and faith that came to her as an undeserved gift from God.

Michel de Montaigne

SOUTHWESTERN France and northeastern Spain make up one of the classic borderlands of Europe, a meeting place of adjacent cultures. Here Basques, Gascons, and Catalans live in close proximity, and the sea on two sides prevents the redoubtable barrier of the Pyrenees from blocking the mixture of peoples. To this day the natives are known for their independence, especially from the distant capitals of Paris and Madrid to which they pay reluctant allegiance. It was not surprising that, when revolts erupted against central governments throughout Europe in the middle of the seventeenth century, some of the most bitter and radical acts of resistance to royal authority should should have erupted in the two great cities of the region, Bordeaux and Barcelona. Gascony regularly provided sanctuary for Catalans, and Catalonia for Gascons; moreover, this area of France was unique in its ties to England, and the area of Spain unique in its ties to Italy—not to mention the Basques, linked by Celtic origins to Cornwall and Wales.

Traditions of political and cultural distinctiveness were, of course, linked to unorthodoxies of other kinds. In the Middle Ages, for example, the Pyrenean village of Montaillou was an extraordinary center of heretical and eccentric ideas, a target of the Inquisition unlike any other. The region was also the setting for *The Song of Roland*, the famous story of crusade and of encounter between Christian and Muslim. If one recalls, in addition, the refuge it offered, both to Jews expelled from Spain in the 1490s and to the Huguenots, the Protestants persecuted by the French crown in the next century, one can understand its reputation as a home for multiple and rarely conventional beliefs. And indeed, it was a woman of Marrano origin—descended from a Jewish family that had been forced to flee Spain—who gave birth in 1533, in a château near Bordeaux, to the most famous of the intellectual dissenters of these borderlands: Michel de Montaigne.

Remarkably, amid the hundreds of pages he was to write about himself, Montaigne never once mentioned his mother, though he was always to be fascinated by Jewish culture, and was to visit synagogues on his travels. He apparently just did not get on well with her, and the one personal document she left, her will, suggests that, although she gave birth to nine children—of whom Michel was the oldest to survive infancy—she had a hard time with all of her family, except for one daughter. It may also be that, as something of a snob, her son was more interested in his father's lineage, which (according to his exaggerated claim) had enjoyed long-standing noble status. In fact, it was his prosperous great-grandfather, a herring and wine trader in Bordeaux, who had bought the country estate which conferred a minor title on its owners, and where Michel was born. What would not have embarrassed him, however, was that there were Jewish and Huguenot tinges in the family—through his mother, and through two Protestant siblings—while he and his father remained loyal to the Roman Church. The clash of opinion was to be one of the fuels of his life's work.

Yet it remains noteworthy that only his father drew from Montaigne expressions of open and unrestrained admiration:

This anonymous portrait of "Lord Montaigne," with his splendid robes and family crest, created the aristocratic image that the essayist was fond of claiming for his recently ennobled family.

> I have had the best and most indulgent father there ever was, who descended from a line famous for brotherly love. His manner was grave, mild, and modest. He was most careful to be neat and decent, and he was adroit in all manly sports. He seldom mounted the stairs without bounding up three or four steps at a time. He spoke little and well. He received learned men in his home like saints; he collected their words like so many oracles. Never was there a more charitable and public-spirited soul.

Such affection might seem strange when one recalls the educational plan this father laid out for Michel, and then followed without compromise. Its central purpose was to make sure that the boy would be entirely at home with the classics which, so Renaissance humanism taught, were the best model for a virtuous life. Accordingly, until he was six, he heard nothing but Latin. For the father this may have been easy: he was an excellent linguist, fluent in Spanish, Italian, and French. But he now imposed his standards on the entire household, and this episode alone may go far to explain his wife's discomfort with life at the château. For Michel, however, as he later noted, the result was that "without artifice, books, grammar, rules, whipping or tears, I learned to speak a pure Latin. What they gave to others in French for translation, they gave to me in bad Latin to turn into good."

Following that start, which took him far ahead of most of his contemporaries, the boy was sent to a new humanist school in Bordeaux. It was no wonder he found it tedious, for the purpose of most such schools was to teach Latin. Instead, Montaigne spent his time with the writings of Ovid, Vergil, and Terence, starting the extraordinary accumulation of learning on which he was to draw in later years. For schools, however, which he felt inspired a hatred rather than a love of books, he had little but contempt:

> They are a real jail of captive youth. Go in at lesson time: you hear nothing but cries from tortured boys and from masters drunk with rage. What a way to arouse zest for their lesson in these tender and timid souls, to guide them with a horrible scowl and hands armed with rods. There is nothing like arousing appetite and affection; otherwise all you make out of them is asses loaded with books. By whipping, they are given their pocketful of learning. But if learning is to do us good, we must not merely lodge it within us, we must espouse it.

He left school at the age of thirteen, and for the next eight years or so underwent the education in refinement that was expected of a young nobleman. How and where he received it we do not know—possibly at one of the academies that taught manners and the art of war, perhaps at court in Paris. What is certain is that in this period he also received the training in the law, at either Bordeaux or Toulouse, that made possible his public career as a magistrate. It was this that was to occupy him for most of the 1550s and 1560s, until he reached the momentous decision that was to transform his life at the age of thirty-seven.

The life of the law was chosen for Montaigne by his father, but he seems to have taken up the career without complaint. Given his social standing and resources, he became a judge in nearby courts, serving from 1557 to 1570 on the chief court of the region, the Parlement of Bordeaux, one of eight such Parlements which together constituted the highest court in France. Like all such positions, it was bought, and when Montaigne retired, he sold it—a transaction that only confirmed his cynicism about the law's formalities and hypocrisies. Being a magistrate did take him into the larger world of politics as well as the petty details of daily affairs. This was a time of religious war, and the Parlement was caught up in the struggles; moreover, as an important local figure, Montaigne was often at the royal court in Paris in these years. But it was the inadequacy of all legal systems, and the foibles in human behavior they revealed, that drew his chief attention and, as usual, provided the lessons on which he would later comment.

> I was plunged over the ears in law. There is nothing more subject to change than the laws. Men amuse me when they try to give certainty to laws by saying that some of them are perpetual. But our fine human reason confounds the face of things into an image of its own futility and fickleness. It is a pity there is not a closer relation between the laws we have and our capacity to obey them. To whom do we prescribe the laws we expect no one to obey? From the same sheet of paper on which a judge writes his sentence against an adulterer, he tears off a piece to scribble a love-note to his colleague's wife. The most desirable laws are the simplest, the most general, and the least likely to be invoked. In a field of learning so lacking in limits and with so many opinions as law, an endless confusion must result. Our laws maintain their credit not because they are just, but because they are laws.

After well over a decade of such observation, and as he rec-ognized that he was approaching his fortieth year, Montaigne resolved to reorient his life completely, a redirection whose consequences bear comparison with other famous mid-life shifts, from St. Augustine and Luther to Gauguin. What Michel decided in 1570 was that he would retire from the world in order to have time to understand himself.

Not that he became a hermit. He was to take a long trip to Italy ten years later; he was to serve as mayor of Bordeaux in the 1580s; and he was to be consulted about law reform by the future king Henry IV. Nor did the civil wars that swirled through this nonconformist area of France leave him untouched. Although he hated violence, and insisted that his doors always be left open to avert the need for force, on the one occasion when troops arrived, took him briefly prisoner, and robbed him, it was his bravery (though he attributed it to luck) that saved his household from harm. Moreover, that household was by no means a trivial distraction from his writing.

Montaigne had married in 1565 a beautiful young woman, Françoise, twelve years his junior, who had been picked for him by his father from a prominent Bordeaux family. Priding himself on his detachment, and his ability to judge everything dispassionately, Montaigne later claimed that he never saw her in the nude, despite the conception of the couple's six children. He also enjoyed being snide about wedlock, approving the aphorism that the best marriage was between a deaf man and a blind woman. In fact, though, he clearly accepted, understood, and even relished both the ups and the downs of the matrimonial state:

> Whoever sees me at one point cold, and at another point very tender, toward my wife, and believes one or the other to be counterfeit, is an ass.

It is clear that the Montaignes led a full and busy life; yet it is equally clear that Françoise took little interest in the writing that preoccupied her husband during his long retirement, hidden away in the study he created for himself in a tower on their estate. That may perhaps explain Montaigne's laconic comment that marriage was like a gilded birdcage: those on the inside wanted to get out, while those on the outside wanted to get in.

What is unmistakable is that there is nothing in his remarks about marriage to compare with the affection he expressed for the one great friend of his life, the humanist lawyer and poet Etienne de La Boétie. They met when Montaigne was in his late twenties, and they knew each other for only four or five years. Yet the erudite Etienne—married, sedate, and thoughtful—was able in that period to counter the inclination of his friend, younger and a bachelor at the time, to fritter away his days as a loose-living man about town. This was the period when Montaigne showed the first signs of more serious intellectual interests, and it is apparent that his anxious bedside vigil during the last days before La Boétie's unexpected death at the age of thirty-two influenced him profoundly. He recalled the events many years later:

> Toward evening, he began to show the unmistakable image of death. He said to me, "My brother, stay by my side." In his distress, he kept calling to know if I were near him. At last he composed himself, and I rejoined his wife. An hour later, after calling my name, he uttered a deep sigh and gave up the ghost. If I compare all the rest of my life with the four years in which I enjoyed his sweet companionship, it is nothing but smoke and a dark and tedious night.

His reaction to the loss was to throw himself even more intensely into his former wild life, until his father brought the tumult to an end by arranging his marriage. But death stalked Montaigne in these years, removing not only La Boétie but also a brother (killed by a tennis ball), his beloved father, and his first two children. Indeed, only one of his six daughters was to survive beyond a few months. These were also years of plague and of civil war, and there is no question that it was the oppressive presence of death and loss that persuaded Montaigne to retire to his tower. Here he would try, or essay, to understand himself, his fear of dying, and how he could respond to the terrifying world around him. Thus was born a new form of literature, the essay—informal, meandering, and capable of addressing any subject its author chose. Rarely, however, has it been as penetrating as it was in the hands of its inventor.

The audacity of the enterprise was stunning. Montaigne's avowed purpose was simply to pick a subject, and then allow his mind to roam through it, following whatever trains of thought it suggested. Thus an essay on cannibals takes up ancient geography; the purposes of war; the story of the Spartan Leonidas at Thermopylae; appropriate quotations from Vergil, Juvenal, and others; and the quality of songs. There are subtle unifying threads, and none of the essays is as artless as it looks, but the aim always is self-analysis and self-revelation, rather than definitive statements about the subject at hand. Montaigne is exposing how he thinks, how he feels. Without preaching—in fact, by exposing frailties—he suggests that his exploration of himself offers, in microcosm, an insight into human nature in general. He may know only one person, but if he follows, ruthlessly and honestly, every element, every strength and shortcoming, of that person's mind and emotions, he will have something to say about all people. As he put it, "I may contradict myself, but I always speak the truth."

Initially, Montaigne's concern was to find ways of coming to terms with death. He took comfort from the advice of the ancient Stoics: exercise self-discipline and remain calm in all circumstances. He would doubtless have applauded Philip II of Spain who, it was said, died so serenely that it was almost as if he had done it before. But he was never comfortable with the acceptance of pain that the Stoics required, and gradually he moved on from other people's answers to his own. Driven by the evidence of human weakness that was all around him—at one point he spoke of "being disgusted with the world I frequent"—he turned toward skepticism. This, too, was a position with roots in antiquity, which he gladly acknowledged. Indeed, since radical skepticism—a total refusal to see truth anywhere—is fearsomely difficult to sustain, there often seems more in common among skeptics of all ages than between the individual skeptic and his own times. Not that Montaigne was alone. Thanks to the humanists, the ancient skeptics had become well known, and the uncertainties and clashes of rival authorities of the sixteenth century had encouraged a number of writers to adopt their views. One contemporary, Sánchez the Skeptic, was so reluctant to assert anything that he published a book consisting entirely of question marks.

For Montaigne, however, skepticism was ultimately a means of achieving self-understanding and discovering moral truths. At one level it entailed a profound dissent from all received opinion, and certainly from all pretension. Even kings, he said, sit on their thrones with their rear ends. And in intellectual matters, pride and certainty were merely foolish:

> The sky and the stars have been moving for three thousand years. Everybody believed it until Cleanthes maintained that it was the earth that moved. In our day Copernicus has grounded this doctrine so well that he can use it systematically for all astronomical deductions. What are we to get out of that, unless that we should not bother to decide between the two? Who knows whether a third opinion, a thousand years from now, will not overthrow the preceding two?

On the other hand, there seemed no point in challenging one's religious inheritance, since one could never be sure about an alternative.

> It seems to me great presumption to place one's opinions in such high esteem that one overthrows public peace in order to establish them. Knowing my own shifting nature, I have cultivated a steadfast belief, which has hardly changed from its original form. Since I am incapable of choosing for myself, I have stayed in the place where God has put me.

What he was leading toward was a way of accepting a turbulent world, not by relying on shoddy certainties but through self-knowledge.

For Montaigne, that knowledge could be gained only through experience. If certainty was impossible, one could not even say, "I know nothing." His motto was "What do I know?" But experiences, and one's reaction to them, could offer guidance. The essays, therefore, focus on the events, the anecdotes, and the ideas that enable their author to define what seems natural. Presumption is the enemy; honest reaction is the source of all hope. And so he must tell us everything he can about himself, in the hope that we will recognize something of ourselves as we learn about him.

Much of the essay "On Vanity," for instance, is given over to the reasons he decided to leave his family in 1580 and take a year-and-a-half journey, for sheer pleasure, through Italy.

> Among human characteristics, this one is rather common: to be better pleased with other people's things than our own. This greedy appetite for new and unknown things fosters in me the desire to travel, but other circumstances contribute to it. I gladly turn aside from governing my house. It is too monotonous and mingled with bothersome thoughts. There is always something going wrong. When I consider my affairs from a distance, I find they prosper beyond my calculations. But when I am in the midst of the job, a thousand things give me reason to fear. It is pitiful to be in a place where everything you see concerns you. Absent from home, I strip off all such thoughts. At home I am responsible for all that goes wrong. When I travel I have only myself and the use of my money to think about.

The larger implications emerged only from the particulars of attitude and behavior.

Nor did Montaigne shrink from accumulating new experiences, like the trip to Italy, during his "retirement." Soon after he returned, he agreed to serve as mayor of Bordeaux, and threw himself into political life. The dominant princely family of the region were the Bourbons, whose leader, Henry of Navarre, was soon to become king of France. That they were Huguenots was of no concern to the irenic Montaigne, who had already tried, in the 1570s, to reconcile them with their enemies in the civil wars of the time. Secure in his own allegiance to the Roman Church, and associated, since his days at the royal court, with the peacemaking efforts of the Catholic queen mother, Catherine de' Medici, he was delighted to accept her invitation to help mediate between the two sides in 1588. Indeed, he could take pride that both Catherine and Henry had nominated him for the mayoralty of Bordeaux. He now headed for Paris on a mission that was to last for over a year, but he soon discovered that in the capital's politically fevered atmosphere his middle ground merely aroused suspicion. Regarded as a friend of the Huguenot Henry, he was thrown into the Bastille by the leaders of the Catholic cause in Paris. Catherine rushed to intervene, and within four hours had him released. Montaigne, expressing more concern for his health than his safety—he was suffering his first attack of gout—had only one comment on the episode: "This was the first prison I had ever seen. I escaped, but it grieves me to think it was more by luck than by justice."

It was while he was in Paris that the fifty-five-year-old met a female admirer more than thirty years his junior who was to be one of the joys of the remaining four years of his life, until his death in 1592.

> I have taken pleasure in making public the hopes I have for Marie de Gournay, my *fille d'alliance*, whom I love more than a daughter of my own, and cherish in my retirement and solitude as one of the best parts of my own being. She is the only person I still think about in the world. If youthful promise means anything, her soul will some day be capable of the finest things. The judgement she made of the *Essays*, she a woman, and in this age, and so young, and the remarkable eagerness with which she loved me and wanted my friendship, simply through the esteem she formed for me before she had seen me, is a phenomenon very worthy of consideration.

This determined bluestocking had lost her father, and she was able, in effect, to persuade the essayist to become his adoptive replacement. She was an extraordinary example, a generation before the *salons* made such a career more common, of the well-born female who devoted herself to the world of letters. Montaigne made her his literary executor, and after his death she stayed for over a year with his family, and became the principal editor and advocate of the *Essays*. There is no doubt that the relationship between the famous old man and his enthusiastic young admirer gave him considerable comfort in his last years, as he pondered the final lessons he could draw from his life.

What he had cherished, above all, was his freedom as an individual:

> I so love freedom that, if someone forbade me access to the remotest corner of the Indies, I should feel myself a little hemmed in. If the authorities under whom I live should so much as wag a finger at me, I would immediately go in search of others, no matter where.

In some respects, this was the credo of the ultimate dissenter. Unlike

LES
ESSAIS
DE MICHEL SEI-
GNEVR DE MONTAIGNE.

*EDITION NOVVELLE, TROVVEE APRES
le deceds de l'Autheur, reueüe & augmentée par luy d'vn
tiers plus qu'aux precedentes Impreßions.*

A PARIS,

Chez ABEL L'ANGELIER, au premier pilier
de la grande falle du Palais.

CIƆ.IƆ. XCV.

AVEC PRIVILEGE.

The magnificent title page of the 1595 edition of Montaigne's *Essays* was a fitting
tribute both to the author and to the efforts of his disciple, Marie de Gournay, who
worked tirelessly to have this corrected edition published three years after he died.

the famous rebels of his age—the Luthers, the Calvins—who detested what they were told, but did not hesitate to tell others what to do or think, Montaigne wanted nothing imposed on anyone (PLATE VII). The beginning of wisdom, he argued, was doubt. Every received opinion, every authoritative pronouncement or custom, had to be regarded as suspect. The only guides to behavior, feeling, and thought lay within; the external could never be trusted. But even when some degree of assurance could be reached, one had to embrace it with absolute modesty. Heroics were always questionable; the acceptance of limits was the antidote to the inflated claims and passions of his discordant age.

> Greatness of soul is not so much pressing upward and forward as knowing how to set oneself in order and circumscribe oneself. It regards as great whatever is adequate, and shows its elevation by liking moderate things better than eminent ones. There is no knowledge so hard to acquire as the knowledge of how to live this life well and naturally.

If in some respects Montaigne was arguing against the very qualities of determination and commitment that had created Renaissance culture, his critique of his times, like Petrarch's, became a powerful influence on the generations that followed. For scientists like Bacon, Descartes, and Pascal the quest for certainty took on a new urgency; and for moral philosophers down to the existentialists of our own time it has been impossible to explore the nature of ethics or truth without reference to Montaigne. He, of course, would have found such celebrity mere fancy:

> What is more fortuitous than reputation? It is chance that attaches glory to us by whim. He who first saw the resemblance between a shadow and glory did better than he intended.

PART V

The Search for Order

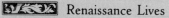

Clouet, Catherine de' Medici. This somber yet vivid portrait shows Catherine simply dressed in widow's black. The face, on which all attention is focused, reflects the intelligence, the thoughtfulness, and perhaps even the persistence of an often troubled queen.

A Prince

B Y THE 1550S AND 1560S, it was becoming clear that the conflict spawned by the Reformation was undermining political stability and threatening to tear European society apart. Religious wars had become part of the scenery, and the struggles between competing orthodoxies were inspiring ever fiercer confrontations. For a Montaigne, the solution was to reject all sides and resort to a skeptical tolerance. But for governments, which saw their authority crippled by rebels who claimed a higher loyalty—faith—neither escape nor perfect compromise was possible. Their need was to reestablish some semblance of order, so that the political and social hierarchy could resume control and reimpose stability on Europe's divided and strife-torn states. ❨No monarch of the late sixteenth century felt that need more urgently than Catherine de' Medici, queen and queen mother of France. She knew and admired Montaigne, but her agenda could not have been more different. Like all the rulers of her day, she sought to extend her own powers and those of her dynasty. To achieve that goal in a time of such turbulence, however, was well-nigh beyond hope. Yet she persisted, and the effort itself, doomed though it often was, revealed much about the preoccupations and ambitions of the rulers of society:

the members of the order of princes, both male and female, in Renaissance times. For whether they were queens or kings, all were seen as the heirs, in this age of growing interest in the possibilities of power, of the character whom Machiavelli had fashioned as their epitome, *The Prince*. And for Catherine that heritage was both immediate and direct.

Catherine de' Medici

NO family is more closely identified with the Renaissance than the Medici. Starting with the austere and remote Cosimo, known in Florence as *pater patriae*, father of the fatherland, they produced a galaxy of leaders of European politics, finance, trade, religion, and artistic patronage that perhaps only the Habsburgs, who were both emperors and kings of Spain, could match. Their eye for talent and their reputation for political shrewdness were legendary. Cosimo himself had emerged out of the struggles of powerful rivals as the dominant figure in Florence in the early fifteenth century, and he had wielded his authority cannily and unobtrusively, although (as he admitted) not merely "by saying pater nosters." But he also put his stamp on Florence by supporting Donatello, Brunelleschi, Fra Angelico, and others who were transforming the face of the city as well as the art of the time.

Cosimo's grandson, Lorenzo, nicknamed "Il Magnifico," exercised his control over Florence more openly in the 1470s and 1480s. At the same time, he used his patronage (of artists like Botticelli and Michelangelo, and renowned scholars who clustered at his court) to exalt the name of Medici both for his contemporaries and for all ages. It was the combination of art and politics, each serving the other, and continuing to do so in the sixteenth century, when Medici popes made Rome the center of High Renaissance art, that gave the family its unique aura.

The Medici women were no less redoubtable than the men, as they demonstrated when the family entered a difficult period following the death of Lorenzo. After a series of weak and incompetent leaders, a lack of male heirs brought his line to an end, and Florence was eventually to be ruled by a collateral line, the descendants of Cosimo's brother. During this period it was primarily the women who held the family together, notably Lorenzo's imposing daughter-in-law, Alfonsina Orsini, herself the member of one of Italy's great families, his daughter Maddalena, and his granddaughter Clarice, who married into the Strozzi, another potent clan.

It was Clarice who was the heroine of one of the most extraordinary scenes in the family's history. It took place in 1527, shortly after Rome was sacked by the troops of the Emperor Charles V. The pope at the time, Clement VII, was a nephew of Lorenzo, and one result of the defeat was the expulsion of his family from Florence. Clarice, however, refused to flee. She denounced her pusillanimous relatives, including the pope, as unworthy of their Medici ancestors, and encouraged the remaining men to leave with the ringing taunt: "The Medici Palace is not a stable for mules." Though they could depart with the family name, she said, she would stay on to defend the family honor. She was still scolding when a mob entered the palace, and drove her out.

The whole episode was reminiscent of the actions, a few years before, of an earlier Catherine, a distant kinswoman and ally of Florence named Caterina Sforza. She had been left in charge of a fortress besieged by the notorious Cesare Borgia. When Cesare threatened to kill her sons, she climbed on the ramparts, lifted her skirts, and called out to the besieging army: "Behold the forge from which I can stamp out more sons!" This heritage of indomitable females, unshakable and determined even in the most perilous of circumstances, was as essential to the Medici as the legendary traditions of artistic patronage and political acumen. And few were to have a more consistent need for those qualities of endurance than the young Medici named Catherine whom Clarice, her aunt, spirited away to the family's country home when the mob invaded the palace in Florence in 1527.

Born eight years before to a grandson and namesake of Lorenzo Il Magnifico, Catherine had become an orphan at the age of three weeks, when fever carried off both her parents; she herself had nearly died twice in early childhood. For her first year she had been raised by her ambitious grandmother, Alfonsina, who was also famous for maintaining the family's backbone amidst male pusillanimity. When the old woman died, Catherine passed to the care of a great-aunt, Lucrezia, the last of Lorenzo Il Magnifico's surviving children, and, most important, to her aunt Clarice. The famous scene of 1527 swirled around the impressionable child, and for the next three years she was to endure the first of the many difficult situations that demanded a full measure of the determination and the instinct for survival that were her legacy.

The republican government of Florence, seeking a Medici hostage, had insisted that Clarice return the child to the city, where she was placed, first in a hostile, and then in a more friendly, convent. Though her treatment varied, it was decidedly not what a young princess was used to. An ambassador who saw her at this time reported: "I have never seen anyone of her age so quick to feel the good and the ill that are done her." In 1528 Clarice died, and a year later, as Medici troops besieged Florence, threats were made to expose the ten-year-old Catherine on the walls of the city or even to cast her into a brothel. Her nuns protected her, and so the council decided to move her back to the less friendly convent. When the emissary arrived, he discovered that the girl had cropped her hair and announced her wish to become a nun. The device gained her a brief reprieve, but for most of the remaining year of the siege, she was to be under the strict regimen of the less friendly convent.

The final victory of the Medici, in 1530, made the eleven-year-

Valois Tapestry, Festival with Tournament. This magnificent tapestry, one of a series, depicts a knightly joust at the pageant that Catherine sponsored in Bayonne. For all the color and commotion of the spectacle, the festivities are dominated by the figure of the queen, clothed as usual in her widow's weeds.

PLATE IX

Walter Ralegh and Son. This carefully posed portrait shows Ralegh dressed in the high fashion that he favored (note the bows on the shoes, matching the outfit). Next to him is his equally elegant son, Wat, who was to die in Guiana. The boy's sword indicates the family's knightly status, and the doffed hat is a mark of the respect for his father that, in reality, Wat did not always show.

PLATE X

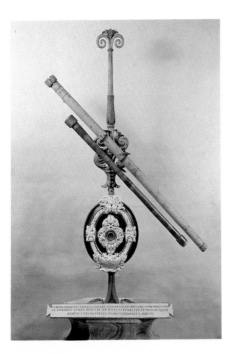

Galileo's Telescope. Galileo's skills as an instrument maker—an occupation that supplemented his income during the Padua years—are evident in the telescope he made for his revolutionary observations in 1609. With the smaller sighting scope alongside it, the instrument has lenses that recent tests have established to be virtually perfect optically.

Caravaggio, The Supper at Emmaus. The immediacy and drama with which Caravaggio transformed the art of painting permeate this scene: the supper in Emmaus, at which disciples suddenly recognize the resurrected Christ. The craggy faces, the almost touchable food, the sharply defined light, the moment of high emotion, and the theatrical gestures are Caravaggesque trademarks that enlivened the work of his many followers in Artemisia's generation.

PLATE XI

Artemisia Gentileschi, Judith Slaying Holofernes. The most gruesome of Artemisia's depictions of this scene shows the biblical heroine at the moment when she is decapitating the enemy general. The gushing blood and the dramatic light create an immediacy and power worthy of Caravaggio.

PLATE XII

old heroine a considerable celebrity. Her distant cousin, Pope Clement VII, brought her to Rome, where he listened to her tales of mistreatment, pampered her, and gave all to believe that "she is what he loves best in the world." Within a year he had arranged for her one of the finest matches in Europe: to Henry, second son of the king of France. It was a marriage the French accepted only to cement a papal alliance, for Catherine was penniless, and a contemporary description was not exactly flattering: "She is small and thin; her features are not delicate, and she has bulging eyes, like most of the Medici." But the pope himself accompanied the young bride to her wedding in France in 1533, and he stayed long enough to pay (as was customary at the time) two visits to the bedchamber on the nuptial night— together with his host, King Francis I—in order to make sure that the two fourteen-year-olds were indeed coupling.

Once again, Catherine was essentially alone. Her mother had come from a fine French family, but they were of little consequence at court. The princess's task now was to learn to survive in the labyrinth of faction that surrounded her. During the next ten years, however, the hostility was palpable, especially after her brother-in-law died and Henry became heir to the throne. For Catherine seemed unable to have children, despite the ministrations of astrologers and magicians, and the prayers of all. In this age of dark speculation, that failure was enough to condemn her as evil and warped, and to raise the specter of divorce. The example of Henry VIII, across the Channel, disposing of a plethora of wives in the 1530s, simply because they failed to provide him with a son, was obvious and alarming. But then, in 1544, Catherine did at last give birth, in great pain, to a son, Francis—a future king, but one who would always be weak and sickly. Once the floodgates opened, though, a veritable torrent of pregnancies followed: nine more over the next decade, all brought to full term. For a mother merely to survive a birth in the sixteenth century, especially when surrounded by the doctors of the time, was a considerable achievement; to do so ten times was little short of miraculous, and a remarkable testimony to Catherine's resilience and determination.

Seven of the ten children lived into adulthood, but even so there is little evidence until late in his life that Henry showed much affection for his queen. His father had grown fond of the young princess, but the great love of Henry's life was a woman over twenty years his senior, Diane of Poitiers, with whom he had already had a child before his official heir was born. The situation called, once again, for Catherine's abilities as a survivor, and she managed to make an ally of the mistress, even at moments when leading courtiers were calling for the barren wife to be divorced. And she also made a staunch friend of the most formidable of the women in the French royal family, Marguerite of Navarre, Henry's aunt.

Catherine was used to powerful females—her adaptability and persistence made her one herself—but no one in her Medici experience or at the French court could have equaled the compelling figure of Marguerite. Long committed to Protestant beliefs, she gave John Calvin and other young reformers crucial encouragement and support. Her own family was brought out of the Church of Rome, and her daughter's marriage to a prince of Bourbon was to set in motion the fateful events that were to place a new dynasty, sympathetic at first to the Protestants, on the throne of France. Her grandson was to found that dynasty as Henry IV, but that was far in the future. In the meantime, she kept up her proselytizing. She persuaded both Catherine and Diane de Poitiers to begin reading the Bible for themselves, and her hopes for them did not dim even when an archbishop intervened, removing the Bibles that, he said, posed the same dangers as the Tree of Knowledge in the Garden of Eden, and banishing the reformed confessor who had been attached to the princess. Catherine's admiration for the *grande dame* who always included her in her prayers—and who claimed that it was only her pleas to the God of the reformed faith that had finally cured the princess's barren womb—never flagged. Catherine even named a daughter after her, though everyone agreed that there was only one "flower of the Marguerites."

Gradually, Henry's trust in his wife grew, especially after he succeeded to the crown as Henry II in 1547. He made her regent of the realm in the early 1550s, and gave her special responsibility for supplying his army when he left for Italy on a military campaign. Catherine took her duties with great seriousness, working tirelessly, attending to endless administrative details, and soon gaining a reputation for overzealousness. The king was impressed, and over the next few years the queen made her views increasingly known, especially on foreign-policy matters having to do with her native Italy.

This may well have been the happiest period of her life. Courtiers remarked on the king's increasing attention to her; she spent much of her time at the lovely royal châteaux along the Loire, where she could indulge her love of gardens and of decorations in the Italian style; and she doubtless pursued her passion for good cooking, which she was later to make an essential part of grand royal spectacles, thus helping to add refinement to the traditions of French dining.

But the good times did not last long. Henry was killed in a jousting accident in 1559, and her sickly oldest son, now Francis II, died little more than a year later. Her daughter-in-law, the eighteen-year-old Mary Queen of Scots, was as moved as anyone by the older woman's grief at Henry's death:

> She is still so troubled, and has suffered so much during the sickness of the late King, that, with all the worry she has had, I fear a grave illness. I believe that if the King her son were not so obedient that he does nothing but what she desires, she would soon die.

Catherine was now forty. During her remaining thirty years, she was to be a major figure on the international scene. For long periods she was to be the virtual ruler of France, and at all times she wielded significant influence over the government of the most populous country in Europe. But these were perhaps the most difficult and destructive decades in French history—over thirty years of vicious civil war, the longest the country ever had to endure—and there is little indication that Catherine, who knew so little gladness in her life, enjoyed any of them.

Just about all of the remarkable females who were her contemporaries seemed to tower over her: her heroic aunt Clarice, the devout

Marguerite, the dazzling Diane de Poitiers, the glamorous Mary Stuart of Scotland. Only the dour Mary Tudor of England, "Bloody" Mary, seemed less appealing; her younger sister, on the other hand, the famous Elizabeth I, showed a command of image making and self-promotion that made her a legendary monarch even to her contemporaries. It was hard enough to win a high reputation, let alone succeed in political affairs, with such comparisons near at hand. The task was made well-nigh impossible by Catherine's position as a foreigner, as a widow at a male and misogynist court, as a female in a country whose law forbade women from inheriting the crown, and as a ruler who kept shifting positions while seeking stability, compromise, and the middle ground amid the fanaticisms of civil war. Nor did she ever have the slightest chance of winning the esteem of the two great families, the Protestant Bourbons and the Catholic Guises, who struggled over the throne as it gradually became clear that the Valois line of Henry II was coming to an end.

It was small wonder, then, that she was disliked and distrusted by both sides in the wars. Recalling that the most notorious book of the century, Machiavelli's *Prince*, had been dedicated to her father, her contemporaries delighted in blaming all their ills on Catherine, denouncing her as cunning and untrustworthy, and assuming that every conspiracy and misfortune was the work of her hands. So common were the libels that the queen took to collecting them as they were published and making corrections in the margins, though she doubtless realized that the average reader probably believed everything they said. But the king who brought the civil wars to an end, the Bourbon grandson of Marguerite (and also Catherine's son-in-law), Henry IV, knew better:

> What could the poor woman do, with five little children on her arms after the death of her husband, and two families in France, ours and the Guises, trying to encroach on the Crown? Was she not forced to play strange parts to deceive the one and the other and yet—as she did—to protect her children, who were able to reign in succession by the wisdom of a woman so able? I marvel that she did not do worse!

That Catherine was mother to three kings of France, not to mention a king of Poland and a queen of Navarre—a record unique in the history of the French monarchy—may have consoled her little in her troubles. Yet the welfare of that progeny did indeed, as Henry IV so shrewdly observed, animate her policies and her life as a widow. Although the lack of male grandchildren doomed her family's hold on the throne, she consistently sought some degree of equilibrium amid the turbulence. As the embodiment of that policy, which she felt was in the best interests of the country as well as her children, she became the principal architect of a political outlook which, for all its novelty and unpopularity at the time, was to shape the future of European states.

In France the position that Catherine took was called *politique*, and this was by no means a term of approval. What the *politiques* stood for was the peace and stability of the realm above all else, and especially above the demands of religious belief. In an age of fierce devotion and uncompromising ideological commitment—when Catholics and Protestants pursued a murderous civil war for decades because those of each faith believed their enemies polluted the earth—this alternative, which relegated individual conviction to a secondary role, was intolerable. Yet despite the difficulties of maintaining the *politique* position, Catherine became its most persistent advocate, and thus, more than any other ruler of her time, the figure who most clearly pointed to a future in which religious diversity would not be allowed to tear a state apart.

She was by temperament well fitted for the task. Adaptability and perseverance had been second nature to her since childhood, and she had long known what it meant to be alone and have to fend for herself. As for her religious faith, that was determined by her family's traditional loyalty to the Roman Church, and it never became more than conventional. Yet her sympathy for the Protestants seems to have been genuine, prompted at first by her affection for Marguerite, and then reinforced as she witnessed their sufferings as a persecuted minority. A Protestant noblewoman who asked her to intercede on their behalf noted that

This engraving depicts one of the first of the violent incidents that precipitated over thirty years of religious war in France. Catholic soldiers (one of whom is depicted as stealing from the poor box, labeled "Donnez aux povres") interrupt a Protestant service in 1562, and the congregation flees out of windows and through the roof.

she understood nothing of their doctrine, and what had moved her to favor them was compassion and pity rather than any desire to be informed or instructed as to whether their doctrine was true or false. When she reflected that these poor people were so cruelly massacred, burned, and tormented, not for thieving, larceny, or brigandage, but simply for maintaining their opinions, and that because of them they went to death as to a marriage, she was moved to believe that there was something in it which surpassed natural reason.

Not that this daughter of the Medici rejected violence. She was prepared to take extreme measures when her own position, or that of her family, seemed threatened. Although her responsibility for the notorious St. Bartholomew's Day massacre—perhaps the most treacherous instance of the savagery of the civil wars—was probably exaggerated at the time (and has never been determined), she certainly condoned bloodshed when it served her purpose. Yet her prime instinct was to maneuver, to tolerate, and to find ways of advancing her aims that did not invite retribution.

For some, like Henry IV, the moderation and the dynastic purpose were understandable. For most, however, they seemed the product of a cynical and Machiavellian self-interest. If that was how she was characterized by the majority of her contemporaries, and indeed by the preponderance of historians ever since, her own judgment was very different, and she put it (not without good cause) in terms of gender:

> I hope it will be recognized that women are more inclined to conserve the kingdom than those who have put it in the condition in which it is. I trust you will show this statement to those who discuss the question, for it is the truth spoken by the mother of the King, whose only affection is for him and for the conservation of the kingdom and his subjects.

To conserve and to settle—that was what she struggled to do for nearly thirty fruitless years. If she considered it an ambition peculiarly associated with women, that may have been a result not only of her open relationship with the devout Protestant Marguerite but also of the efforts of her Catholic sister-in-law, another Marguerite, to advance religious toleration in her husband's Duchy of Savoy, on the border of that sink of Protestantism, Geneva. Compromise was Catherine's basic aim from the moment she proclaimed herself regent—after Francis II's death in 1560—and for as long as she controlled policy (during most of the fourteen-year reign of his brother, Charles IX). With the last of her sons, Henry III, she had less influence, though the presence at court during his reign of the

Italian financiers whom she patronized only intensified the unpopularity of the royal family. Through it all, however, she struggled to find the religious and political middle ground that might end the hatreds and the destruction. The record was quite astonishing, and was unsurpassed in this century of ideological loathing and confrontation.

It began in 1561, before the outbreak of war, when she organized a colloquy of Calvinists and Catholics at Poissy—the last time there was a serious discussion between leaders of the two faiths anywhere in Europe. It continued when she drafted an edict of toleration the following year, and then, a year later, engineered a "pacification" of France after the first months of devastating civil war. In 1570 she brought about another "pacification," and in 1577 an edict of peace. To enforce the latter she worked strenuously for two years at internal diplomacy, traveling throughout southern France to calm fears and urge compromise.

She had undertaken such a journey before, in the 1560s, and it was clear to all who saw her that she seemed able to relax during the strains and anxieties of these years only when she approached the palm-tinged warmth of her native Mediterranean. So relaxed did she become that she was known to joke with those who traveled with her, even with the famous "flying squadron" of thirty-five ladies from the finest families of France who accompanied her wherever she went. The ladies would all speak "Huguenot"—that is, with exaggerated seriousness, laced with scriptural quotations—amid gales of laughter. Once, in Marseille, Catherine abandoned the gloomy widow's costume she always wore, which accentuated her bulk and often made her seem older than she was, and dressed up in a Turkish outfit.

In the South, too, the balls, the entertainments, the spectacles, and the hunting that enlivened the court took on a softness and ease that enhanced their function as a meeting ground for aristocratic enemies and factions. The most famous of these spectacles that brought all the warring parties together as a peaceful audience took place on the river at Bayonne (PLATE IX). It featured a ballet on an island, shepherdesses serving a splendid meal, and a boat disguised as a whale (which was stranded by an unfriendly squall). The banquets at these events set new standards of elegance in dining, and became one of Catherine's most subtle legacies to France.

Yet political utility remained essential to almost everything she did. Her patronage of artists, astrologers—including the renowned Nostradamus—and scholars was tailored almost exclusively to that end. Relentlessly, she asked them to demonstrate, through mythological stories or through the testimony of history and law, that women could be effective rulers and that religious toleration was the best course. And they responded, if not always wholeheartedly, at least in quantity. In the process, the lawyers and historians among them helped to create a central tradition of modern political theory which, starting with the *politiques*, has given pride of place to governmental stability and authority (though it has also led to justifications of absolute obedience, such as those in Thomas Hobbes's *Leviathan*).

That Catherine made grievous mistakes was inevitable in so volatile a situation. She did not always change directions at the best time, and at a crucial moment in 1588 her natural preference for compromise prevented Henry III from taking decisive action against his main adversary, the duke of Guise. The result was that the king had to flee from Paris, and never controlled his capital again. Catherine's sense of failure during her last years, when the Valois line was headed for extinction, must have been overwhelming. But the old instinct for survival remained undimmed.

That much was clear when the last of the many dramas of her life unfolded. The royal family was in its château at Blois, on the Loire, for Christmas 1588. It had been a tempestuous year—the flight from Paris at home, and the defeat of the Spanish armada abroad. The latter, however, had diminished the threat to the king of his principal enemies, both foreign and domestic, because the duke of Guise was closely allied to Spain. Henry now felt himself strong enough, at last, to do away with this dangerous adversary. Guise was invited to the château, and murdered. The scuffle took place above Catherine's bedroom, but she was ill and slept through the commotion (Henry himself had asked the assassins to try not to disturb her). The next morning the king came to wake her and give her the news.

"How do you feel, Madame?" "Oh, my son, only fair." "As for me, Madame, I am extremely well. Monsieur de Guise is dead. I have had him killed."

Catherine was furious, for she knew that as leader of the Catholic cause Guise had supporters who would avenge his death, and thus the last of her sons would be killed in turn. That expectation, shared by many, would be fulfilled within a few months, but by then the queen mother herself was gone. Her last act was to promote reconciliation once more, going out in the bitter cold of a January day to tell an imprisoned leader of the Bourbon family that now, with Guise gone, he had been freed. She developed pneumonia, and four days later she was dead.

It had been a sad but exemplary life. In an age when old feudal obligations had died, and new nationalisms had not yet been born, few monarchs were able to achieve long-term goals. Most settled instead for dynastic ambitions, and in this regard Catherine had succeeded beyond expectation. The same was true of the authority she had managed to exercise despite her sex. Other women of the period, notably Elizabeth, may have looked more admirable or effective, but none had a Continent-wide role—dominating the largest government of the day—to compare with hers. And the personal characteristics and public policies that formed Catherine's career, especially her adaptability, her resilience, and her tolerance, made her seem ahead of her time. Her openness was particularly unusual amid the zealotry of the century, and yet nobody ever doubted the force of her presence, or the power she embodied. As the most eminent of sixteenth-century French historians, Jacques de Thou, noted when he heard of her death: "It is not a woman who has just expired, it is royalty itself."

PART VI

The
Discovery of
New Worlds

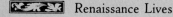

Left: Walter Ralegh. The miniature is associated closely with Elizabethan and Jacobean England, though it was also prized in other times and places (as can be seen in the portrait of Catherine de' Medici on the cover of this book). The delicate exactness of the form inspired a particular brilliance in Renaissance England, which was not otherwise noted for its painting. This example, a tiny portrait by the greatest master of the form, Nicholas Hilliard, captures the splendor for which Ralegh was famous. It was produced, like a snapshot today, as an easily portable memento that he could give to an especially close friend or relative.   *Right:* Sustermans, Galileo. Painted when Galileo was at the height of his powers, and before his eyesight failed, this lifelike portrait has him looking at the heavens that had made him famous.

An Explorer and a Scientist

OWEVER STRONG THEIR INCLINATION to look to the past for guidance, many of the writers and philosophers of the Renaissance, from Petrarch to Montaigne, were in fact saying things that were new. Despite their protestations that they were merely rediscovering the old, they could not deny that at least in two areas—geographic exploration and the study of nature that we call science—information was appearing that had never been known before. For all the reluctance of the discoverers to make such claims, it was this achievement in uncovering the new that eventually persuaded them that they had indeed exceeded the ancients. Open acknowledgment of such superiority was not common until around 1700, and its emergence can be taken as an indication that the Renaissance, the period of rebirth, was over. But the heroic discoveries had been made much earlier. ⦅ In the year 1600, for example, two men were at work with schemes that involved the crossing of old boundaries. The older of the two, the Englishman Ralegh, was a soldier, poet, and courtier who exemplified what has come to be called the Renaissance man: a dazzling talent in many and diverse fields, equally at home in the active and the contemplative life. His great dream, however, was to discover fabulous new lands overseas, to join the ranks of the great explorers of the age. The younger, the Italian Galileo, sought nothing less than to reveal secrets of nature that no previous investigator had been able to unlock.

Walter Ralegh

DEVON is the most distinctive of England's counties. It is not alone in having all of its territory within a few miles of the sea, but in just a few decades its seafarers gave it a special identity as a home of sailors and explorers that it retains to this day. One has but to name its most famous families—Drake, Gilbert, Grenville, Hawkins—to evoke the county's unique leadership at a decisive moment in English history. None of its progeny, however, has had as strong a hold on the imagination of succeeding generations as Walter Ralegh. Perhaps because he was much else besides a mere sea dog, or perhaps because he captured the heart of the queen who gave her name to the age, he has come to epitomize the image of the explorer.

Ralegh was born into the family of a respectable squire who owned a few acres near the sea. Related to the Grenvilles, the Drakes, and the Gilberts, the young Ralegh determined, like them, to make a name for himself far beyond his native county. The only way to do that, however, was to get to the seat of all favor and opportunity, London. His stepping-stone was the life of a student at Oxford, where he studied Latin, theology, and rhetoric, but earned no degree, a casualness that did not prevent him from becoming one of the most learned men of his time, author of a *History of the World* that shows an astonishing command of ancient and contemporary writings. Ralegh was even less diligent at his next stop after Oxford, the Inns of

Court, England's law school. Here (so he said) he never looked at a word of law; instead, he gained a reputation as a wit, a poet, and a swordsman.

For Ralegh, like many other young blades, Oxford and schools of law were social badges, not serious pursuits. He did not need a degree to be able to exchange Latin phrases and references to the classics with his fellow gentry; but he did need the Inns of Court's location in London as a base from which he could make an impression in the capital, and above all at its heart, the royal court.

Ralegh had Devon connections both at the Inns and at court, but what drew attention was the figure he cut. He was in his mid-twenties, and already he combined the dash, the multiple talents, and the cleverness that set him apart from other adventurers. High skill on the high seas might be expected of him: as his relative Francis Drake noted, "If any such there be, that thirsteth after fame, / Here a means to win himself an everlasting name," and Ralegh was nothing if not a thirster after fame. But the facility in poetry and repartee were not common skills, and they were much prized at court. The queen may have put her trust, and the task of governing, into the hands of earnest or austere bureaucrats like Lord Burghley and Francis Walsingham; but for public display, and in her private life, she pre-ferred such glamorous, if sometimes feckless, characters as the Earls of Leicester and Essex, who made up in handsomeness and wit what they lacked in steadfastness. Her need was to be surrounded by lively intelligences to match her own. After all, she was widely read; she had an excellent library, not to mention a good ear for music and a fine eye for the arts; she spoke four languages; and she inspired a knowledgeable observer to call her "learned, her sex and time con-sidered, beyond common belief."

That was the Elizabeth to whom Ralegh would appeal. First, however, he had to prove his worth as a man of action. And this was a good time to do it: the late 1570s, when tension with Spain was on the rise, and England's navy, small and in disrepair, was starting a crash program of refurbishment and growth under a shrewd Devon seaman, John Hawkins. One of its first major expeditions—ten ships, over three hundred fighting men—set sail in 1578, bent on piracy and possible colonization in the New World. The fleet included one ship owned by the queen herself, the *Falcon*, commanded by her brave new courtier, Ralegh, who alone rode out a gale that sent the other ships scurrying home to port. But that was not enough of a display of mettle to win much glory. Ralegh therefore remained at sea, on the lookout for a chance to exhibit the derring-do that would win him undying renown. What he found was a Spanish convoy, which he attacked single-handed in a gesture of sheer bravado. Remarkably, he survived, but he lost a number of men and badly damaged his ship in the process. The stingy queen was furious, and Ralegh had his first taste of the disfavor that always lurked at the edges of his career.

This time, however, the disgrace was minor and did not last long. For the Catholics of Ireland were rebelling against their English Protestant rulers, and Ralegh was sent as an officer to help put the uprising down. If Devon was the nursery of explorers, Ireland was to the Elizabethans the nursery of colonizers. Here they won their spurs in the subjugation of natives and the settlement and administration of strange and hostile lands. For Ralegh, who built himself a fine estate, it was an apprenticeship in a lifelong vocation. His new neighbor, Edmund Spenser, made the point when he described the younger poet, out in the countryside and surrounded by sheep, as "the shepherd of the ocean."

The Irish have a less lyrical memory of Ralegh. The cruelties visited on them are an irremovable part of the Elizabethan scene— the beginning of the blight that has covered Anglo-Irish relations ever since. In one province that Ralegh commanded, 30,000 people are estimated to have died of starvation in a year. After he captured a small town that refused to surrender, his 200 soldiers slaughtered all 600 of its inhabitants. Whether the victims were men, women, or children, he told his troops, one had to avoid bones so as to keep sword blades sharp—it was best to slash the neck, or, to increase the agony, to jab the belly.

For the many back in London who regarded such behavior as

brave and glorious, Ralegh returned from Ireland as something of a hero. Secure as a warrior, he could cultivate his image as a clever dandy, notorious for the fine clothes and jewels that now caught the queen's eye. This was when (it was said) he spread his "new plush cloak" over "a splashy place" in the garden to keep Elizabeth's shoes dry. Though the story was first told much later, it has the ring of truth, especially its moral: that this was the way the newly knighted Sir Walter got the queen to give him even more clothes.

Arrogant, talked-about, the new favorite was called the best-hated man in England. But Elizabeth did not care. She loved the verses he wrote her:

> She is neither white nor brown,
> But as the heavens fair.
> There is none hath a form so divine
> In the earth or the air.

And their repartee was famous. Elizabeth: "How long will you remain a beggar?" Ralegh: "So long as Your Highness remains a benefactor." Scratched on a window with their diamond rings:

RALEGH: "Fain would I climb, yet I fear to fall."
ELIZABETH: "If thy heart fail thee, climb not at all."

And yet, for all the acclaim he won—whether by introducing the new fashion for tobacco smoking, or by being appointed as captain of the queen's personal guard—Sir Walter had too restless and probing a nature to be satisfied by the glitter. "The court," he wrote, "glows and shines . . . like rotten wood." In an extraordinary poem, "Farewell to the Court," the melancholia and unease take over:

> Like truthless dreams, so are my thoughts expired.
> And past return are all my dandled days;
> My love misled, and fancy quite retired,
> Of all which past, the sorrow only stays.

Increasingly, he was spending time in the fine house Elizabeth gave him in London, so that he could keep in touch with the intellectual excitements the capital offered. Ralegh was at the heart of a lively company that was discussing the most advanced ideas of the time—physical experiments, alchemy, astrology, mathematics, and the magical theories of Hermeticism, Cabala, and other wonders. The famous Italian speculative philosopher, Giordano Bruno, who believed that the universe was infinite, and that hidden magical formulae would allow investigators to strip "the veils from the face of nature," visited England in the 1580s, and he was an inspiration to the group.

Their patron was a great aristocrat, the Earl of Northumberland, known as the "Wizard" Earl, who assembled at his home, Syon House near London, the finest scientific library and the best scientific minds in England. Among them was Elizabeth's court astrologer, John Dee, a disciple of Bruno and a master of arcane knowledge, who was dismissed as a conjuror by his enemies, but who was consulted by royal ministers when, for example, a picture of the queen was found with a pin stuck through its heart. Also at Syon was the most accomplished student of the new learning in England, Thomas Hariot, a mathematician, alchemist, experimenter, and naturalist as well as an astronomer. In later years, Ralegh was to be famous not only for patronizing Hariot, but for his own chemical, botanic, and medical experiments. Another member of the coterie, the playwright Christopher Marlowe, described Hariot with an irreverence that did not always stand the group in good stead: "Moses was but a juggler, for Hariot, one of Ralegh's men, can do more tricks than he."

But the exuberance and optimism was always tempered by a more introspective, even pessimistic streak, noticeable especially in the poetry. To Marlowe's famous "Come Live with Me and Be My Love," for example, Ralegh replied:

> But could youth last and love still breed,
> Had joys no age and age no need,
> Then these delights my mind might move
> To live with thee and be thy love.

In 1585 the devotion to experiment and the fascination with colonies came together when Ralegh sent a small fleet under Richard

Their rype corne.

Their greene corne.

Corne newly sprong.

Their sitting at meate.

The place of Solemne prayer.

The house wherin the Tombe of their Herounds standeth.

SECOTON.

A Ceremony in their prayers wth strange restures and songs danssng about posts carued on the topps lyke mens faces.

John White, The Town of Secota. Although commissioned primarily to satisfy Ralegh's scientific curiosity, White's paintings during the Roanoke expedition remain a unique record of Native American life at the dawn of the colonial era.

Grenville to deposit three hundred settlers on the island of Roanoke, off the North Carolina coast. In honor of the Virgin Queen, they named the place Virginia, and nearby they were to found the city of Raleigh. But this was no mere quest for glory. A painter, John White, was sent along expressly to observe and portray the new land, and his pictures remain the most vivid evocation we have of Indian life before the coming of the white man. And Hariot himself joined the company in order to write a description of the flora and fauna; it was to become the most famous account of the Virginia of its day. Hariot amazed the Indians with tricks using a magnet and a magnifying glass, but sadly, his friendship with the native Americans was unusual among the settlers. Tensions rose, a number of Indians were killed, and when Francis Drake stopped off on his way back from a Caribbean raid to see how the colony was doing, the entire community clambered aboard his ships and went home.

Ralegh at once sent out a new group of settlers. Grenville was supposed to resupply them, but he never left. A huge armada was making its way up the Channel, and every boat and sailor was needed for England's defense. Elizabeth, worried about her favorite, refused to let Sir Walter go to sea, and instead put him in charge of organizing land defenses in Devon and the West Country. When he was finally permitted to set sail, it was only with a message to the English commander to ask why the fleeing Spaniards had been allowed to escape. As he knew, it was a pointless question. The English had won precisely because they had avoided engaging the giant armada while it was destroyed by fire, sea, and wind. But at least his quick excursion into the Channel gave him a small part in the Elizabethans' most celebrated seafaring achievement.

As soon as the armada was gone, Ralegh hurried to send relief ships to Roanoke. What they found has remained one of the most baffling mysteries of the age of exploration. Night was approaching as they drew alongside the island, but they thought they saw one sign of life, a column of smoke. To reassure their countrymen that they were not Spaniards, they sang English songs and made appropriate noises, but when they landed the next morning, they found the settlement abandoned. A single word, "Croatoan," was carved on a tree, but no Englishman ever saw the 113 colonists again. Over twenty years later the settlers in Jamestown heard stories of an Indian massacre, and of seven survivors living some fifty miles up the James River. They made a feeble attempt at a search, after which even the rumors of white men and women vanished without a trace in the vastness of the land.

At home Sir Walter's luck was no better. As a courtier commented, "Ralegh was one that it seems fortune had picked out to use as her tennis ball, for she tossed him up from nothing, and to and fro to greatness, and from thence down to little more than wherein she found him." He had fallen in love with Bess Throckmorton who, as a lady-in-waiting at court, was technically a ward of the queen. Fearful of Elizabeth's jealousy (though there is little to suggest that her relationship with Ralegh was ever more than flirtatious), Bess and Sir Walter got married in secret, and then, thanks to the voluminous dresses of the day, managed to become parents of a baby boy without the queen knowing. When at last she found out, she was livid, not only at the personal betrayal but also because Ralegh had neither asked for the permission that protocol demanded nor apologized when he was discovered.

The result was imprisonment in the Tower, where he languished, sulked, and wrote sad poems, to no avail. Even his sardonic wit did him little good. Looking over the small zoo that was kept nearby, he asked the queen if he "might feed the Tower's lions as I go by, to save labor." She finally released him as a Christmas present, but not in London. While she had an accounting made of his debts to her, Ralegh was banished to his new home in the West Country, at Sherborne—a lovely house in beautiful grounds, but very far from the whirl of the capital.

The exile was hard on him, because for all his versatility—his delight in both action and contemplation, and the instinctive breadth of interest that made him a genuinely universal man—he found it hard to be isolated from the political and intellectual company that kept him on his toes. Not until much later in his life was he to come to terms with confinement and the exercise of contemplation alone. Now, bored and at loose ends, he poked fun at a local parson in a manner that confirmed his reputation for irreverence and revived the charges of atheism—the standard libel against skeptical minds—that had been cast at him and friends like Christopher Marlowe, members of a supposedly wicked "school of night."

RALEGH: I have been a scholar some time in Oxford, yet in this point, what the reasonable soul of men is, have I not been satisfied.

PARSON: It is a spiritual and immortal substance breathed into man, whereby he lives.

RALEGH: Yes, but what is that spiritual and immortal substance, etcetera?

PARSON: The soul.

Now another old passion came to the fore. Years before, Ralegh had heard of a Spanish soldier who had blundered into the depths of Guiana, far up the Orinoco River, and been taken blindfolded to a fabulous city built entirely of silver and gold: El Dorado. He got royal permission for an expedition, and at last set out himself for the continent to which he had sent so many ships. He reached Guiana, and in five open boats he and a hundred men began rowing up the Orinoco. These were not the conditions he was used to—cramped, unwashed, and eating dreadful provisions—but he did not flinch. "I never saw a more beautiful country, the deer crossing in every path, the birds towards the evening singing on every tree with a thousand different tunes, and every stone promised either gold or silver." The Indians welcomed him, told stories of El Dorado and of extraordinary humans who had eyes in their shoulders, and kept promising that the end of the journey was just around the next bend in the river. Ralegh became convinced a major colonizing effort would be needed, and returned home to write a description of what he had seen, *The Discovery of the Large, Rich, and Beautiful Empire of Guiana*, that became a classic of the promoter's art; but he proved unable to persuade the queen.

For the age of the sea dogs was passing. Ralegh's half brother Sir Humphrey Gilbert had disappeared in a storm at sea. Last seen on deck calmly reading a book, he had called out, "We are as near to heaven by sea as by land." Drake and Hawkins had died on a futile privateering venture in the Caribbean while Ralegh explored Guiana. The two old men's voyage was a disaster, but they preferred death at sea to returning home empty-handed. Drake's despairing cry, "We must have gold before we see England," could have been the motto of Elizabeth's adventurers. But none stirred the spirit so deeply as Sir Richard Grenville, overwhelmed in a lone ship by a Spanish fleet, and immortalized by his cousin Ralegh in a masterpiece of stunning prose, *The Last Fight of the "Revenge,"* that has drawn tears from generations of English schoolboys ever since:

> Sir Richard, finding himself in this distress, and unable any longer to make resistance, having endured in this fifteen hours fight, the assault of fifteen several Armadas, and eight hundred shot of great artillery, besides many assaults and entries; and that himself and the ship must needs be possessed by the enemy, who were now all cast in a ring round about him (the *Revenge* not able to move but as she was moved with the waves), commanded the Master Gunner to split and sink the ship; that thereby nothing might remain of glory or victory to the Spaniards: seeing in so many hours fight, and with so great a Navy, they were not able to take her.

During these twilight years of Elizabeth's reign, Ralegh was the last surviving master of such panache, and he slowly came back into the queen's good graces. He showed great bravery on two military expeditions led by her new favorite, the earl of Essex, and he was once again made captain of the royal guard. But he was responsible, in that capacity, for executing the earl, who had rebelled against Elizabeth, and the old dislike of Ralegh revived as he came to be seen as the chief enemy of the popular Essex—the dashing young man who had replaced him in the queen's affections.

It was a dangerous time to be losing friends, because Sir Walter's great protectress, Elizabeth, was dying. Fittingly, it was he who wrote the most gallant of her epitaphs—though it could also have applied to himself. "Her Majesty," he said, "was a lady whom time surprised."

For now, with all of the old sea dogs dead, Ralegh stood out, in the subdued atmosphere of the new reign, as the last personification of a dashing and glorious age. The contrast with the pacifism, pedantry, and caution of the new monarch, James I, founder of the Stuart dynasty, was unmistakable. Naturally, James resented the frequent comparisons with the glamour of Elizabeth's time—exemplified by the continued celebration of the queen's birthday as a public holiday—and he countered the nostalgia by crushing the man who was its most visible focus.

Ralegh did not do well at the Stuart court, and he made some stupid mistakes, but the retribution was cruel: the ringing patriot, famous for his hatred of Spain, was accused of plotting treason with the Spaniards. The trial was a travesty, a blot on the career of the great lawyer who prosecuted him, Sir Edward Coke, who simply ranted at the prisoner, refused him permission to speak, and asserted his guilt instead of proving it. Ironically, Coke was always suspect at court thereafter, while Ralegh's unpopularity faded away. But James got his conviction, and in a show of mercy sent the prisoner to the Tower in 1603, though the sentence of death was left hanging over his head.

Sir Walter remained in confinement for thirteen years, but he was far from uncomfortable or invisible. His wife and two servants joined him in his ample quarters, Bess gave birth to another son, and their household became the talk of London society. He started a botanic garden, converted a chicken house into a chemical laboratory, and concocted medicines that brought him a stream of visitors. Sixty years later people still spoke of his elixir, but in James's reign the consultations with this last of the Elizabethans also had political implications. The king's heir, Prince Henry, set himself apart from his father by calling on the famous prisoner, and even his mother the queen occasionally stopped by.

Fortunately for Ralegh, he was soon joined by an old friend: the "Wizard" Earl, condemned to prison for his part in the Gunpowder Plot against King James. Hariot came to stay with them, and the three companions created in the Tower what was probably the first society for scientific experiment in England. It was in these years, as his instinct for the exploration of nature kept him in the public eye, that Ralegh became the symbol of all that had been lost when Elizabeth died: the living embodiment of a golden legend. For he stood for adventure overseas, which now was curtailed; for war with the old enemy, Spain, which now was ended; and for the kind of speculation about nature which James dismissed—when a scientific treatise was dedicated to the King, he likened it to "the Peace of God, which passeth all understanding." By contrast, Ralegh, together with Northumberland and Hariot, established in the Tower the last outpost of the ever-curious Elizabethans. And when, at last, a settlement took hold in Virginia, he could be revered as the prophet of English colonization, as well as the shrewd promoter of the country's commercial destiny: "Whoever commands the trade of the world," he wrote, "commands the riches of the world, and consequently the world itself."

As Ralegh came to be seen as the epitome of the qualities of Elizabeth's brilliant reign, James changed course and tried to attach to himself the aura of glamour and overseas venture that his famous prisoner symbolized. He let the old man out of the Tower in 1616, and gave him permission to sail once more for Guiana—to discover El Dorado at last. This time, however, the catastrophe was final and total. Ralegh did find an old Indian who had guided him before, but he came no closer to the city of gold. And, despite the express command of the pacifist king not to interfere with the Spaniards in Guiana, he got into a fight and destroyed a Spanish fort. Worse yet, his own son was killed in the fight.

Young Walter, nonchalant yet aggressive, had had his father's spark (PLATE X). A well-known story had the old man telling him he was ashamed to have "such a bear" with him at a distinguished dinner table, and warning him to behave. When they sat down, the lad "was very demure at least half dinner time. Then said he, I this morning, by the instigation of the devil, went to a whore. I was very eager to enjoy her, but she vowed I should not, 'for your father lay with me but an hour ago.' Sir Walt, being put out of his countenance at so great a table, gives his son a damned blow over the face. His son, rude as he was, would not strike his father, but strikes the gentleman that sat next to him, and said, 'box about, 'twill come to my father anon.' " This was the boy who was now dead, and on the way back to England Ralegh wrote Bess a letter worthy of his grief:

> I never knew what sorrow meant till now. My brains are broken, and 'tis a torment for me to write. As Drake and Hawkins died heartbroken when they failed in their enterprise, I could willingly do the like, did I not contend against sorrow, in hope somewhat to comfort and relieve you. If I live to return, it is the care for you that hath strengthened my heart.

Like the true Elizabethan he was, Ralegh did return, though it was to certain death. For the king, enraged by the skirmish with the Spaniards, was determined to apply the fifteen-year-old sentence of death (for treason with Spain!) that had never been lifted. Sir Walter's friends urged him, when he landed in Devon in 1618, not to go back to London, but he shrugged off their fears.

Execution held little terror for him now. While in the Tower he had written the first massive volume of a monumental *History of the World*, whose mordant view of those who held power was to become an inspiration to generations of revolutionaries. Through the book he became a tangible reminder of a golden age that Oliver Cromwell and his contemporaries were to regard as betrayed by the Stuarts. It was the only reading Cromwell recommended to his sons, perhaps because of its final paragraph, a hymn to Death the great leveller, superior even to kings:

> O Death! Whom none could advise, thou hast persuaded; what none hath dared, thou hast done; and whom all the world hath flattered thou only hath despised.

The night before his execution Ralegh returned to the poetry that had always been his solace, and added two lines to a verse written many years before:

> Even such is Time, which takes in trust
> Our youth, our joys, our all we have,

> And pays us but with earth and dust;
> Who in the dark and silent grave,
> When we have wandered all our ways,
> Shuts up the story of our days.

To which he appended:

> But from this earth, this grave, this dust,
> My God shall raise me up, I trust.

And so the soldier, sailor, poet, experimenter, skeptic, historian, and courtier—the quintessential explorer of the age, the embodiment of its tensions and its hopes, the blend of the active and the contemplative life who was the era's closest real-life model for the vigorous but melancholic Hamlet—came to the scaffold. Even here his jauntiness did not desert him. When the executioner hesitated to show him the ax, Ralegh chided him: "Dost thou think I am afraid of it? This is sharp medicine, but it is a sure cure for all diseases."

Sir Walter may once have seemed "damnable proud," but to the huge crowd that gathered around the scaffold, his life held a different meaning. In the hush—instead of the usual cheers—that greeted the executioner's raising aloft of the severed head, a lone voice expressed the feelings of all: "We have not such another head in England."

Galileo Galilei

To the people of the time—and most historians have agreed with them—the golden age of Renaissance Florence appeared to be over by the middle of the sixteenth century. When Michelangelo died in 1564, it seemed that the last of the giants was gone. His younger contemporary, Giorgio Vasari, certainly thought so, and said as much in his pioneering history of art. Nor was it easy to disagree. Florentines no longer made up the main vanguard of new artistic movements; the scholarship inspired by humanism had moved to new centers; and the literary and intellectual legacy of Dante, Petrarch, Machiavelli, and the historian Guicciardini had found other homes. Not surprisingly, the period that began at this time has been called Florence's "forgotten centuries." And yet the major Florentine contribution to one area of central importance to European culture—natural philosophy, which we now call science—still lay ahead.

That contribution is associated primarily with a man who was born in the very year that Michelangelo died: Galileo Galilei. His family had fallen on hard times by 1564, though they had distinguished roots in Florence's past as leaders of the city's government and society for over two hundred years. But Galileo's father Vincenzio, a talented composer and musician, had not prospered in his native city, and so had entered the world of trade and had moved to Pisa. It was here that he got married and started a family that eventually numbered seven children. Galileo, the eldest, was always to feel responsible for his siblings—a heavy burden, even though his father's fortunes did revive slightly, and they were able to move back to Florence. Especially after Vincenzio's death, in 1591, the young man saw himself as the head of the family and assumed financial obligations he could ill afford.

The return to Florence took place when Galileo was ten years old. But it was hardly a dramatic change from Pisa. Both places were part of the larger territory that had gradually emerged from the one-time city-state. The expansion had been gradual during the previous two centuries, and now he was a citizen not just of Florence but of the entire region of Tuscany. Yet the government was still run, as it had been on and off for some 150 years, by the Medici family, who had risen from the status of leaders of a powerful city faction to the title of grand dukes of Tuscany. And their patronage was to be as crucial to Galileo as it once was to Michelangelo.

Vincenzio was a remarkably cultivated man, adept not only in music but also in literature and mathematics. He moved in the leading intellectual circles of his day, but he wanted a more secure life for his son. When the boy was sent to the University of Pisa at the age of seventeen, therefore, it was as a student of medicine. Very soon, however, other interests asserted themselves. On a visit home in 1583, Galileo, to his father's dismay, began to study mathematics intensely, and performed his first experiments on the regularities of the movement of a pendulum. He returned for two more years at Pisa, but he never completed his medical degree. Instead, mathematics and physics became his preoccupation. Unable to resist, his father allowed him to change fields when the twenty-one-year-old returned to his family in 1585, and he spent the next four years investigating natural phenomena: he invented a hydrostatic balance, and he investigated the properties of solids.

Yet Galileo was by no means a narrow mathematician or natural philosopher. He inherited from Vincenzio a love of music, an enjoyment of discussions of literature and philosophy, and a fondness for the humanist study of the classics of ancient Rome. It was during these years that Galileo even gave two lectures on the poetry of Dante. His was a breadth of learning and an engagement with many areas of intellectual life that was characteristic of the great students of nature in this period—from Bacon to Pascal, from Kepler to Descartes—before the subject became professionalized, self-conscious, and distinct.

For Galileo, however, this indulgence in wide-ranging interests during his early twenties was something of a luxury. He was living with his parents and earning no more than a pittance by teaching occasional mathematics lessons. Yet he was making useful contacts in Florentine society. One of his pupils was Cosimo de' Medici, future grand duke of Tuscany. And his liveliness and intelligence drew to him an aristocrat who was an early dabbler in, and patron of, science: Guidobaldo del Monte, a marquis and the brother of a cardinal. It was Guidobaldo who helped his young protégé land the academic position that was essential to the further pursuit of his interests. Galileo had applied unsuccessfully for a number of openings, but at last, in 1589, Cardinal del Monte persuaded the grand duke to appoint him to the chair of mathematics at his alma mater, Pisa.

It was not a particularly distinguished post in the academic

PARS INTERIOR GYMNASII PATAVINI

Galileo is reputed to have given lectures from the upper level of this splendid colon-
naded courtyard at the University of Padua, because the throngs who wanted to hear
him could not fit into a regular lecture hall. On the left, in cross-section, is an
indication of the structure of the famous anatomy theater, where students stood in
rows, looking down, as the dissection was performed below.

hierarchy of Italy, and Galileo was soon hoping for advancement,
especially after his father's death in 1591, when his meager salary left
him hard put to care for his mother, two sisters, and a feckless
brother. Over the ensuing decade he was to have to provide two
dowries for the sisters, as well as the expenses of the brother. After
just three years at Pisa, therefore, Galileo once again turned to
Guidobaldo for help, and the marquis interceded with the authorities
in Venice who oversaw the nearby University of Padua. The chair
of mathematics was vacant, and in 1592 it was offered to the twenty-
eight-year-old Florentine.

Padua's university was far more renowned than Pisa's. It was
the premier medical school in Europe, and its fame as a training
ground for such subjects as mathematics and medicine attracted leading students of natural philosophy and anatomy from many countries.
The Polish astronomer Nicolaus Copernicus, the Flemish anatomist

Andreas Vesalius, and the English doctor William Harvey, discoverer of the circulation of the blood, were merely the most celebrated of the galaxy of students and professors who spent time at the university during and before Galileo's lifetime. In one area in particular—the combination of observation with theory that was characteristic of its faculty of medicine—Padua was virtually unique. Breaking with tradition, the teachers in its anatomy theater dissected cadavers themselves while they lectured. Previously, the man of learning, who imparted wisdom by reading a book or notes, was sharply distinguished from the manual laborer, the barber-surgeon, who cut up the body and produced its parts to illustrate the lecture. Direct observation made possible new discoveries, and it happened also to be an approach that Galileo had pursued from his earliest days in the study of nature, in his pendulum and other experiments.

The move to Padua provided another encouragement to the blending of experience with theory. One of the jewels of Venice was its enormous arsenal, a remarkable industrial complex that employed a labor force of thousands, with dozens of skills, who were capable of building and arming a ship within twenty-four hours. The arsenal was essential to Venetian naval power, and the government therefore regarded its well-being as a particular obligation. Its employees had their own welfare system, and experts were regularly brought in to advise its administrators. As a well-known and readily available investigator of physics and the problems of motion, Galileo was naturally someone to whom the arsenal looked for advice. He was consulted frequently, though he felt that he learned more about mechanics from the artisans who moved huge weights and found new ways of using levers and pulleys than they ever did from him:

> Frequent visits to the famous Venetian arsenal open a large field for philosophizing on the part of speculative minds, especially in a field which requires mechanics. For a large number of artisans there constantly use every sort of instrument and machine. Among them there must be some who are real experts and capable of the most acute reasoning, because of the observations made by their predecessors and those which they themselves are continually making.

But Padua and Venice offered far more than endorsements and opportunities for Galileo's inclination to experiment. The republic in which he now lived had a unique tradition of open discussion and unorthodox opinion, thanks to its long history as a meeting place of many different cultures, and the most famous of its philosophers in the previous generation, Giordano Bruno, had shocked traditional authorities with his views. Bruno was a former monk who argued that the universe was infinite, and he also questioned the doctrine of the Trinity. Such heresy could not be defended, even in tolerant Venice; Bruno was handed over to the Inquisition, which condemned him and had him executed in Rome in 1600. What Galileo made of the case we do not know, and indeed his silence prompted reproaches from contemporaries—notably the German mathematician Johannes Kepler—and also from historians, who have seen it as evidence of his timidity early in his career. There is little doubt that Galileo's reluctance to come out openly in support of Copernicanism was reinforced by the fate of Bruno, who had used the Copernican view to argue for the rejection of Aristotle and much else in standard philosophical thought.

Yet the openness and liveliness of Venice's intellectual life clearly appealed to Galileo. He became friendly with the republic's leading theologian and historian, Paolo Sarpi, who was soon to attack the authority of the pope and to orchestrate a major confrontation with the papacy. (It was in a letter to Sarpi that Galileo outlined his earliest theories about falling bodies.) Through the work of Tintoretto and Palladio he encountered painters and architects who inspired all Europe (El Greco, for instance, was trained in Venice). And the University at Padua was perhaps the most stimulating blend of the traditional and the new in the academic world of the time.

Galileo also made friends among Venice's political leaders, notably a patrician named Francesco Sagredo, whose palace on the Grand Canal was to be the fictional setting for his most famous book. And his circle even included a Paduan professor named Cesare Cremonini who was one of the principal defenders of the very Aristotelian theories of physics that Galileo was to undermine. It was a heady and open atmosphere, energized by the liveliness of its intellectual exchange, and he later said that the eighteen years he spent in Padua, up to the age of forty-six, were the happiest of his life.

For all the excitement, however, and the regular salary increases he received, Galileo still found the earning of an adequate living a struggle. He had to give private lessons, and took some of his students as paying boarders in his house. In addition, he opened a small shop, where he and an employee made scientific instruments, such as proportional compasses, which not only served his own researches but also provided a small income. He had additional obligations, because for some ten years he maintained a liaison with a Venetian woman who lived in Padua, Marina Gamba. There was no wedding, but they did have three children, and they became Galileo's responsibility when Marina got married after his departure from Padua. Though his son remained with him, he placed his two daughters in convents, because increasingly—especially during his frantically busy last years in Padua—his concern was to find enough time, amid his many commitments, to pursue his work:

> My thought is to get enough leisure and quiet to bring to a conclusion, before my life ends, great works that might be published, perhaps with some credit to me. More leisure than I have here I do not believe I could have elsewhere so long as I am forced to support my household by public and private teaching. The freedom I have here does not suffice, since I am required to consume many hours of the day at anybody's request. To obtain a salary from the Republic, however splendid, is not possible without public service; and so long as I am able to teach and serve, nobody in the Republic can exempt me from that duty.

It was the professor's perennial complaint about teaching interfering with research, and although it deserved no more sympathy in the seventeenth century than it does now, Galileo did keep struggling to find a remedy until, in 1610, his work brought him sufficient recognition and patronage to free him from the demands of his academic position.

The two major problems that were Galileo's main concern at Padua had preoccupied students of the physical world since the time of the ancient Greeks: motion and the structure of the heavens. Since Aristotle it had been assumed that all bodies were naturally at rest. To the extent that there was any "natural" motion, earth and water went down, and fire and air went up; but basically motion was unnatural, and had to be explained—for example, by saying that a moving object slowed down and eventually came to rest because it was trying to return to its natural state. As for the heavens, the standard description—the so-called Ptolemaic system—accounted for what one saw in the sky by placing the earth at the center of the universe, surrounded by revolving transparent spheres, to which all stars and planets were attached.

Galileo was moving in new directions on both these fronts. Starting with the pendulum, he spent much of his life devising experiments—such as rolling balls down inclined planes—that would enable him to describe motion in mathematical terms. His observations were approximate at best: he had neither perfectly smooth balls nor frictionless inclined planes. Moreover, the crucial variable was time, and his means of measuring its passage were far from precise: a water clock he developed that dripped water at regular intervals, or his own pulse beats, which became unreliable when he grew excited. Yet it is clear that, for Galileo, thought experiments (in which he imagined perfect conditions) could be as important as real experiments, and that definitive proofs were the product of mathematics. Gradually, he was moving toward a view that downward motion was as "natural" as rest, and his work in Padua concentrated on the measurement of free fall. In a letter to Sarpi in 1604, he suggested that "the body in natural motion increases its speed in the same proportion as its departure from the origin of its motion." Eventually, he was to conclude that the determinant of the speed was time, not distance. His discovery—a mathematical formula that described the process of acceleration—was virtually complete by 1609, but he was then distracted by astronomy, and he did not publish his findings until 1637, in *The Two New Sciences*, the masterpiece on physics which defined a new principle of motion, inertia:

> Any velocity, once imparted to a moving body, will be rigidly maintained as long as external causes of acceleration and retardation are removed. If the velocity is uniform, it will not be diminished or slackened, much less destroyed.

Although it did not appear in print for thirty years, much of the work on which this startling conclusion was based had been done in the Padua years—and, significantly, the setting for the dialogue that makes up *The Two New Sciences* was Venice's arsenal.

To his contemporaries, however, it was his investigations of the heavens that were his most sensational achievement. Galileo had become convinced by the 1590s that the Ptolemaic system was wrong to place the earth at the center of the universe. He had concluded that the alternative theory, placing the sun at the center—published fifty years earlier by Nicolaus Copernicus—was correct. There was no proof either way, and none was to be forthcoming for decades; but a number of astronomers were taking the Copernican line.

The most charismatic was the brilliant German astrologer, mathematician, and speculative philosopher Johannes Kepler. Unlike Galileo, Kepler avoided academic posts and led a restless but independent career, which at times got him into trouble with both Catholic and Lutheran authorities. What he never had to fear, however, were the conformist impulses of the academic establishment or the disapproval of professors who did not want to change their lectures. In 1597 he sent Galileo the manuscript of a work on astronomy that, in a typically bold act of faith, adopted the Copernican view. The Italian, aware as always of the precariousness of his livelihood, replied that, although he had reached the same conclusion, he dared not state it openly for fear of being "derided and dishonored." Kepler's response was the classic exhortation of the pioneer:

> I could only wish that you, who have so profound an insight, would choose another way. You advise us to retreat before the general ignorance, and not expose ourselves to the violent attacks of the mob of scholars. But after a tremendous task has been begun in our time, first by Copernicus and then by many learned mathematicians, and when the assertion that the Earth moves can no longer be considered

something new, would it not be much better, with powerful voices, to shout down the common herd? Be of good cheer, Galileo, and come out publicly. If I judge correctly, only a few of the distinguished mathematicians of Europe would part company with us, so great is the power of truth.

It was an appeal that seems ironic in retrospect, especially in its invocation of the power of truth, and its suggestion (later in the letter) that Galileo publish in the Protestant north if he was afraid to do so in Italy. At the time, however, Galileo was unmoved.

What finally persuaded him to come out publicly, more than ten years later, was a new set of observations. He had heard that a Dutch lens maker's invention made distant objects seem closer, and he copied the device in his workshop (PLATE XI). At first, though, he regarded it as a means of enlarging his income from the Venetian authorities, who quickly perceived how useful it could be at sea. But he then made the revolutionary move: he turned his spyglass toward the heavens, and what he saw—satellites orbiting Jupiter, dark spots that came and went on the sun, mountains and shifting shadows on the moon—transformed astronomy forever.

It took someone who knew the meaning of his observations—and extraordinary eyesight—to be able to explain his discoveries. Despite his confident espousal of Copernicanism in the years that followed, however, Galileo had not yet proved that the world was heliocentric. Most of what he described could have fit into a Ptolemaic picture. Indeed, it was a work just published by Kepler, based on nontelescopic observations, that posed the main threat to Ptolemy. For Kepler showed that the orbits of planets were ellipses, a discovery Galileo, who believed in the esthetic perfection of the circle, was never able to accept. His own findings were in fact a threat to an entirely different assumption about the universe.

For centuries theologians, reinforced by Aristotelian teachings, had claimed that the heavens were pure precisely because they were not subject to the change and decay that were visible on the vile and flawed Earth. The results of Galileo's observations challenged that assumption directly. The satellite moons that orbited Jupiter were

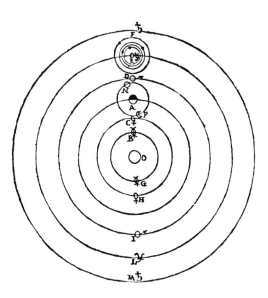

Galileo's own drawing of the heavens, published in his *Dialogue* in 1632, shows a Copernican system with the sun at the center. The Earth is orbited by its moon, and is dark on the side away from the sun. Circling Jupiter are the four satellites Galileo had discovered and named the Medicean stars. Significantly, the orbits remain circular, for Galileo had not been convinced by Kepler's conclusion that they were elliptical.

just like the Earth's moon (and they also resolved the anomaly in the Copernican system that only the earth seemed to have a satellite); the passing spots on the surface of the sun revealed change in the heavens; and, most devastating of all, the shifting areas of light and dark on the moon were caused, he said, by the moving shadows of mountains (which blocked sunlight in the same way they did on Earth). Indeed, the shadows enabled him to estimate the height of lunar mountains by normal surveyors' techniques. Where now was the essential distinction between heaven and Earth?

Galileo published the observations of Jupiter and the moon in 1610, in a book he called *The Starry Messenger*. It was the climax of the extraordinarily productive Paduan years, when, for all the distractions he complained about, he had laid the foundation for his principal scientific achievements and had made the discoveries that now propelled him to fame. For the book caused an immediate sensation, and Galileo became the most celebrated professor in Europe. Moreover, *The Starry Messenger* also enabled him to leave the obligations of academic life. He dedicated it to Cosimo de' Medici, grand duke of Tuscany, his former pupil, and astutely named Jupiter's moons the Medicean stars. Within a few months he had an invitation to become court mathematician in Florence, with a handsome salary and no teaching obligations.

His benefactor, the grand duke, wished to ensure that he could continue his researches undisturbed, and Galileo took up the offer with alacrity. Indifferent to the offense he might be causing, he packed up at short notice and left Venice, abandoning Marina and even (for a while) his children. A year later he was being lionized by the most prominent social and ecclesiastical circles in Rome, and invited to become a member of a pioneering society devoted to the study of nature, the Academy of the Lincei. A life of celebrity and achievement seemed to lie before him.

Already, however, Church authorities were expressing unease. At the very time that Galileo was the talk of Rome, the head of the Inquisition, a distinguished and cultivated Jesuit theologian (and future saint), Robert Bellarmine, was asking his fellow Jesuits whether they accepted the new findings and whether there did not seem to be too much fondness for innovation in Galileo's work. Bellarmine himself had looked through the telescope, and the Jesuit order was well known for its scientific interests. Indeed, when Kepler had wanted to find out, a few years earlier, how the extent of a solar eclipse might vary by geographic region—the first international scientific experiment in history—the only uniform group of qualified observers in different countries he could rely on were the Jesuits. In general, Bellarmine felt that studies of nature ought not to be a concern of the Church: they did not affect essential dogma, and they had long been thought of as "matters indifferent." After all, Copernicus had been a respectable cleric, and his great work had been dedicated to a pope.

But the world was changing. The Church was engaged in a fierce struggle with Protestantism, and for the previous half century or so it had been increasingly concerned to stamp out any ideas or practices that might threaten the traditional beliefs it was seeking to uphold. Only seventy years before, it had established both the Roman Inquisition that Bellarmine headed and the listing of unacceptable literature known as the Index of Forbidden Books. It had also issued regulations for works of art on religious themes, and now it was beginning to worry that new scientific ideas might be seen as challenges to orthodox views. Did the Bible not say that Joshua ordered the *sun* to stand still?

Galileo was infuriated by such concerns. Emboldened by his newly won eminence, and never blessed with tact—twenty years before, he had briefly hurt his career with a disparaging comment about a technical invention that had been made by a member of the Medici family—he decided to explain why theological niceties were irrelevant to scientific work. His outburst took the form of a "Letter" to Duke Cosimo's mother, the Grand Duchess Christina, a cultivated aristocrat with whom he had discussed his discoveries. Written not in scholarly Latin but in Italian and completed in 1615, the "Letter" was not published for over twenty years, but it did circulate widely in manuscript copies. As a statement of the emerging self-consciousness and distinctiveness of natural philosophy, it is a remarkable document, a landmark in the history of science. At the time, however, it was an invitation to trouble, because the assertion of science's independent claim to truth forced Galileo to adjust religion to his own purposes. To anyone who read the "Letter," the crucial passages attacking his critics suggested that he was practicing theology without a license:

These men have resolved to fabricate a shield for their fallacies out of the mantle of pretended religion and the authority of the Bible. Contrary to the sense of the Bible, they would extend its authority until even in purely physical matters—where faith is not involved—they would have us abandon reason and the evidence of our senses in favor of some biblical passage. I think that discussions of physical problems ought to begin not from the authority of scripture but from sense-experiences and necessary demonstrations. I do not believe that that same God who has endowed us with senses, reason, and intellect has intended us to forgo their use. Truly demonstrated physical conclusions need not be subordinated to biblical passages, but the latter must rather be shown not to interfere with the former. To banish the opinion in question it would be necessary to ban the whole science of astronomy. It would also be necessary to forbid men to look at the heavens.

The reaction soon followed. In 1616 Galileo was summoned by the Inquisition to Rome to answer his critics. At the end of the investigation Bellarmine, seeking the middle ground, stated that Copernicanism should be taught only as a theory. The cardinal had little choice, because members of one of the powerful orders of the Church, the Dominicans—long known as upholders of orthodoxy—were dismayed by the implications of the new astronomy and demanded action. Copernicus's book was placed on the Index, and a warning was issued to its most famous advocate. Only Bellarmine's reluctance to intervene in "matters indifferent" prevented a sterner response.

Yet the rumormongers who flourished in Rome were quick to describe the confrontation as a total repudiation of Galileo's ideas. "The disputes of Signor Galileo have dissolved into alchemical smoke," one of these gossips, Monsignor Querengo, wrote. "So here we are at last, safely back on a solid Earth, and we do not have to fly with it as so many ants crawling around a balloon." Resentful of the publicity, Galileo asked Bellarmine for a certificate confirming that he had not been condemned in any way, but had been told only not to defend Copernicanism. Bellarmine agreed, and gave him a document that Galileo later believed would protect him from further attack.

For the next few years the astronomer lay low on the subject of Copernicanism, but his self-confidence—indeed, arrogance—and the biting wit that came naturally to him, were leading him into new difficulties. A brief earlier argument with a Jesuit over sunspots notwithstanding, he was still on friendly terms with that influential order. But between 1619 and 1623 he kept up a running battle on the subject of comets with one of its most erudite astronomers, Orazio Grassi, who wrote under the pen name of Sarsi. The sarcasm and humiliation that were Galileo's main weapons as he demolished Sarsi's arguments earned him enmities he would come to regret:

> Note the great confidence which Sarsi places in the sense of sight, deeming it impossible for us to be deceived by a spurious object whenever that may be set beside a real one. I am more like the monkey that firmly believed he saw another monkey in a mirror, and discovered

his error only after running behind the glass to catch the other monkey. If simple appearances can determine the essence of a thing, Sarsi must believe that the sun, the moon, and the stars seen in still water are true suns, real moons, and veritable stars.

With the Dominicans already against him, it was self-destructive of Galileo to offend his Jesuit friends. As one of them later noted, "If Galileo had known how to retain the favor of the Jesuits, he would have been spared all his misfortunes, and he could have written what he pleased about everything, even about the motion of the Earth."

For the time being, however, there seemed to be no reason to worry about the offense he had caused. In the very year his final statement on comets appeared, 1623, the man to whom it was dedicated became the pope. Cardinal Maffeo Barberini had long been an admirer of Galileo, and as Urban VIII he was to be one of the most sophisticated patrons of learning and the arts the papacy had ever seen. Now, if ever, the astronomer was surely free to write his major work, especially since Urban himself encouraged the idea, with the proviso that to mention Copernicanism as anything but a hypothesis "would be tantamount to constraining the infinite power of God within the limits of your personal ideas." And so, between 1625 and 1629, in his early sixties, and at leisure in Florence, Galileo composed his most famous work, *Dialogue on the Two Chief World Systems*.

Written in a lucid Italian that attracted an audience far beyond the scholarly world (and soon translated into French, Latin, and English), the *Dialogue* is one of the few masterpieces of science that can still be read for pleasure to this day. The dialogue form enabled Galileo to identify the Ptolemaic and the Copernican positions with specific characters, and thus to claim that he took no sides. Yet the first was represented by a slightly dim-witted figure called, appropriately, Simplicio, both for his naïveté and because his namesake had been a noted Aristotelian commentator. Simplicio is outargued again and again by Salviati, the Copernican, named after one of Galileo's disciples. Questions are put to them by the third figure, Sagredo, the layman, who was named after Galileo's Venetian patrician friend. It is unmistakable that Simplicio's role is to lose every

The frontispiece of Galileo's *Dialogue*, dedicated to his patron, the Grand Duke of Tuscany, shows the three men who conduct the discussion in the book. The questioner, Sagredo, is on the left, and as a layman he is hatless. The Ptolemaic in the center wears the turban commonly given to ancient or exotic figures; and the Copernican, on the right, wears a doctoral hat and carries a little model of the heliocentric system. Since they are walking along Venice's canals as they talk, there are ships in the background.

argument, and Galileo was rash to put into his mouth, at the very end, an echo of the pope's warning about limiting God's power to construct the world in any way he wished.

The book ranged over the nature of scientific reasoning as well as specific problems of astronomy, and both topics served to reinforce not only the Copernican view but also the insistence that heaven and Earth were subject to the same physical laws:

> SAGREDO: Resolve, Simplicio, to produce the reasons that may serve to persuade us that the Earth differs from the celestial bodies.
>
> SIMPLICIO: On the Earth there are continual generations, corruptions, alterations, etc., which neither our senses nor the traditions of our ancestors ever saw in heaven.
>
> SALVIATI: But if you content yourself with these "seen" experiences, you must account China and America among the celestial bodies, for you never beheld in them the alterations you see here in Italy. And if you believe the alterations in Mexico on the report of those who come from there, what intelligence have you from the Moon to assure you that there are no such alterations on it? . . .
>
> SAGREDO: Make the Earth turn round its axis in twenty-four hours and, without imparting this same motion to any other planet or star, all shall have their risings and settings.
>
> SIMPLICIO: The business is, to make the Earth move without a thousand inconveniences.
>
> SALVIATI: All the inconveniences shall be removed as fast as you propound them. It is a shorter and easier way to move the Earth rather than the Universe. A most true maxim of Aristotle teaches: "That is done in vain by many means which may be done with fewer." This renders it more probable that the diurnal motion belongs to the Earth alone rather than to the whole Universe, with the exception of the Earth.

Galileo's citation of Aristotle was ironic, because he was undermining the view of the universe that had its roots in Aristotelian teachings. Yet his own arguments were by no means flawless. Just as he could not accept Kepler's ellipses because of his esthetic preference for circles, so he refused to acknowledge magnetic attraction. He was so determined to remove magical interpretations from the study of nature, and so convinced that magnetism was an occult property, that he refused to acknowledge attraction between bodies as a means of explaining physical phenomena. The result was that he came up with a completely mistaken theory about the cause of tides, which he attributed to the shaking of the oceans as the Earth spun. Yet the overall impact of the book was unavoidable: it dealt a devastating blow to the Ptolemaic system and other traditional ideas.

The *Dialogue* was published, after some delay, in 1632, complete with the Church's imprimatur. But if it was a bureaucratic error that provided the book with formal approval, that alone could not deter Galileo's enemies from taking advantage of the opportunity he had now given them. Later that year he was once again summoned to Rome by the Inquisition, and in the face of such a request his patron, the grand duke, was unable to protect him. Pope Urban, unwilling to take on the powerful orders who were now ranked against his old friend, piously affirmed that it was "best to go along with the common opinion," raised no objection, and even urged a rigorous interrogation. The sixty-eight-year-old Galileo, after a lifetime of peering through telescopes and watching nature's ways, was almost blind, but he undertook the arduous journey, confident that the certificate from Bellarmine, now long dead, would absolve him.

It was not to be. He was confined in an Inquisition prison and interrogated; and when, after two months, he finally faced his tribunal in April 1633, his defense was brushed aside. Against his certificate, which left open the possibility that Copernicanism could be discussed as a theory—hardly a case he could have defended in the best of circumstances—the inquisitors produced a document (unknown to Galileo and possibly a forgery) that represented Bellarmine as forbidding any discussion of Copernicanism at all. The old man now realized his danger. Still jaunty just a few weeks before coming to Rome, he understood at last that he was in mortal danger of excommunication, a terrible punishment for the traditional and unquestioning

Christian that he was. His only recourse was to recant, and to do so with a wholeheartedness that would convince his inquisitors of his sincerity:

> Whereas I wrote and printed a book which has caused me to be vehemently suspected of heresy, that is to say, of having held and believed that the sun is the center of the world:
>
> Therefore, to remove from the minds of your Eminences, and of all faithful Christians, this strong suspicion, reasonably conceived, with sincere heart and unfeigned faith I abjure, curse, and detest the aforesaid errors and heresies.

The recantation went against everything he had stood for, and legend (though implausible) has it that, as he left the hall, he said below his breath, referring to the Earth, *"Eppur si muove"*—"And yet it does move." Indeed, during the remaining nine years of his life, he was anything but cowed. Although placed under house arrest in his home outside Florence, he had both the "Letter" to the grand duchess and his great work on physics, *The Two New Sciences*, published abroad, beyond the reach of the Inquisition.

Kepler had been prophetic—appropriately for an astrologer— when he had suggested to his colleague that Protestant publishers would enable him to be bold. Yet the boldness had gone far beyond anything even Kepler could have predicted. Although Galileo may have brought much of his misfortune on himself, and the retribution was as much political as religious, there is no question that, like Socrates, he was a martyr for new ideas, and in his case the first martyr of science. If his enemies thought they had done more than frighten a sickly old man, however, they were mistaken. The reaction to the condemnation was dismay rather than fear, and although the French mathematician René Descartes briefly considered burning his manuscripts, in the end he, too, published, and saw his books placed on the Index for their theological implications. Galileo had said long before that one could not forbid men to look at the heavens, and even earlier he had been reassured by Kepler—though it was not a position he himself espoused until his livelihood was secure—that good ideas had to be proclaimed, and would eventually succeed, "so great is the power of truth."

Remarkably, he was able to remain true to that cause even during the years of house arrest. But now he could also give more attention to the family that he had largely neglected during the twenty years of celebrity and court life. His younger daughter never forgave him for putting her in a convent, but the older one had become a devoted nun and stayed close to her father, especially as his difficulties mounted. "You know I am with you in your troubles," she wrote him in the Inquisition prison, "which should be of some comfort to you. Since you are fully aware of the instability of all things of this world, you must not pay much heed to these storms." It was a consolation to him to return to her company late in 1633, but a terrible blow—as hard as the Inquisition trial—when she died just four months later, at the age of thirty-three.

The other children were never particularly close to him, and Galileo's last years were spent essentially in blindness and solitude. But one last relationship did stir some of his old enthusiasm. The brilliant sister-in-law of his son, Alessandra Bocchineri, was in her thirties, though she had already been widowed twice. She had been a dazzling figure at the Gonzaga court in Mantua and at the Habsburg court in Vienna. Now married to a Florentine diplomat, she kept up a lively and coquettish correspondence with the famous scientist: "I often wonder to myself," she wrote to the seventy-seven-year-old in 1641, "how I shall be able before I die to find a way to be with you and spend a day in conversation without scandalizing or making those people jealous who have made fun of us for this wish." Appropriately, it was to her that Galileo wrote the last letter of his life, and its debonair ending reveals how little his love of the world around him had diminished, even in his lonely final days: "Your letter is a great consolation, for I have been confined to bed for many weeks. My cordial thanks for your kind affection, and for your sympathy. I beg you to excuse my involuntary brevity, and with most warm affection I kiss your hands."

PART VII

The New Professional

Artemisia Gentileschi, Self-Portrait. One of the allegories Artemisia produced for the
Queen's House in Greenwich was a female figure representing Painting. It was entirely
appropriate, therefore, that the figure should have been a self-portrait.

An Artist

Y THE FIRST HALF of the seventeenth century, the ability of artists to bestow immortality on their subjects was widely acknowledged. Thanks to Vasari's writings, especially about Michelangelo, artists were considered to have the special, God-given quality known as genius; and they had achieved a level of respect and honor that they had last known in the ancient world, which the Renaissance had now revived. And yet they still struggled, as had Dürer a century before, to establish their autonomy, to win for themselves an independence of mind and freedom of action that the patrons on whom they relied were reluctant to grant. In essence, they were seeking the status of professionals: practitioners of a skill with its own procedures and its own standards of judgment. ❨ Although there were a number of leading figures who found dramatic ways of making that claim around 1600—notably the deliberately outrageous Italian painter Caravaggio—the emergence of this new self-image, this new identity, is seen with particular clarity in the career of the Roman artist Artemisia Gentileschi (herself a disciple of Caravaggio). For her triumph over the double disabilities of her vocation and her gender suggests how far-reaching were the changes in the status of the artist during the Renaissance.

Artemisia Gentileschi

FOR those who shaped the Renaissance, ancient Rome was an essential model for politics, education, literature, and the arts. In the mid fifteenth century the city also became a more immediate inspiration, as a source of patronage for artists, scholars, and musicians that endured longer and covered a wider range than any other center of patronage of the time. Generation after generation of popes, cardinals, and powerful aristocratic families brought the finest architects, sculptors, painters, writers, and composers to the holy city, making it a place of cultural pilgrimage that eventually outshone even Florence and Venice. For all the brilliance of the papal court, however, it was not until the age of the Baroque—from around 1600 onward—that Rome recovered its ancient role as the birthplace (rather than the borrower) of a new style that swept through Europe. It could be argued that the city of these years, adorned as it was by the works of Bernini, Caravaggio, and the Carracci, and serving as it did as a mecca for foreigners, enjoyed what may well have been the most dazzling and creative century in its long and distinguished artistic history.

A dramatic new vision of the possibilities of art has more than once crystallized, quite suddenly, in a particular place and time—whether it be the turn to antiquity of Masaccio, Donatello, and Brunelleschi in the Florence of the 1420s, the cubism of Braque and Picasso in the Paris of the 1910s, or the abstract expressionism of Pollock and de Kooning in the New York of the 1940s. The Rome of the 1590s was another such place. Here the Carracci brothers and Caravaggio began to create a powerful immediacy in painting that was to inspire at least two generations and to make the churches and palaces they decorated objects of artistic pilgrimage that bore comparison with Masaccio's frescoes or Michelangelo's marbles in Florence. Over the next few decades, Rubens, van Dyck, Poussin, and Velázquez were only the most famous of those who came to the city to study the pioneers of the Baroque as closely as they examined the relics of the classical age.

It was in this Rome that there had been living, since his teens in the 1570s, a well-respected, though not quite front-rank, painter from Pisa named Orazio Gentileschi. And it was here, in 1593, that his first child and only daughter, Artemisia, was born. Artemisia alone, among his four children, chose to follow her father's footsteps, and that very determination already marked her as unusual, because in sixteenth-century society no trade requiring apprenticeship was formally open to a woman. Indeed, had Orazio not trained her himself, there would have been no way for her to have qualified as a recognized artist, eligible to receive commissions in Rome and elsewhere.

Artemisia lost her mother at the age of twelve, and thereafter she seems to have been caught up entirely in the world of men—with her three brothers and her father's artist friends constantly in the studio-cum-house that was her home. Caravaggio himself, who is known to have borrowed props from Orazio, was a visitor, and the child would doubtless have seen the powerful and unprecedented depictions of biblical subjects that he created both for secular patrons (PLATE XI) and for the churches of San Luigi dei Francese and Santa Maria del Popolo, not far from where she lived. Although his influence took hold of her work only slowly, she had completed her first known painting by the age of seventeen, in 1610, the year of Caravaggio's death. That its subject should have been *Susanna and the Elders*, however—that timeless story of woman's vulnerability in a male world—was sadly prophetic.

For it was only a few months later, when Artemisia was still seventeen, that she endured the traumatic experience that was to shadow, though by no means to redirect, her life. Her own account, given at the trial which ensued in 1612, has a directness and immediacy that remain vivid even after the passage of nearly four hundred years.

My father has had imprisoned the tenant who lives in our upstairs apartment, named Tuzia. In the disgrace and betrayal that was perpetrated by the said Tuzia against me, she acted as procuress to have me deflowered by a certain Agostino Tassi, a painter.

Last year, when my father lived on the Via della Croce, he rented the apartment upstairs to Tuzia. My father was a close friend of Agostino Tassi who, because of this friendship, began to visit our house often and to become friends with Tuzia. One of the times he came Tuzia tried to persuade me that Agostino was a well-mannered young man, courteous to women, and that we would get on well. She pushed so much that she convinced me to speak to Agostino, having said he would let me know what scandal a servant named Francesco was spreading about me. Since I wanted to know what Francesco had said, I decided to talk to Agostino, who had been let into the house by Tuzia. He told me Francesco was boasting I had given him what he wanted. I replied it didn't matter to me, because I knew I was a virgin. He told me he was upset by these things, because of his friendship with my father and because he valued my honor, and he left.

The following morning, when I was in bed and my father had left the house, Agostino came again, with an orderly named Cosimo, and Tuzia let them in. When I heard people walking up the stairs I threw on my dress and went upstairs. Cosimo came toward me and tried to persuade me to be nice to Agostino. When I showed I was disgusted with the way he was treating me, he added: "You have given it to so many, you can give it to him as well." Enraged, I asked him to relieve me of his presence, and turned my back on him. Finally they left. I was upset by these words for several days, and my father was distressed because I didn't want to tell him the reason.

Tuzia took this opportunity to tell my father to send me out for walks because it was bad for me to stay home all the time. The following morning my father told Tuzia to take me out as far as S. Giovanni, believing that she was a respectable person. We went to S. Giovanni, where I saw Cosimo and Agostino close by. As I left the church Agostino followed me, coming closer and closer. But because I complained about it, he followed me at a distance all the way home.

While I was at home, the parish Fathers dropped by, and left the door open. With that, Agostino took the opportunity to come into the house. He then left, but as soon as the Fathers had gone, he came back and complained that I behaved badly toward him, saying I would regret it. I answered "Regret what, regret what? He who wants me must give me this," meaning marry me and put a ring on my finger.

On the same day, after I had eaten lunch, I was painting an image of one of Tuzia's boys for my own pleasure. Agostino stopped by and managed to come in because masons had left the door open. When he found me painting, he said: "Not so much painting, not so much painting," and he grabbed the palette and brushes and threw them around, saying to Tuzia, "Get out of here." When I said to Tuzia not to go and leave me, she said, "I don't want to stay here and argue."

Before she left, Agostino put his head on my breast, and as soon as she was gone he took my hand and said: "Let's walk together a while." While we walked around the room I told him I was feeling ill and thought I had a fever. He replied: "I have more of a fever than you do." After we had walked around two or three times, when we were in front of the bedroom door, he pushed me in and locked the door.

There follows a detailed, graphic, and shocking account of a sickening assault, during which the overpowered Artemisia screams out for Tuzia in vain. Feeling utterly helpless, she throws a knife at Agostino after her ordeal is over, but manages only to draw a little blood. And then, overcome by her shame and her fear of discovery, she allows herself to be mollified by his promise that he will now marry her, and even permits further visits in the expectation that he will make everything right in the end.

The revealing details of this depressing recollection, of which only a small portion has been quoted here, may seem all too familiar. A young woman with talents far beyond the ordinary somehow brings out the worst in those around her. Lacking female company at home, she seeks out a neighbor who betrays her while a busy father is away, and the terrifying result proves only how alone she is. Perhaps the most heartbreaking of the particulars in Artemisia's account is that the final horror begins when Agostino finds her painting "for my own pleasure." It is precisely her talent, so out of place in his world, that he finds so threatening, and infuriates him to such a degree that he has to grab her brushes and paints and throw them away.

But Agostino did not reckon with his victim's independence and determination. He probably expected that, as has always been the case—but especially in early modern times, when a woman's rights (to say nothing of her veracity) were more easily questioned than accepted—it would be difficult for her to convince the authorities to take her accusations seriously. At worst, he could (and did) resort to the standard response, for which the comments of Francesco and Cosimo had already prepared the ground, that she was known to be of loose morals and therefore unfit to charge anyone with misconduct. Indeed, Artemisia could not even bring her complaint herself. Following the procedures of the time, it was her father who had to sue Agostino for damages, while the real plaintiff had to relive her experiences—which she did, with remarkable calm and lucidity—as the prime witness.

The trial lasted for seven months, during which the assaults on Artemisia's character came thick and fast, not only from Agostino and his friends, but also from Tuzia. Orazio defended her shrewdly, revealing to the authorities how shady most of her accusers were. It turned out that Agostino had already been imprisoned for incest with his sister-in-law, and had had children with her. One of Agostino's friends, named Stiattesi, broke ranks, and finally the court concluded that Artemisia's was the correct version of the events. If this was vindication of sorts, the society of the time seemed unable to take the matter too seriously. Agostino spent eight months in jail, but he was then released.

For Artemisia, at the age of nineteen, the central concern now was to return to the painting she loved. First, however, she had to leave Rome: though a source of inspiration, the city, and even the walks through its streets, had become too immediate a reminder of disgrace. Although Orazio had taken up her case largely in order to defend his own honor, and relations between father and daughter were never to be the same again, he was instrumental in her relocation and her return to respectability.

One of Orazio's contacts was with the Medici court, home of the grand dukes of Tuscany in Florence, and in 1612, during the trial, he wrote to the mother of Duke Cosimo, the Grand Duchess Christina, about his family's tribulations. The Medici mother and son were distinguished supporters of the arts and letters, famous to this day for their patronage of Galileo. Florence may not have been what it was in the age of Lorenzo the Magnificent, but it was still an artistic center of major importance. Moreover, it was a Florentine artist, Pietro Stiattesi—probably a relative of the friend of Agostino who had turned against him at the trial—who married Artemisia (possibly at her father's urging) and thus, in the eyes of the time, restored her respectability just a month after the trial ended. The couple seem to have produced two daughters over the decade that followed, both of whom apparently followed their mother into careers as painters, though little more is known of them. What we do know is that at some point in the early 1620s Artemisia and Pietro separated, and that by the 1630s they had lost all contact with each other.

Artemisia's instinct for independence, even though now accompanied by two daughters, seems to have reasserted itself as her life stabilized. She was determinedly self-reliant, and when she absolutely required male help—for instance, in transporting her work to distant patrons—she employed one of her brothers. The estrangement from her father certainly continued, perhaps because, his own honor satisfied, he became reconciled with Agostino a few years after the trial. In any event, it became clear in the 1610s that Artemisia was embarking on a public career, with international recognition: a remarkable achievement for a nonaristocratic woman of her time.

The subject of her art, moreover, was distinct. Of the nearly sixty paintings she is currently believed to have completed, over forty had women in central roles. Her most common subjects were taken from biblical and classical themes. To a degree unique among the artists of the time, however, they focused on stories that had women as leading characters. This emphasis doubtless reflected her own interests as well as those of her patrons, and was abetted by the fact that she had easier access to female models than did her male colleagues. Artemisia had a particular fondness for allegorical figures, a genre that relied heavily on female embodiments, such as Inclination,

Artemisia Gentileschi, Madonna and Child. The warmth that flows between mother and child in this painting reveals Artemisia at her most tender, capable of using strong contrasts of light and dark, not for drama, but for subdued effect.

various Muses, Poesia, and Painting. And although the Madonna and Mary Magdalene, standard themes of the age, did appear in her paintings, they were only a small part of a roster that included Lot's daughters, Potiphar's wife, Bathsheba, Esther, Susanna, and Judith from the Old Testament and the Apocrypha, and Diana, Galatea, Lucretia, Minerva, Andromeda, and Persephone from classical myth.

It is hard to think of anyone else in the history of art who painted the biblical heroine Judith five times in ten years (PLATES XII AND XIII). And yet, given what she had lived through, one can understand why Artemisia returned to the theme that often during the first decade of her career. Indeed, in one version, Artemisia makes the figure of Judith, holding both the sword that has cut off the head of Holofernes and the head itself, suggest a self-portrait. What is arguably her most powerful painting, alive with so much immediacy, drama, violence, and slashing contrasts of light and dark as to make it entirely worthy of Caravaggio himself, is a *Judith Slaying Holofernes* that rivets the attention to the half-severed head and the blood gushing from the wound. This was a sufficiently famous image to inspire engraved copies for wider distribution. Nor is the theme of a woman's struggles (and rare triumphs) in a man's world hard to find in the other stories she depicted: Esther, Bathsheba, Susanna, Lucretia, Cleopatra, and Persephone.

And her talent was soon recognized. Within a short time of settling in Florence, she had become an official member of its artistic academy, the Accademia del Disegno, the first woman ever to receive that honor. The great-nephew of Michelangelo, a leading figure in the city's artistic circles, promoted her work and gave her a major role in the decoration of the Casa Buonarroti, a house that he was turning into a shrine to his great-uncle. She became friendly with Florence's most famous citizen, Galileo, who was also a member of the Accademia del Disegno, and she reminded him, in a letter twenty years later, that one of her Judiths "would have been lost to memory if it had not been revived by your assistance," an intervention about which nothing else is known. Most important of all, she received commissions from the Medici themselves. It was to the grand duke

Artemisia Gentileschi, David and Bathsheba. During Artemisia's last years in Naples, the style of her paintings became more subdued. But the themes remained dramatic. Her scene of Bathsheba bathing is less a celebration of the female form, as was often the case in other depictions of the time, than an illustration of the incident that begins a biblical story of lust, adultery, and death.

that she wrote in early 1620 to make sure it was all right for her to leave the city:

> So that you will not be displeased by a short trip to Rome that I have decided to take, I wish to inform Your Most Serene Highness of it with this letter. The many minor illnesses I have suffered, as well as the not inconsequential worries I have had with my home and family, have led me to this decision. In order to recover from my troubles, I shall spend a few months there with friends. During that time, I assure Your Most Serene Highness that you shall have what you ordered, for which I received an advance of fifty *scudi*.

The troubles here referred to may well have been Artemisia's difficulties with her husband. Since the grand duke died just two weeks after this letter was written, however, she probably felt that her obligation to return was at an end. Well established in the world, and with Rome now seeming less threatening, she apparently decided to stay in the city of her original inspiration. Except for brief trips to Genoa (with her father, with whom there was apparently a reconciliation in Rome) and to Venice, she remained there throughout the 1620s. She became part of a lively and famous group of artists, many of them foreigners, who occupied her old neighborhood and in one form or another elaborated the inspiration of Caravaggio. One of them depicted her hand, holding a paintbrush, as the very essence of their craft; others created her likeness in engraving and medal. And she herself considered it appropriate to use a self-portrait to embody Painting, a choice obviously approved by one of Rome's leading patrons, who commissioned the work, and by one of Europe's greatest collectors, King Charles I of England, who bought it a few years later (see page 176).

Around the time this picture was completed, in 1630, Artemisia moved to Naples, where she was to remain, except for a three-year interlude in England, for the remaining twenty-two years of her life. She never liked the city, which seethed with social unrest and a resentment of its Spanish rulers that erupted into a major revolt in 1647. Her constant hope was to return to Rome, or, as she put it in a letter to the Medicis' secretary of state, her main contact in Florence, to some other source of patronage:

> Whenever you have the opportunity to talk to His Most Serene Highness, please do not forget what I mentioned in my last letter, as I have no further desire to stay in Naples, both because of tumults and fighting, and because of the hard life and the high cost of living.

And yet, for all of her efforts, and commissions from princes and patrons not only throughout Italy but also from abroad, she remained in Naples. The appeal, despite the less congenial living conditions, was probably twofold: style and patronage. Ever since Caravaggio's stay there, following his departure from Rome over twenty years earlier, Naples had become a prime location of his influence. Moreover, as the largest city in Italy (and possibly in all Europe), it had a wealth of buyers of art in religious orders and monasteries, and among court aristocrats, that outshone even Rome, with its cardinals, papal families, and patricians. If these two attractions—style and patronage—were indeed the reasons Artemisia remained in Naples, despite its discomforts, she was demonstrating her unique sense of independence yet again, placing her commitment to her profession above all else.

That she felt secure enough in the Naples years to poke fun at her own work is apparent in her comment to a patron that "the painting is coming along well, and will be finished by the end of this month, with eight figures and two dogs, which to me are even better than the figures." But she defended herself fiercely against what she regarded as slights:

> I was mortified to hear that you wanted to deduct one third from the already very low price I had asked. I must tell Your Lordship that this is impossible, and that I cannot accept a reduction, both because of the value of the painting and my great need. Were this not so, I would give it to Your Lordship as a present. And I am displeased that for the second time I am being treated like a novice. It must be that in your heart Your Lordship finds little merit in me. I thought I was serving you well to charge less. However, so that you are not

Inigo Jones, The Queen's House, Greenwich. This exquisite building introduced the English to the classical Palladian style, which dominated large-scale architecture in England for the next two centuries. Commissioned originally for the queen by James I, and completed by his son Charles I for his queen, it had a magnificent central hall whose ceiling was decorated by the Gentileschis.

left with the wrong impression, I think it would be a good idea for you to have it appraised.

And she clearly had the standing to make such claims with confidence. In 1638 she was called to London, to join her father in a major decorative project, by one of the most lavish and discriminating patrons of the day, Charles I.

A wonderfully elegant house had been built for Charles's mother in Greenwich some twenty years earlier by England's leading architect, Inigo Jones. If any one building can be said to have introduced the Palladian style to a nation that was to be its ardent disciple for two centuries, the Queen's House was that building. For Charles, devoted as he was to things Italian, it seemed only fitting to complete the interior in the manner of the villas it was echoing, and the best way to do that was to import artists familiar with the Palladian tradition. It was a tribute to both Gentileschis that they received the commission, and even more of a tribute that they were able to adapt their art to lyrical depictions of mythological themes that brought to life in England the Venetian atmosphere of Veronese and his followers. Artemisia also sold more than half a dozen paintings to Charles; but once the Queen's House was finished, and a civil war loomed, she moved back to Naples in 1642.

Her painting now displayed more delicate qualities—a softness and a sensuality in depictions of Lot, Galatea, and Bathsheba that muted some of the drama and harsh contrasts of her earlier work. But the themes of vulnerable womanhood remained strong, and the shift toward a less overtly Caravaggesque style reflects her continuing artistic development and also her ability to respond to changing tastes. That she was eagerly sought after was clear, as was her ability to set her fees, like other major talents, according to the number of human figures in a picture. Yet she was never able to rest in the struggle to win equal treatment. Just two years before she died, she was still protesting to one of her patrons, Antonio Ruffio, because a friend of his wanted a drawing to confirm that she would produce a *Galatea* similar to the one Ruffio owned:

> I have made a solemn vow never to send my drawings, because people have cheated me. Just today I found that, having done a drawing of souls in Purgatory for the Bishop, he, in order to spend less, commissioned another painter to do the painting using my work. If I were a man, I can't imagine it would have turned out this way, because once the concept has been realized and defined with lights and darks, the rest is a trifle. Therefore, this gentleman is very wrong to ask for drawings, when he can see the design of the *Galatea*.

A few months earlier she had complained in similar vein that Ruffio thought her worthy of pity, "because a woman's name raises doubts until her work is seen."

Artemisia would doubtless not have been surprised to learn that soon after her death in 1652 her work fell into obscurity. Occasional mentions aside, it took three hundred years before she again attracted significant interest. Yet her own estimate must have left her content. As she wrote to Galileo, "I have seen myself honored by all the kings and rulers of Europe." And the paintings themselves, as she correctly predicted, would eventually serve to "provide the evidence of my fame."

PART VIII

The
Mastery of
Power

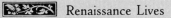

Van Dyck, Albrecht von Wallenstein. This painting of the generalissimo in armor, holding the commander's staff, suggests why Van Dyck was regarded as the greatest portraitist of the age, because even in its unfinished state it suggests the imperiousness for which Wallenstein was notorious.

194

 # A Warrior

HE RISING COSTS AND DESTRUCTIVENESS of warfare following the invention of gunpowder were an inescapable feature of Renaissance society. If on the one hand they added a grim tinge to the enthusiasms of the age—while at the same time creating new opportunities for exploitation and profit—they also had profound effects on social relations. In particular, the leveling of military prowess by the humble handgun caused aristocrats to rethink their traditional emphasis on military valor as the justification for their exalted status. A gentleman came to be set apart by taste, patronage, and elegance, as well as bravery. But even the value of courage was put in question by the rising levels of atrocity, especially during the vicious conflict known as the Thirty Years' War. ℭ That military success was essential to power could not be denied. But what sort of person should a warrior be in this new era? One model was offered by the most spectacular and meteorically successful general of the Thirty Years' War, Albrecht von Wallenstein. A minor Bohemian nobleman, master of logistics, brilliant speculator, and fastidious patron, he dazzled all of Europe both by his rise and by his fall. What he made unmistakable, however, was the fascination of warfare, and its central place in Renaissance society.

Wallenstein

LONG after its sensational appearance on the European stage as a hotbed of dissent in the days of Hus, Prague remained a refuge for the unorthodox. The tradition has continued into our own century, through Kafka and Havel, but the galaxy of fantastic and exuberant figures—magicians, mystics, and rebels—may have shone at its brightest two hundred years after Hus, during the eccentric reign of Rudolf II. This Holy Roman emperor, who ruled from 1576 to 1612, made Prague his capital, and turned it into a haven for the unconventional and even the bizarre, for the most probing but also the most unexpected ideas of his time.

His contemporaries regarded Rudolf as a melancholy man. Like his cousin in Spain, Philip II, he was sober, dignified, and remote. He dressed in black and rarely smiled. Unlike Philip, though, who was famous for his self-control, Rudolf suffered fits of depression, and was less interested in practical, day-to-day matters than in ideas, symbols, and the supernatural. It pleased him, for example, to have a pet lion, which brought to life in his palace the emblem of the Habsburg emperors. To some observers this seemed a sign of madness, no less incomprehensible than his collection of oddities, his patronage of arcane art, and his tolerance of religious as well as intellectual diversity.

Yet there was a method to Rudolf's madness. Fascinated by the ingenious magical speculations of his day, which sought the hidden, mystical keys that many believed could unlock all knowledge, he tried to put the new ideas into practice. He brought leading theorists of the occult to his court—not only the leading astronomer-astrologers of the time, the Dane Tycho Brahe and the German Johannes Kepler, but even a local rabbi, Judah Loeb, who dabbled in Cabala and mysticism and was later said to have fabricated an artificial man, the Golem. Rudolf also put together a cabinet of curiosities, the ancestor of the modern museum, in which he sought to reflect symbolically all

Jan Brueghel the Elder and Adriaen Stalbemt, The Archdukes Albert and Isabella in a Collector's Cabinet. This scene, showing two rulers of the day visiting a "cabinet" of marvels, documents the new passion for collecting. Like the best-known pioneer of such enterprises, Emperor Rudolf II, this collector has assembled works of art, plants, animals, globes, instruments, and other objects in an enterprise that is the ancestor of the modern museum.

of creation by assembling not only works of art but also exotic objects like a tiger's tooth. The purpose was to suggest that the emperor could now comprehend, and thus rule, a representation of the entire world. The Italian painter Arcimboldo paid tribute to Rudolf, one of the great patrons of the age, by depicting him quite literally as the image of fruitfulness and fertility (PLATE XIV).

Albrecht von Wallenstein, the only son who would survive child-hood in a family of minor Bohemian nobles, was born during Rudolf's reign. Both his parents died before he reached the age of twelve, in 1595; but despite a meager inheritance, he was brought up by relatives to the life of a young aristocrat. He had a fine humanist education, an introduction to court life, a Grand Tour of Italy, and an exposure to the variety of religious beliefs that still flourished in Bohemia. Wallenstein was always to wear his faith lightly, showing no great personal commitment either to the Protestantism of his closest relatives or to the Catholicism of the distant but more prominent relatives who eventually persuaded the ambitious young man that the future, in Habsburg lands, lay with those who identified with the Roman Church. He had already started on the military career that was the standard means of livelihood for poor noblemen when, around 1606, at the age of twenty-three, he formally became a Catholic. Where the supernatural was concerned, however, it was always clear that he was far more interested in the magical world that, in those years, was centered in Prague.

The first public indication of Wallenstein's lifelong fascination with astrology came in 1608, when he asked Rudolf's principal astrologer, the great astronomer Johannes Kepler, to cast his horoscope. Although he was not told the identity of his subject—only the time and date of his birth—Kepler's assessment was uncannily accurate and prophetic.

> This lord is of an alert, assiduous, restless temper, with a keen appetite for novelties, striving always after the new and untried. He has an inclination to alchemy and sorcery, contempt for human practices and all religions, and an assumption that all actions are suspect and deceitful. This will give him grievous hurt and disparagement, so that he will be considered aloof and disdainful. His character will lack mercy and love, but be devoted to himself alone, harsh, rapacious, fickle, vehement, and intrepid. With age, his exceptional nature will be suited to perform great and important deeds. [He will marry] a widow, not beautiful, but rich in lands, buildings, cattle, and coin.

The client, committed to the truth of astrology, may have set about ensuring that the prophecies would be fulfilled, and Kepler may have found out who had commissioned the horoscope. Nevertheless, it is by no means easy to dismiss the document (of which only a small extract is quoted here, and not one of whose details proved wrong) as fakery or fluke. Within a year, for example, Wallenstein made exactly the kind of marriage—loveless, but hugely rewarding financially—that Kepler had predicted, and the young nobleman noted in the margin of the horoscope: "In May 1609 I entered into this marriage with a widow as described here to the life."

The union proved to be the turning point of his career. Lucretia was perhaps the richest woman in Moravia, the province neighboring Bohemia. Widowed but childless, she was four or five years older than her new husband, and immediately made him the joint administrator of her fortune and her sole heir. Within four years she was dead, and Wallenstein, now thirty years old, could use his formidable inheritance to pursue a spectacular military and political career.

Wallenstein's early background as a soldier had been primarily in minor skirmishes with the Turks, where he had been slightly wounded and, as befitted a nobleman, had risen to the rank of colonel, in command of a regiment. He had not particularly distinguished himself, but he had gained experience, and in one respect this was to be significant, for he had also served as a commissioner of supplies. In this second role he began to gain a familiarity with logistics, requisitions, funding, and pay that was to stand him in good stead. His mastery of precisely this aspect of warfare would in later years set him apart as a general. What counted now, however, was making a name for himself, and that he was at last able to do in 1617, four years after Lucretia's death.

Up to this point most of the fighting in central Europe had been prompted by the struggle, now more than a century old, between the Christian West and the Turks. In those campaigns, the Habsburgs, rulers of the areas in the Balkans and to the west that formed the frontier with the Turks, were in the front line. In 1617, however, an intra-Christian dispute erupted between Venice and one of these Habsburgs, Archduke Ferdinand of Styria, a cousin of Emperor Rudolf. Ferdinand was clearly the man of the future in the family—its most vigorous administrator, and also its staunchest advocate of Catholicism, beloved especially by the Jesuits. It was to him, therefore, that Wallenstein offered his services. "Lord Albrecht will of his own account place 180 cuirassiers and 80 musketeers at the Archduke's disposal." A well-equipped corps of good size was raised, and the paymaster himself led it to battle in Italy where, so the report went, he "especially distinguished himself by intrepid daring and valor." The campaign was soon over, but it had been a highly astute investment. As the promotions Wallenstein received from Ferdinand (who was indeed the rising star of the Habsburgs, and soon to be emperor) multiplied over the next few years, they were regularly accompanied by a mention of the Italian campaign and the soldiers "he placed at our disposal on his own account."

Albrecht was betting on the up-and-coming Ferdinand at the very moment when a crisis was brewing that would turn central Europe upside down and provide ample opportunities for the brilliant maneuvering, backed by Ferdinand, that would transform his life. The problem began in Wallenstein's homeland, Bohemia. Here the tradition of unorthodoxy and dissent that went back to Hus had resulted, during the sixteenth century, in a widespread commitment to Protestantism. That inclination had been accepted during Rudolf's tolerant reign, and even under that of his brother Matthias, who succeeded him in 1612. Next in line for the Bohemian crown, however, was the fiercely Catholic Ferdinand, who was determined to eradicate heresy from his lands. Indeed, when he became emperor in 1619, he set up his capital in Vienna rather than suspect Prague. The nobles of Bohemia, however, had the right to elect their kings, and when it became clear that Ferdinand intended to abolish the religious toleration they had enjoyed, they deposed him, threw his representatives out of a window, and elected a German Protestant prince in his place.

This seemingly local revolt precipitated thirty years of war throughout most of Europe, a struggle in which Wallenstein was to play a crucial part. At its outbreak, as a leading Moravian landowner with military experience, he was put in charge of the province's small band of troops, which were committed to Ferdinand, but he had only peripheral responsibilities in the campaign that followed. What did catch the eye was that he commandeered Moravia's treasury, after personally killing an officer who refused to cooperate, and sent it off to Vienna for war expenses. Ferdinand returned the treasure as illegally confiscated, but the gesture only confirmed the impression of fierce loyalty from Wallenstein. It did not take long for Albrecht to convert his resulting good graces into substantial personal gains.

The opportunities arose when the Bohemians were crushed, late in 1620. The army that conquered the kingdom for Ferdinand was provided by a devout Catholic ally, the duke of Bavaria, since the emperor did not have the resources to field an army of his own. As soon as the victory was won, however, it was the loyal nobility of the area who were put in charge of reestablishing Habsburg control. Here Wallenstein came into his own. When the rebels were condemned, and in many cases executed, their estates were forfeited. In the frenzy of confiscations, sales, and speculation that followed, the shrewd and ruthless Wallenstein emerged as the most successful profiteer of the age. He invested in banking, in the minting of coins, and above all in land, and within two years he had become the richest and most powerful figure in Bohemia.

In 1622 he became the owner of one of the great estates of central Europe, the duchy of Friedland north of Prague. As its lord, he was recognized as a prince of the empire and, even more elevated, as an imperial duke. Henceforth, he was to be known as the duke of Friedland, and it was in this capacity that Ferdinand, late in 1622, made him commandant of Prague and, in effect, the military governor of Bohemia. Wallenstein now built for himself, in the Italian style, with a lovely garden, one of the most magnificent palaces Prague had ever seen, a place that became a center of patronage for the leading artists of the day. Here he brought the new wife he married in 1623—a beautiful young woman eighteen years his junior, with whom, however, he was rarely at home. His second wife brought him an important family alliance, and was a splendid hostess, but there is little evidence that she falsified Kepler's prediction that Wallenstein would have a life lacking in love.

What took his attention, instead, was the application of his entrepreneurial skills to the rebuilding of towns in his duchy, so that

The magnificent classical loggia, and the gardens decorated with sculptures and a grotto in the Italian style, are the most spectacular features of Wallenstein's palace, which remains to this day an exceptional work of architecture in a city—Prague—that is by no means deficient in remarkable architecture.

he could make the area an enormously prosperous agricultural producer. Identified now with the Catholic cause, he was a leading supporter of the Jesuits, who poured into Bohemia to crush the last vestiges of Protestantism. He set up a college for them in his duchy, and to it he attached a boys' school that he supervised as closely as any of his properties.

Send me a list of nobly born boys who are at the school, how many they are, and give me the name of each, how old he is, and what hopes are placed in him for the future. Let the doctor who is to heal them be liberal with his medicines. Since they are liable to have scabs

202

from sheer dirtiness, see that they are kept clean and that the doctor heals with baths and other remedies those who have scabs. See that they learn everything my endowment specifies.

The grandeur and the magnificence were all very well, but they were exercised within narrow confines: to be a great man in Bohemia did not satisfy Wallenstein's ambitions. And so in 1625 he offered, in return for appointment as commander in chief, and permission for a novel form of financing, to raise an army for Ferdinand to fight the Protestants who were still trying to overturn the defeat of the Bohemian rebels. The emperor's limited resources notwithstanding, he would now have his own army and no longer be dependent on allies like the duke of Bavaria. Yet it was Wallenstein who sounded imperious as he described the offer:

> His Majesty must not temporize while the enemy daily musters more soldiery. That is why there is not a minute to be lost. I have offered to be of service to His Majesty, but if I come to see that a chance for boldness is missed, and recruitment intended only when the enemy is at our throats, then I shall not venture into such a labyrinth.

Within two months Ferdinand accepted.

Ever since the application of gunpowder to battle some two centuries earlier, the costs of warfare had been rising relentlessly. Equipping troops with cannon and guns was far too expensive an undertaking for anyone but a central government. Moreover, seventeenth-century tactics depended on ever-growing, disciplined bodies of soldiers, organized into massive formations that confronted one another on the battlefield with a constant stream of gunfire. To gain the advantage, one needed more men, and so recruitment and costs spiraled yet again. For a ruler like Ferdinand, whose small personal territories yielded only modest taxes, raising a significant army was well beyond his means. Wallenstein's offer thus seemed a godsend.

Wallenstein's recommendation, unprecedented in its scope, was that his troops be allowed to support themselves entirely "off the land"—to appropriate everything they needed in the way of food, housing, supplies, and even cash from any hostile territories they traversed. Previously, requisitions had been supplementary windfalls. Now they accounted for the totality of the army's support. As Ferdinand's commission put it, "We sanction the levy in conquered places and territories of sufferable contributions [whatever that meant!] and loans." Since much of the empire, following the defeat of Bohemia, feared and hated Ferdinand and offered havens for a succession of Protestant armies, it was not going to be hard to locate hostile lands. Moreover, Wallenstein reasoned, as long as his army kept moving, it would not drain an area of the means to support it. Equally important, he could convert his own domains in Bohemia into a huge source of provisions—food, beer, timber—for the army, and thus enrich himself even as he kept his troops supplied. This required a transportation and communication system of the highest order, and he set about creating it with the exemplary efficiency he had shown in all his enterprises. It could be said that Wallenstein became the greatest quartermaster in history (PLATE XIV).

Within a few months he had an army of over 50,000 men at his disposal. It was a polyglot force, for he never worried about the nationality or religion of his troops, so long as they served him well. To ensure their loyalty, he made certain that—almost uniquely in the Europe of his day—his soldiers were paid and fed regularly. That, after all, was the purpose of the high-powered logistical system he had put in place.

During the previous century, and as late as the 1650s in Cromwell's England, religious zeal often served to unite and rally a body of troops, though it was not as dependable as leaders would have liked. In the decades to come, and already in the army of Wallenstein's great adversary, the Swede Gustavus Adolphus, national allegiances were beginning to offer a means of inspiring soldiers. But no ideological cause was likely to be as effective or as predictable, in this age of perennial shortages of funds, as regular pay and victuals.

Over the next five years Wallenstein swept all before him, building for Ferdinand a level of power the emperor could never have expected. For centuries the Habsburgs, though titular rulers of an area that extended from the Baltic to the Alps, had been able to exercise direct control over only a small region centered on Austria. Now Wallenstein handed them what was in effect all of modern Germany, and more. Obsessive administrator that he was, he threw himself into details ranging from the supply of boots to the administration of military justice, not to mention larger questions having to do with strategy and tactics. He complained constantly, but his exertions had their effect, as opponent after opponent was defeated and fear of his troops steadily grew. Already in 1626 people were deploring the "singular character of this cruel man and his ambitious plans—nobody even wants to hear the name of Wallenstein."

The duke himself was undeterred, secure in his feeling that he was a pillar of the Habsburg cause:

> If people want me to retain my appetite for these affairs, then they should leave me alone, for I certainly neglect nothing that may benefit His Majesty. Were I to pay as much attention to the safety of my soul as I do to the service of the Emperor, I would surely have to spend no time in purgatory, much less suffer the pains of hell.

There were reasons for the suspicions. He was notoriously short-tempered; he was haughty and dictatorial; and he was brooding and distant, often wrapped up in his astrological speculations. A second horoscope by Kepler, now aware who his client was—he was later to enter Wallenstein's service for a while—predicted great things for the late 1620s, though it warned of dreadful prospects for early in 1634. The horoscope seemed to make the duke even more overbearing. He carved out a second dukedom for himself in northern Germany, took the title of generalissimo, or supreme commander, and began to act independently on the international scene.

There was constant diplomatic negotiation during this period, both with neighboring states and among leading princes of the empire, including the seven most important, the electors, with whom Wallenstein actively pursued his objective of securing a favorable peace. As he informed Ferdinand, the size of his army had diplomatic as well as military purposes:

> This great force at the disposal of Your Majesty will help bring about within the Empire a good and lasting peace, which I most humbly commend. I believe that when the Electors assemble, they will strongly espouse the cause of peace, which again I most humbly beg Your Majesty not to reject.

For all his protestations, Wallenstein hardly ever behaved humbly. And it was clear that some of his discussions, notably with representatives of Sweden, were being conducted quite independently. He was a long way from Vienna, and it seemed that he was talking about peace terms and the future of the empire without consulting, or even informing, the imperial court. Rumor suggested he was aiming to become emperor himself.

What infuriated the princes of the empire most of all, however, was that their own autonomy had been seriously impaired. This Bohemian upstart had subjected them to unprecedented control by the emperor. In 1629, in fact, Ferdinand ordered that all the Church property they had confiscated over the previous seventy years be returned. He was imposing his fierce Catholicism on them, and there was little they could do to resist. The following year, however, the seven leading princes had their revenge. They were known as electors because they had the power to elect each new emperor, and in 1630 Ferdinand asked them to bestow the title "king of the Romans" (in essence, heir to the imperial crown) on his son. The electors refused, saying they would vote for him only if Wallenstein were dismissed. Feeling he had no choice, the emperor capitulated.

In little more than a year, however, the generalissimo was back in command. He had not enjoyed retirement. His only son had died a few weeks after birth, and his surviving child, a daughter, seemed to be of little interest to him. He craved the great world of affairs, and even out of office he maintained his old contacts, prompting the rumormongers to suggest ever more insistently that he was plotting against his old master. There was never the slightest evidence of treason, or even of a wish to avenge his dismissal. Wallenstein simply liked to be at the center of events. Eventually, the repeated stories were to have their effect, even on his old patron Ferdinand, but for the time being they were ignored as a desperate need arose for the generalissimo's services.

The origin of the new crisis in fact antedated Wallenstein's dismissal. A few months earlier Gustavus Adolphus, increasingly worried about the rise of Habsburg and Catholic power across the Baltic from Sweden, had landed in northern Germany and had begun an invasion of the empire. The Swedish king was one of the most brilliant geniuses in military history, a master of mobility, swift strikes, and technical innovation. He had his engineers develop the first easily movable battlefield cannon, and it was he who had the idea of mixing small-arms fire with artillery at a siege (to protect the besiegers by making the defenders keep their heads down). With a huge army, most of them either fiercely loyal Swedes or dedicated Protestants, he swept through the empire in a campaign that transformed the Thirty Years' War and ended Habsburg ambitions in Germany forever. As Gustavus headed south, the danger to Ferdinand became palpable, and so, late in 1631, little more than a year after he had dismissed him, the emperor asked Wallenstein to resume command of his army.

What ensued over the next year was one of the most extraordinary cat-and-mouse games in the history of war. Two great armies, led by commanders of high intelligence and experience, shadowed each other across central and southern Germany. There were skirmishes, and in September of 1632 a pitched battle at which Wallenstein repulsed a major Swedish assault. Nearly sixty of his officers were killed, but he was able to report to Ferdinand:

> I can on my honor assure Your Majesty that all our officers and men behaved with a bravery I have rarely experienced. In this encounter the King [Gustavus] has blunted his antlers. This battle has given us further confidence by seeing that the King has been repulsed and that the title "invincible" belongs not to him, but to Your Majesty.

According to standard practice, that was the end of the campaigning season. With winter approaching, and conditions deteriorating, it was taken for granted that generals would retire to camp and resume fighting the following spring.

The execution of a criminal among the soldiers is one of the many powerful engravings in which Jacques Callot described the sufferings caused by the Thirty Years' War. Widely distributed, the pictures focus on the lawlessness and violence that disrupted European society. Here the discipline that the troops were supposed to maintain—visible in the orderly pikes on the left—is contrasted with the indiscipline that in fact marked the behavior of soldiers.

But not Gustavus. He decided on a bold strike in early November. He suddenly marched south, caught Wallenstein unawares, and forced an open battle on his terms near the village of Lützen on November 16. Never had a major battle taken place so late in the year, and few had been so brutal—a seven-hour bloodbath, according to one observer, which made casualties of half of the participants, leaving over 9,000 men dead, and even more wounded. The outcome was a standoff, though in forcing a large-scale retreat at the end of the day, the Swedes could claim victory. The decisive loss they suffered, though, outweighed any advantage they might have gained: Gustavus had been killed, and without his leadership his troops never again posed a mortal threat to the Habsburgs.

From this moment of ultimate triumph stemmed the tragic final act of Wallenstein's life. Just sixteen months after Lützen he was dead, assassinated on the orders of the emperor, and his fall has fascinated generations of playwrights, poets, novelists, and historians, from Schiller to Ranke. To some he has been the lost hero of Bohemian independence, the only man in the dark centuries before Masaryk who could have freed the Czechs from foreign domination. To others he represents the last effort to unite Germany before Bismarck. He has also been regarded as the one force for peace amid a ghastly war, and as a megalomanic traitor seeking nothing but his own ends. Unfortunately—perhaps fortunately—the record during these crucial sixteenth months is so murky that we will never know for sure.

We do know that he spent a good part of the time seeking to resupply his army; that he was often not well, and may in fact have suffered periods of depression, or at least of melancholy; and that he engaged in discussions (some of which have remained secret ever since) with just about every significant actor in the war theater: German princes, Swedes, French, fellow generals, even Bohemian exiles. There was talk of making him king of Bohemia, of finding a way to peace, of ridding the empire of the Jesuits, of armistices, of Spanish reinforcements, of the old enmity of the Bavarians (long resentful because his army had replaced theirs), of a vast Catholic-Protestant alliance to expel all foreign troops, of papal and other plots. Finally, however, Ferdinand was persuaded that his generalissimo was indeed plotting treason, that he was about to join the enemies of the Habsburgs, and that the only solution was to order his murder. Whether the contacts with the other side were quests for peace or not, the emperor had no doubt:

> His design was to drive Us and Our House from Our hereditary kingdoms, lands, and peoples, to usurp Our crown, to which end he proposed to attach Our faithful generals, letting it be heard how he would utterly exterminate Us, with perjured disloyalty and barbaric tyranny.

It seems clear that these accusations were nonsense, but by this stage accuracy no longer mattered. Wallenstein had too many enemies, and was too widely feared. He was also in sufficient ill health for Ferdinand to gamble that, unlike the situation in 1631, little would be lost if the generalissimo were removed from the scene. Nor was there any compunction about assassination: this was wartime, it was an age of public murder (including two kings of France during the previous fifty years), and emperors had their rights. The order was given, and in March of 1634 (the spring that Kepler had warned of) Wallenstein was savagely put to death by a company of assassins. For the victim, though, this fate would have been accepted as a destiny told in the stars, or by an even higher authority.

A few years before, a mystic named Christina Poniatowska had visited Wallenstein's wife. While there, she had fallen into a trance, and then described what she had seen:

> Wallenstein entered in a bloody gown and sought to climb a ladder swiftly into the clouds. It broke, and so he fell to earth. As he lay on the ground, his heart was pierced by a bolt from heaven, and an angel said: "This is the day when this wicked man, wholly without pity, shall perish."

The generalissimo's response to the story was jocular, but may well have reflected his deepest beliefs. "My Lord the Emperor," he said, "gets letters from Rome and Constantinople, Madrid and Paris, but I receive them from Heaven!"

PART IX

The Pragmatist in Changing Times

Glückel of Hameln. No authentic likeness of Glückel has survived, but this nineteenth-century imaginary portrait is labeled a memorial to her, and it may have been commissioned by one of her many descendants. The clothing and the gold betrothal ring she wears as a pendant (a common practice at the time) suggest a person of standing, and the quill and paper recall the remarkable memoirs for which she is now remembered. Since the painting itself vanished during World War II, even this link is now distant and indirect—a fate that would not have surprised Glückel, who thought herself unremarkable and regarded all human accomplishments as ephemeral.

A Merchant

AS EUROPE'S POPULATION GREW, and overseas empires provided new markets and resources, the pace of economic change quickened. The Renaissance was the period that saw the birth of modern capitalism. Rapid urbanization would create, by 1700, over a dozen cities larger than 100,000, and three (London, Paris, and Naples) that approached or exceeded half a million inhabitants. Major financial and industrial enterprises were being established, and governments were launched on their long history of trying to devise policies that would promote prosperity. ℭ Then as now, however, much about economic behavior remained unknown. The result was, for all the expanding opportunities, an unpredictability and volatility that was only aggravated by the plagues, famines, and wars that regularly devastated huge areas. And yet, even amid the uncertainty, an indomitable breed of traders and entrepreneurs gradually forged new levels of wealth for Europe and laid the foundations for the transformations that were to follow in the age of industrialization. We have caught some of the flavor of their lives in the biography of Thomas Platter. For a closer look, a century later, and in those same Germanic lands, one can do no better than to follow the fortunes of an obscure woman named Glückel. Her experiences can give us a better sense of the struggles and achievements of these early capitalists than can the exploits of more prominent representatives of the world of commerce.

Glückel of Hameln

SCATTERED throughout Renaissance Europe, often in small communities, was one distinctive group of perennial wanderers, the Jews. In the early days of our period, in the 1400s, they were most abundant and visible in Spain, where they provided leading figures in the intellectual and professional circles of the day, such as the royal finance minister, Isaac Abarbanel. Elsewhere in Europe, they were to be found in occasional isolated concentrations (for instance, in Prague) and in significant numbers only in Italy. By 1700, however, the pattern was very different.

Their largest gathering now was in Poland. Here they inhabited a distinct area, known as the Pale, where contact with gentiles was limited. The Italian community remained noteworthy, but its members now lived in ghettos. And in Spain, Judaism was but a memory, recalled only by the traditions of the *conversos*—those who had converted to Christianity in order to remain in their homeland. In two countries where they had been virtually unknown for centuries, however, England and the Netherlands, newly arrived groups of Jews were flourishing in relatively open societies. And in area after area of the German-speaking territories of Europe, pockets of Jewish life had reappeared after a major forced exodus on the eve of the Renaissance. Indeed, they were given a sizable boost in the mid seventeenth century by the usual stimulus to their population growth—persecution elsewhere. A large section of the kingdom of Poland, the Ukraine, seceded, and the terrible pogroms that marked the ensuing civil war drove thousands of Jews westward. If the pressure for constant movement was one of their most distinctive experiences, it had certainly not diminished by 1700.

Even in the best of circumstances they functioned under severe disabilities. There was no host regime that allowed Jews the rights even the humblest Christian could take for granted. In most regions, for example, they could neither own land nor enter the basic trades of the time, from shoemaking to weaving, all of which were controlled by guilds or other corporations that were open only to members of the Church. But the ingenuity and risk taking the Jews required to survive, combined with their enforced aptitude for travel and international connections, gave them a unique and emblematic role in the transformation of Europe's economic life during these centuries.

It was no wonder that William Shakespeare, perhaps the most acute observer of the age, should have made a Jew the symbol of the profound commercial revolution that was overtaking his society. *The Merchant of Venice* is a play about the new moral universe created by capitalism, and Shakespeare, by making Shylock its exemplar, signaled his view that its values were the antitheses of such standard Christian virtues as charity. If to notable contemporaries like Christopher Marlowe the Jew epitomized evil, and to others like Jean Bodin or Francis Bacon he embodied the wisdom of Solomon, to Shakespeare he was the new *homo economicus*, with horizons that reached far beyond traditional localities and occupations, with links to distant places, and with means of livelihood that exposed him constantly to risk. Nor is this insight contradicted by the historical record. Even the hectic life of one of the few Jewish women whose story we can trace in detail reveals the consequences of her people's position and how their response contributed to the shaping of Europe's new international and entrepreneurial economic system.

Her name was Glückel ("little piece of luck" in German), and she was born in the old Hanseatic port city of Hamburg in 1646. For most of this period Hamburg housed one of the three fairly large

Der Jüd.

Bin nicht vmb sonst ein Jüd genannt/
Ich leih nur halb Gelt an ein Pfandt/
Löst mans nit zu gesetztem Ziel/
So gilt es mir dennoch so viel/
Darmit verderb ich den loßn hauffn/
Der nur wil Feyern / Fressn vnd Sauffn/
Doch nimpt mein Handel gar nit ab/
Weil ich meins gleich viel Brüder hab.

These two engravings give the flavor of public attitudes toward Jews in the German lands during Glückel's lifetime. The page from Jost Amman's *Ständebuch* (see page 88) devoted to the Jew (*above*) characterizes him entirely by his financial extortions, by the many religious festivals and the gluttony which somehow do not interfere with his profits, and by the large numbers of his brethren. Given the hatred the Jewish community (which in fact was tiny) managed to arouse, we can guess it is an account book that one of the "people of the book" is holding in this picture. The persistent hostility deteriorated all too readily into assaults like the one portrayed (*right*)— an invasion of the Frankfurt ghetto during a vicious persecution in 1614.

settlements of German Jews. Yet Jews were by no means city dwellers in general, like their Italian cousins. Less than 10 percent of them lived in the three major centers—Hamburg, Breslau, and Frank-furt—while the rest were scattered throughout the villages and small towns of rural Germany. And no place was secure. When Glückel was two, all Jews were expelled from Hamburg. Some forty households settled in the adjacent town of Altona, ruled by the king of Denmark, but the breadwinners had to travel each day to Hamburg (and leave by the time the gates were shut at nightfall) in order to earn a living. Only ten years later did Glückel's father get permission for the Jews to return.

That same year, 1658, she was betrothed to Chaim of Hameln, the son of a prosperous jewelry and precious-metals dealer in the small nearby town of Hameln, famous now only for the story of its pied piper. The wedding took place in 1660, when Glückel was fourteen (not unusually early for a small and embattled community bent on survival), and the thirty-year marriage that ensued was the happiest period of her life. She did not much like Hameln, "a dull, shabby hole" in her words, with only two Jewish households, which could barely provide the ten men needed for religious services. But she adored her in-laws, who made up for the lost bustle of Hamburg:

> There I was—a carefree child whisked in the flush of youth from parents, friends and everyone I knew, from a city like Hamburg into a back-country town. Yet I thought nothing of it, so much did I delight in the piety of my father-in-law, whose virtues shone in his fine God-fearing children.

There were nine of those, and she had married the youngest. Her devotion to him was unmistakable. She called him "blessed," and at his death her grief was overwhelming:

> Who will now be my comforter? To whom shall I pour out my soul? Where shall I turn? All his life my beloved companion listened to my troubles, and they were many, and he comforted me so that somehow they would quickly vanish. But now, alas, I am left to flounder in my woe.

Indeed, it was to come to terms with her grief that she began to write, in 1690, the extraordinary memoirs, intended as instruction for her children, that are the source of our knowledge about Glückel's life.

What is remarkable about the autobiography—beyond its literacy, which again was not unusual, even among women, in a community that had to live by its wits, and whose faith was in books—is its awareness of the precarious livelihoods of those who peopled its pages. Her husband's oldest brother, while on his way to his wedding, "dowry and all," was set upon by robbers. Among other members of the family, promises of partnerships came to naught; financial resources, though often carefully specified, were rarely what they seemed; advantageous marriages did not always meet expectations; rich estates were frittered away; and homes had to be left empty-handed because of war. But Chaim was adept at trade, and this was a source of great pride to Glückel.

In focusing on these matters, however, she was by no means unique to her age. An Englishman who was a younger contemporary of hers, William Stout of Lancaster, wrote an autobiography that was no less attentive to business transactions and accounts of the ways in which he had prospered. But Glückel was a woman, and in that respect her interests and her expertise have to be seen as quite extraordinary. For there is no question that she was a full partner with her husband in his enterprises and was closely consulted in all his dealings. As she noted, "My husband took advice from nobody else, and did nothing without our talking it over together." When he died, leaving his affairs in her hands, she was up to the responsibility:

> I went over the books and discovered we owed 20,000 Reichsthalers in debts [a huge sum]. But this was not news to me, and gave me no worry, for I knew I could pay them and still have enough to provide for myself and my children, though it was no light thing for a widow with eight orphans to be weighed down with such debts.

And pay them off she did. She held an auction of some assets, and within a year she had cleared the debts and made a profit, which she loaned out at interest.

The business that occupied the couple was one of the few open to Jews, who always had to operate on the margins of society. Yet the need to find room for maneuver in the interstices between traditional occupations was what set apart the nascent capitalist as well as the social pariah. Entrepreneurship was at a premium, as was the willingness to take risks. And few callings required both skills so relentlessly as the specialty Chaim had learned from his father—the jewelry and precious-metals trade. Extremely valuable small objects, easily stolen, had to be moved great distances, and bought and sold on the basis of a close understanding of international markets. It was no wonder that most Christian merchants chose easier ways of making a living, or that high-risk enterprises like dealing in gold or furs were left to outsiders like the Jews.

A year after their wedding, the young pair moved to Hamburg and "quickly learned how things stood." Jewels were not as sought after as they would be later.

> Instead, it was the fashion to wear solid gold chains; and gifts, if the occasion demanded, were all of gold. Although, to tell the truth, the profits were smaller than in jewels, my husband began dealing in gold. He bought the precious metal, turned it over to goldsmiths, or resold it to merchants about to be married, and thus made a tidy income.

Glückel was not closely involved in these early transactions, for she was having the first of her thirteen children—just eight days before her mother produced a new aunt for the baby. Only one of her brood was to die in infancy—an amazing achievement for the time—and a number were to enjoy both status and prosperity (one son-in-law was to become an East India merchant in London). Yet she was determined never to become dependent on them, and her restless widowhood was to be driven largely by her need to make her own way in the world. As she put it:

> In the heat of summer and the rain and snow of winter, I took myself to the fairs, and stood all day long in my store. I made desperate efforts to keep my footing lest I become a burden on my children and eat another's bread. Though it would have been my children's bread, it seemed more bitter than the bread of strangers, for my children, God forbid, might have cast it in my teeth, and the thought of this was worse than death.

What the trade in gems and metals entailed above all was ceaseless traveling, either by the owners of the business or by their agents. Chaim and Glückel had contacts from France to Denmark, from Holland to Poland. Their dealings depended on events in places as far-flung as Danzig, Copenhagen, Amsterdam, and Vienna. On one trip, to the fairs at Frankfurt and Leipzig, two of Chaim's companions died, and he himself fell ill; when other fellow traders returned to Hamburg, they had no news of his whereabouts. The endless cross-country journeying, on terrible roads, was arduous under the best of circumstances, threatened as it was by bandits, disease, and other dangers (PLATE XV). For Jews, however, it posed the additional burden of having to reach the next contact by nightfall, because only in Jewish homes could they eat or find a roof over their heads. Understandably, Glückel panicked when Chaim failed to return, and sent one of her sons off to look for his father. That he was able to make it home "broken and suffering" was due only to the hiring of a coach, in which he was able to lie on a bed.

Six years later Chaim was dead, leaving eight unmarried children and an encumbered estate. Undaunted, Glückel herself took to the road, and began the dealings with agents and suppliers across Europe that was the heart of her enterprise. She had come to understand its principles long before, and did not hesitate to pass them on in her memoirs. As she recalled, on one occasion

> much of our money was tied up in 300 ounces of seed pearls. It did no good to keep such wares on hand, for the profit was small and likely to be eaten up by interest if they were not sold soon. My husband went at once to the wholesale dealers, especially the Muscovy merchants. But no one made a favorable bid: the gain would have been too little. Since the offers were too low, he decided to mortgage the pearls, and took a loan on them. But war broke out in Muscovy, so the merchants lost all stomach for buying pearls. My husband had to sell the lot for a big loss, with interest to boot. The first offer, I tell you, is always the best; one must watch, and a merchant must know when to say "yes" as readily as "no."

Equally important was the need to use every opportunity to conduct the trade. When a daughter was married in Amsterdam, Glückel took full advantage of the trip. "While we were in Amsterdam, my son and I did business every day in precious stones." She was reluctant to break away even for a visit to relatives, and she "remained in Amsterdam some weeks after the celebration, attending to business" (PLATE XV).

The steadiness of purpose had to survive repeated setbacks and troubles. One of her sons—charming, but a ne'er-do-well—fell deeply into debt, causing hardship throughout the family when he defaulted on loans both from his brothers and from her. Undaunted, he asked for more money, and she launched into him:

> How can you think of committing such a wrong? You know that your brothers have already come to grief because of you; in fact, they can no longer support their losses. Now, when a small amount of tear-stained money, alas, returns to them, you want to snatch it from their bitterly aching hearts.

They screamed and quarreled for an hour, but he was unshakable. Turning on the charm, he prevailed on his brothers once again for loans that would never be repaid.

Glückel's response, typically, was to work even harder.

> I busied myself in the merchandise trade, selling every month to the amount of five or six hundred Reichsthalers. I went twice a year to the Brunswick fair, and each time made several thousands in profit, seeking to repair the loss I suffered through my son. My business prospered. I bought goods from Holland; I bought nicely in Hamburg, and disposed of the goods in a store of my own. I never spared myself: summer and winter I was out on my travels, and I rushed about the city. I maintained a lively trade in seed pearls, selected them and sorted them, and resold them in towns where there was a good demand. My credit grew by leaps and bounds.

But the effort was taking its toll. After ten years of this life she accepted her children's pleas—especially the recommendation of one daughter, Esther, who had settled in the French city of Metz and had identified a suitable widower—and in 1700, at the age of fifty-four, she reluctantly decided to remarry so as to avoid what seemed dire prospects:

> Despite all my pains and travelling about and running from one end of the city to another, I found I could hold out no longer. Though I had a good business, and enjoyed large credit, I was in constant torment lest goods go astray or a debtor fail me. I might fall, God forbid, into bankruptcy, and be a shame for my children and my pious husband, asleep in the earth.

And so she accepted the proposal of a rich widower, Hirsch Levy of Metz, one of the leading bankers of the duchy of Lorraine.

Finance was another of the risk areas in which Jews were forced to operate. Banking had long been one of the pillars of burgeoning capitalism, and it created some of the great fortunes of Europe, from the Medici to the Rothschilds. At the same time, however, it was acutely vulnerable to the whims of royal borrowers, or the unforeseeable shifts of volatile economies, and it spawned some of the most spectacular bankruptcies of the age. Yet its appeal was obvious to the risk taker, and Glückel had known a number of so-called court Jews, who achieved considerable prominence as governmental financiers. But she also knew how unpredictable any enterprise could be, let alone one as exposed as banking. Not for nothing had she always feared one of the period's perennial problems, the unrecoverable debt. For its effects could be more devastating than the other strokes of misfortune she had seen: agents killed by robbers, partners swindling her husband, illness, and even the effects of pirates on the high seas.

Yet her weariness, and the prospect of a comfortable old age, overcame her doubts. She moved to Metz, prepared for the best. But soon she found herself quoting ominous passages from Proverbs and Psalms:

> Alas, although "there are many devices in a man's heart," "He that sitteth in heaven shall laugh at them." God laughed at my plans. He had long before decreed my ruin and disaster, to punish me for the sin of relying on my fellow-men. For I ought not to have thought of taking another husband.

She had paid off all her debts in Hamburg, but in Metz she was to "suffer the very shame I feared," namely, to "fall to the care of my children." For although she was received magnificently, and was able for a little more than a year to enjoy all the comforts she had expected the marriage to bring her, disaster then struck. As she put it, her husband Hirsch "crashed on the rocks and all was lost."

Almost overnight a lifetime of prosperity and financial success evaporated. A business slump and bad debts combined to plunge Hirsch into bankruptcy, and he had to flee creditors who sought his arrest.

> When his creditors discovered he was gone, they sent three bailiffs to our house. They made an inventory of everything, down to the nails on the walls, and wrote it down and sealed everything up, so that I did not have food enough for a meal. I lived together with my housekeeper in one room. The bailiffs made themselves master of this as well, and no one could enter or leave. Once when I sought to leave, they searched me, lest I had hidden something on my person.

After three weeks of this existence a settlement was reached, but thereafter the couple "lived in the direst misery, and time and again there was no bread in the house."

There was no real impoverishment, because Glückel continued to mention family business dealings, including her stepson's transactions as provisioner and master of the mint to the duke of Lorraine. But that position became hostage to the conflict between the duke and King Louis XIV of France, in whose territory Metz was situated, just across the border from Lorraine. The troubles were too much for Hirsch, who died in 1712, leaving Glückel alone once again, "sitting with my cares and woes."

She was now sixty-six years old, but for three more years she insisted on living alone. Finally, however, in 1715, she had to give way.

> Once, when I was sick, my son-in-law visited me and said I had to come and live with him. He wanted to give me a room on the ground floor, to save me climbing stairs. But I refused his offer, for I had many reasons for wishing never to live with my children. But as things went, I could hold out no longer, Life grew very expensive in Metz, and I had to keep someone to take care of me. So I finally yielded, and moved into the house of my son-in-law.

Glückel lived another nine years, and died in 1724 at the age of seventy-eight. For all her fears, she was treated wonderfully by her children, and could spend her last days taking pleasure from her ever-

Artemisia Gentileschi, Judith and Her Maidservant with the Head of Holofernes. Painted five years after the blood-drenched "Holofernes" (see plate XII), this scene shows what followed after the assassination. Judith and her maid echo the figures in the earlier painting, but now, as they prepare to move on, Artemisia uses the light and shadows cast by the single candle to make even the wary Judith a powerful and dramatic presence.

PLATE XIII

Giuseppe Arcimboldo, Rudolf II as Vertumnus. Among the many unusual interests pursued at Rudolf II's court was a fascination with analogy and the connectedness of all creation. That interest was made visible by one of the court's leading artists, the Italian Arcimboldo, who depicted a number of figures as assemblages of recognizable objects. Appropriately, he portrayed Rudolf as Vertumnus, god of orchards and gardens (and thus fecundity), made up entirely of fruits, grains, and flowers.

Sebastian Vrancz, Siege of Ostend. Vrancz's picture captures the atmosphere of military life during the age of the Thirty Years' War, notably its variety and complexity. The scale of the enterprise—the equipment, the servicing, the accommodations for those who accompanied the soldiers, and the skills and crafts that were required—indicates why Wallenstein's logistical skills were so important.

PLATE XIV

Hendrick Avercamp, Travelers. This scene of life on the road in the seventeenth century would have been all too familiar to Glückel and her family.

Emanuel de Witte, Portuguese Synagogue in Amsterdam. Glückel may well have visited this great synagogue when she was in Amsterdam for the marriage of her daughter. Its sumptuousness contrasted sharply with the tiny houses, or mere rooms, of worship she would have known in much of Germany. Indeed, this very painting, produced by a prominent artist and echoing the depictions of churches that were common at the time (see St. Odolphus Church, plate XVI) reflects the integration of the prosperous Jewish community into the tolerant society of the Netherlands.

PLATE XV

David des Granges, The Saltonstall Family. This charming portrayal of a contemporary English family (around the deathbed of the grandmother) gives us a glimpse into the domestic world of Josselin's time. It is a scene that he would have found entirely recognizable.

P. J. Saenredam, Interior of the St. Odolphus Church in Assandelft. Although St. Odolphus's is in the Netherlands, we can see in this unadorned church the austere setting for worship that an English Puritan like Josselin would have approved. He would have been delighted, too, by the soberly dressed congregation, and by the emphasis in the service on the preaching of God's word.

PLATE XVI

expanding list of descendants (who were to encompass some of the leading figures of German and Jewish life, including, later in the century, the poet Heinrich Heine). Even amid this good fortune, however, her innate pessimism resurfaced: "The best of everything was put on my plate, more than I wanted or deserved, and I fear that God might count these rewards against my merits, which, alas, are few enough."

To the end Glückel's powerful personality shone through everything she said or did. At one level she appeared as an indomitable matriarch, tireless in her efforts to ensure that all her children would marry well and thrive. At another, she was a remarkable teller of tales, drawing on the wisdom of folklore to point morals for the children whom she hoped the memoirs would guide and instruct. And at all times she conveyed the deep respect for piety, religious practice and study, and ethical behavior that she considered the touchstones of her faith.

Again and again Glückel emphasized the primacy of traditional values, noting for example that her husband often missed excellent business opportunities because he could not be interrupted while he was at his thrice-daily prayers. In this respect she bore little resemblance to the image of the new capitalist that Shakespeare formed in *The Merchant of Venice*. Yet there was nothing inherently inconsistent in a commitment to both morality and commerce. Their seeming incompatibility was more a product of the personality of individual capitalists, and the comments of social critics, than the result of a necessary conflict. That her life provides this revealing sidelight, among many others, into the day-to-day character of the economic revolution that overtook Europe in these years—from the significance of its high-risk ventures to the importance of its international scope—is but one more tribute to the ways in which a whole world could be seen in the one little room of Glückel of Hameln.

PART X

The Response to Revolution

Left: Ralph Josselin. This appropriately unadorned portrait of Josselin by an unknown painter is still owned by his descendants.   *Right:* John Milton. The aging Milton in this portrait is not yet blind, but the face that emerges from the simple clothes and setting does not mask the cares and troubles of his life.

A Believer
and a Dissenter

HE REVOLUTION THAT SWEPT ENGLAND in the 1640s
and 1650s was in some respects the final great act of the
drama of the Renaissance. It pitted past against present,
traditional structures of government, church, and society
against agents of change. And some of the issues—whether the world
needed to be reformed, whether religious authority ought to be
challenged—still echoed, albeit faintly, the concerns of the age of
Petrarch and Hus. But lines were blurred. Even the most famous of
the revolutionaries, for example—Oliver Cromwell himself—could
be radical in matters of faith yet deeply conservative in politics.
Nevertheless, when the revolution ended and the reforms it either
promoted or resisted came to be generally accepted, a crucial divide
seemed to have been passed. The changes associated with the Renaissance had been integrated into society, and a new era was unfolding.
⟨ Those who lived through this final seismic disturbance reacted to
it as diversely as had their forebears to the transformations of the
preceding centuries. Just as Teresa had faced the upheavals of the
Reformation with confidence and calm, so did another believer,
the Protestant minister Ralph Josselin, draw on his faith to survive
his own tumultuous times serenely. The dryness and flatness of his

life is a testament to the power of such steady assurance. The poet and pamphleteer John Milton, by contrast, saw his age as a renewed opportunity for excitement, new ideas, and bold dissent. The ideals he strove for, in many cases unrealized for centuries to come, are among the most powerful legacies of the Renaissance.

Ralph Josselin

DURING the Renaissance, as for centuries before, no European village was without its clergyman. In many places he was indistinguishable from most of his parishioners—nearly as poor as any of them, sometimes not much more literate, and often no less fearful or more aware of the larger world. And yet he did have the wider experience of his education, however minimal it had been, and his ordination as a cleric. There was reason, therefore, to regard him as someone special: a villager, yet also a solace in time of trouble, a channel of communication with the mysterious supernatural forces that controlled human existence, a general source of advice, and the preserver of the rituals by which life was measured out.

In one respect, however, the Renaissance witnessed a major change. Under the pressure of religious conflict, the antagonistic faiths placed a new emphasis on education and on a self-conscious understanding of spiritual needs, so that the clergy could promote authentic religious devotion. As a result, priests, ministers, and preachers became far better prepared to explain doctrine and belief. This process has been described by some historians as the Christianization of Europe—as the transformation, for the first time ever, of semipagan peoples into true Christian believers. If that conclusion may reflect an excessive faith in the effects of education, it would not have astonished one of the exemplars of the new learned clergy, an English country vicar named Ralph Josselin.

He was born in 1617, and at some point in his twenties began to keep a detailed diary. By the time he died, in 1683, his enormous daily output—the complete modern edition fills more than six hundred large and densely printed pages—had created a giant kaleidoscope of the personal and public events that he had experienced. Throughout, however, one hears the voice of the devout and earnest clergyman, even in the description of his birth and infancy.

> I was born to the great joy of father and mother, being much desired, as being their third child and, as it pleased God, their only son. I had this happiness in my birth to be the seed of the righteous, both parents being in the judgment of man gracious persons [that is, blessed by grace].
>
> In my infancy, I had a gracious eye of providence watching over me, preserving me from dangers by fire—a remembrance I shall carry to my grave on my right thigh; by knives, being stabbed in the forehead by my second sister—a wild child, but now I hope God hath tamed and sanctified her spirit; falls from horse; water; and many casualties.

The sanguine and steady outlook seems to have been with him from an early age. Although his grandfather had been a well-to-do farmer, his father was not a good husbander of the family's resources. Moreover, Ralph's mother died while he was a child, and the boy knew that a stepmother could be his "undoing, and truly so it proved in respect of estate." But none of these disappointments seem to have oppressed him. He simply decided to get a good education, "so should I be able to live of my self."

> My father, moved by God, yielded to my desires and placed me with [the schoolmaster] Mr. Leigh, a painful man to me whom I have cause to love for his labors. In the school I was active and forward to learn, which contented my master and father. I remember not that I was ever whipped—once for an exercise when my master was passionate. It might be I often deserved it, yet I made it my aim to learn.

And learn he did. By the time he was sixteen, he was enrolled at Jesus Collegé, Cambridge, where again he was "close and diligent."

Ralph was often short of funds at university, and had to come home, to the "somewhat sour spirit" of his stepmother. But already at this age he seems to have been the most mature member of the family. His father had a terrible quarrel with his sister, and threw her out of the house. Apparently in spite, she decided to marry an old widower, but her sixteen-year-old brother talked her out of it and managed to reconcile her with their father. Although the old man often apologized at having squandered the boy's inheritance, Ralph seems not to have reproached him, and indeed to have hoped that he himself might be able to help the family finances. In the event, his father died just before he received his B.A. in 1636, and for the next three years he had to keep himself going with loans, help from an uncle, and a job as a schoolmaster.

When Josselin obtained his M.A. in 1640, at the age of twenty-three, he was ready to settle down. He had been ordained, and he had found a wife. Twice as a teenager he had succumbed to "too much familiarity" with a girl, a lapse that, though regretting, he later was pleased to have experienced, because it enabled him to understand the "wantonness" of the young. Now, on his very first Sunday in his first steady job, as a curate and schoolmaster in a Buckinghamshire village, "was my eye fixed with love upon a maid, and hers upon me." When his uncle offered him a better post, "my affection to that maid that God had laid out to be my wife would not suffer me to stir." It was nearly three months before they met, but then within a month they were engaged. They were married later that year, and soon thereafter, in March 1641, they moved to the village of Earls Colne in Essex, where Josselin was to remain as vicar until his death.

Jane was four years younger than Ralph and was to outlive him by ten years. Their marriage was clearly a love match, and although it had its share of disputes and troubles, especially in the couple's later years, there can be no doubt about the affection that united them. They did farm work together; they seem to have been of one mind on almost all family matters; and on one occasion they even had parallel dreams: "Dreamed I was familiar with the Pope; wife dreamed we were so with the Protector [Cromwell]. Lord lead me not into temptation." They missed each other terribly the few times they were apart, and the devotion shines through the diary entries.

> My dear wife exceeding tender and careful of me, which love of hers I hope I shall never forget. . . .
>
> My dear wife faint; the Lord in mercy preserve her, and sanctify her, as a choice vessel to himself, and comfort unto me. . . .
>
> This day 8 years my dear wife and I were married. Good is God to me, in wife and children, and my comforts in them. . . .
>
> Set apart this day to seek unto God for my wife, the continuance of her life.

The central joint endeavor of their lives was raising children. Between 1642 and 1663 Jane gave birth ten times. Only half of these children outlived them (four girls and a boy), and the Josselins took the losses very hard. In fact, these are the only times when the diary's unrelentingly sober demeanor cracks, and emotion bursts through:

> This day a quarter past two in the afternoon my Mary fell asleep in the Lord. She was 8 years and 45 days when she died. It was a precious child, a bundle of sweetness. She was a child of ten thousand, full of wisdom, woman-like gravity, knowledge, sweet expressions, tender hearted and loving. Thy memory is and will be sweet unto me.

The survivors all married, and Ralph proudly noted that he was able to provide each one of his daughters with a handsome dowry. To his endless regret, his oldest son, much beloved, was always sickly, and died at the age of twenty-nine. The blow was especially hard, because the brother who survived, John, was the exception to the tranquility of the household—a recurring cause of grief for his parents.

This son apart, it was clearly a close family. Births were major events, as a succession of entries over a three-day period revealed:

> At night the midwife with us, my wife thinking she might use her. But being sent for, my wife let her go, that another that was in present need might be helped. Within half an hour, as soon as I had done

family prayer, my wife had so sure a sign of her labor, and speedy, that put us all to a plunge. I sent a messenger after her, and it was at least 4 hours before she came, but she came time enough for us. My wife was wonderfully afraid and amazed, but help was speedily with her. [The next day] her pains ceased, the labor very strange to her. My faith was up for her. Prayer was for her. We commended her to God and her warm bed early. Her sleep was a comfort to her, mixed with pain, fear, which made her quake and tremble. [The third day] By two of the clock this morning I called the midwife, and nurse, got fires all ready, and then her labor came on so strongly and speedily that the child was born. Only 2 or 3 women more got in to her, but God supplied all. My heart was very lightsome and joyful.

Mother and child were then watched anxiously for a number of weeks, though the sturdy Jane always recovered well and nursed her children for at least a year.

For over three decades Josselin had one or more children at home (PLATE XVI). They usually remained until they were between nine and fifteen years old. Then, at a moment presumably determined by their maturity and the situation in the house, they were sent off —the girls to school or as servants in another family, the boys as apprentices in London. What this practice ensured was that adolescence was not spent in the care of parents, who thus avoided the worst of its turbulences. They, in turn, employed teenagers from elsewhere as their own servants, though not always to Ralph's delight. When one of them left the household after struggling with its devout atmosphere, he prayed, "Send me one, Lord, that feareth thy name."

But the absences did not loosen the household's bonds. Well into their married lives the daughters came visiting, as did grandchildren and in-laws. The Josselins traveled to see their offspring, too, and presided over regular family gatherings at Christmas and other occasions of celebration. It took but a hint of Ralph's illnesses in his later years to bring his progeny rushing home. And the interaction with kin extended to a wide network of uncles, cousins, and the like. It was almost taken for granted that, when Jane's elderly father became a widower, he would come and live with the Josselins.

To deal with the one exception to this harmony, the black-sheep son John, Ralph summoned a family conclave when he felt that the relationship was getting out of hand. John was a constant grief to his father: unpleasant, haughty, shiftless, and not above stealing money from both his mother and his sister. When he was twenty-three, his four sisters and mother sat down with Ralph at Christmastime to consider what to do next. Armed with their support, Josselin addressed his wayward son as follows:

> John: set yourself to fear God, and be industrious in my business. Refrain your evil courses, and I will pass by all past offences, settle all my estate on you after your mother's death, and leave you some stock to the value of £100. But if you continue your ill courses, I shall dispose my land otherwise, and make only a provision for your life to put bread in your hand.

According to the diary, "John owned his debauchery," but it was in vain. He was soon back to his old ways, and displayed his disrespect by marrying without his parents' knowledge, let alone consent. Eventually, although his father could not bring himself to disown him completely, his inheritance was significantly reduced. Given the turmoil of the age in which he lived, though, Ralph may perhaps have considered himself lucky that there was but one such cause of distress in his large and close-knit family.

It helped, of course, that he had the financial resources to sustain the connections. Given the hardship of his early days, it was remarkable that he was able to provide so well for his children—bequeathing, for instance, the substantial amount of over £1,000 to each of his two youngest daughters. In this respect, however, Josselin was a classic product of devout Protestantism: attributing all his blessings to God, but in fact working very hard to earn them. He had a good income at Earls Colne, was not averse to bargaining for a raise, and for a while supplemented his salary by serving as a schoolmaster. Moreover, thanks to his wife's inheritance, bequests from relatives, and his own shrewd management, he accumulated a respectable landholding. Sheer hard work, shared by Jane, plus an insistence on saving and careful supervision, eventually enabled Ralph to pass an ample estate on to his heirs. The diary is peppered with the accounts, the records of payments and receipts, and the general assessments of conditions (notably the weather) that mark the new economic self-consciousness of these early days of capitalism. Usually at the end of each March, he reviewed his situation. For example, in 1655:

> I again review my estate. Lands as formerly, and the same personal estate good that was last. There is added this year, £111.10. Though I am unprofitable, God is mindful of me. I wait on the Lord, desirous rather to honor him than to gain money.

The record keeping alone, not to mention the constant awareness of economic benefit and loss, sets Ralph apart from the clergy, and even most landowners, of an earlier age.

But there was no question that he was indeed a clergyman, deeply conscientious and aware of God's hand in everything he did. The diary is full of the baptisms, sermons, marriages, and funerals that were his life's work, and also of the local crises that were his stock-in-trade:

> Alarmed as if Goodman Mathew were dying suddenly. I hasted and found it a fainting fit. He was troubled his estate was not disposed so that his wife should enjoy it, but that we did the next day to his content. He was very cheerful. I judge it is an ague.

He mediated quarrels, arranged marriages, read scripture with parishioners, and made himself available to advise any who needed him. He also had a sharp eye for the village's characters:

> One mother Davy, a butcher's wife aged about 67 years, a town-born child, buried. Who was so miserable, she grudged anything to herself. One instance: she would have no fire in her house in her illness. Thus said she: "money runs away," and spread her hands. She had hid by her in the ground a vast sum of money.

Josselin's concern for the spiritual well-being of his charges never flagged. One can well imagine him as he "pressed persons to be firm to Jesus" (PLATE XVI). He gave generously to charity himself; denounced intemperateness, swearing, and the desecration of the sabbath; and was untiring in urging his congregation to find God's handiwork all around them, repeatedly chastising them when they lapsed. The moral instruction came naturally to him, for his dependence on his faith permeated his own life. The goodness of God, whether in prospering the harvest or restoring a sprained hand, is the leitmotif of the entire diary. And the assurance of his own righteousness was essential to Ralph's self-image:

> Preached at White Colne with my mouth and spirit. One Brett, after prayer, fell on me as no minister, accused me of pride. My heart untroubled, I called to him to charge anything I had delivered of error, but he could not. Lord, it's a glory to be reproached for thee.

And yet, however confident he was of God's grace and beneficent purpose—that the faithful would be taken care of—Josselin was as practical and observant about the turbulent political situation of his time as he was about economics. Here, too, God clearly helped those who helped themselves.

Ralph's position in the religious spectrum of Stuart England was toward its radical end. When the struggle between Parliament and king began in the early 1640s, therefore, there was no doubt which side he would take. Notwithstanding the patronage he had received from the traditional Church, he was unhappy with its outward ceremonies and display—the lack of emphasis on private faith—and he rejoiced in the opportunity to break its authority.

> This Michaelmas, upon an order of the House of Commons to that purpose, we took down all images and pictures, and such like. Thus this winter passed away a time of hopes, and yet sometimes fears. Spinning out my time, I began to be a little troubled with some in [the] matter of separation [from the Church of England].

Yet the disputes that are hinted at here never seemed to disturb his equanimity. Even as religious and political passions mounted, and England began to be torn apart, Josselin's faith led him, not to anger, but rather to a calm self-confidence that was never ruffled. The beliefs that, in others, provoked turmoil, in him merely reinforced the sense of assurance and rectitude. Nevertheless, as civil war approached, Ralph was determined to do his part for the side he supported. He found himself a musket and other arms, subsidized a number of soldiers "beyond my estate," and in general "endeavored others to go forth."

Finally, he went to war himself. Appointed chaplain to a regiment, he joined them for a march across central England in the autumn of 1645, preaching to the troops and living through the experience of combat. Three years later the royalists arrived in his own neighborhood:

> We were all young and raw men, yet God in mercy disposed our spirits to resolvedness. On Monday morning the enemy came to Colne, were resisted by our townsmen. No part of Essex gave them so much opposition as we did. They plundered us, and me in particular, of all that was portable, except brass, pewter, and bedding. When our losses may serve to advance God's glory, we ought to rejoice in the spoiling of our goods.

And yet, although his loyalties were unmistakable, Josselin retained his instinct for moderation, even amid civil war. He was deeply troubled by the execution of Charles I; he disliked attacks on those whom he regarded as God-fearing even if mistaken, like the Presbyterians; and he was fearful of the extreme ideas, notably Quakerism, that England's revolution provoked. When one of the radical groups, the Levellers, was suppressed, he did not hide his delight: it was "a glorious, rich providence of God to England."

In the long run, the moderation may have stood him in good stead. When the monarchy returned, in 1660, he had no hesitation in declaring his allegiance to Charles II and requesting a pardon. But he did not subscribe to the Act of Uniformity required of ministers, hesitated to reintroduce the official Book of Common Prayer, and resisted using the vestments the Church demanded. It may be that his nonconformity was sufficiently mild to save him from retribution. Possibly, the local gentry were comfortable with his presence and protected him; he mentioned his gratitude that they did not report

An English Bible would have been Josselin's most prized possession. Although he probably owned the King James version, it is the title page of an earlier translation that is reproduced here—the Coverdale Bible, published in 1541—because it is such a splendid example of the printer's art. This extraordinary paean of praise to Henry VIII, who began England's Reformation and commissioned the translation, rises in complex iconography from the people shouting "Vivat Rex" ("Long Live the King") at the foot of the page to the enthroned king at the top.

him when he strayed from formal doctrine in his sermons. Whatever the reason, however, and despite a few scares—notably a visit by the bishop of London, which he was relieved to see pass without incident—he survived, and was able to end his days in the vicarage that had been the center of his life.

It is easy to see Josselin as the stern and relentless figure, always at his prayers, that we tend to conjure up with the word "Puritan." And yet his enjoyment of the world was real, and even playful. He relished family celebrations, indulged eagerly in banquets and festivities, loved birdsong, and was tolerant of amusements as long as they did not intrude on the Sabbath. He even records winning a pair of gloves in a wager with one of his parishioners. And the larger world of politics, on the Continent as well as in England, was a source of constant fascination. The major events of the day, and many of the minor, found their way into the diary, from a revolt in Barcelona to false rumors of a siege of Copenhagen.

Ralph's favorite recreation, however, seems to have been reading. One of his happier days was described as a time when he rode to a nearby village, "enjoyed the company of good friends, saw some manuscripts, [and] had there a good bargain of books." Building on the studious habits of his youth, he progressed in Hebrew as well as Greek, and tried to keep up with major theological writings of his day. The purpose of the study was, of course, to make him a more effective minister to his parish, but he could not hide the sheer pleasure his books gave him. Even when relaxing, however, he was steady and precise, recording in one diary entry that he had finished reading "a pretty discourse" of 418 pages and "a learned discourse" of 559.

The hard work, the concentration, and the self-improvement may have been unceasing, but what sustained him above all was his confident belief in his own faith and, as a result, in himself, in his wife, in his family, and in his life's mission. Josselin was never a grumbler, for all the ailments and difficulties that he, like everyone of his time, encountered. Whether merely suffering from a chronically sore navel or grieving deeply over the death of a child, he was able always to react in measured tones, to maintain his fortitude, and to accept without question whatever God had decided. Equally, though, he was quick to attribute all examples of good fortune to the same benefactor. And the genuineness of his sentiments is inescapable, for the diary was clearly intended as nothing more than a private record for its author. The expressions of a constant faith came from within; they were not written to impress, or even to be seen by, anyone else.

Yet the assurance and self-sufficiency did not lead to smugness. They created, instead, a sense of fulfillment, a quiet embrace for all that life might bring. As he put it a few months before he died, having just read in his Bible, "Be of good courage, and he shall strengthen your heart, all ye that hope in the Lord":

> Sensible this day entered my 67th year. I blessed God for his presence thus far with me. I heartily repent me of my sins and hope in his mercy. I read Psalm 31, which was a comfort to me. I commit my soul and all concerns to God.

John Milton

FOR sheer speed of growth, no city in late Renaissance Europe could compare with London. England's capital had maybe 50,000 inhabitants at the beginning of Queen Elizabeth's reign. By 1700, just 150 years later, it had ten times that many, and it had become the largest city in Europe.

The growth may have made for excitement, with the bustle of new people and ideas—as many as one in every six Englishmen spent some part of their lives in the city—but it also exacted a heavy price. Hygienic conditions were horrendous. Deaths far exceeded births each year: as a saying of the time put it, London devoured the countryside. And the widespread poverty of the many who poured into the capital in hopes of a better livelihood, inspired by such stories as the tale of Dick Whittington, was equally inescapable. Crime was rampant, and a number of neighborhoods served as havens for the underworld, immune to outside interference. For most citizens it was impossible to go out at night, in the unlit and unpoliced streets, without a large escort. The vibrant cultural life of the Elizabethan age, exemplified by its theaters, had to be enjoyed during the day-time.

The sheer variety of people and opportunities that London offered made it a breeding ground of nonconformist opinion. Political leaders often thought it ungovernable, and during England's civil war, in the mid seventeenth century, it confirmed their worst fears as a seedbed of revolutionary ideas. Long before then, however, it had been a major center of Puritanism, the unorthodox set of beliefs that posed the most severe challenge to the official Church of England. And its citizens were always close to the events taking place in the Parliaments that met in nearby Westminster. Here were being developed remarkable, and ultimately subversive, notions of liberty and individual rights, which were the talk of the capital's streets and taverns.

If any place in the 1600s was likely to produce dissenting minds—people unwilling to accept received authority without a struggle—it was London. Of its many fiercely independent sons and daughters, however, none asserted the right to act and believe without dependence on traditional norms so powerfully or so movingly as John Milton.

Milton was born in 1608, the middle one of three children who survived infancy in the family of a successful scrivener, the very trade from which another poet, Petrarch, had sprung some three hundred years before. John's father, a professional copier of documents, guarantor of loans, and occasional moneylender, was making a comfortable living at a trade that was flourishing as the capital's economic and legal activity accelerated. The work brought him into contact with the city's elite, but it was his avid love of music and all learning that was to have the chief influence on his son. From an early age he encouraged the boy to spend long hours at his books. "When he was very young," a contemporary biographer wrote, "he studied very hard and sat up very late, commonly till 12 or one a clock at night, and his father ordered the maid to sit up for him." And it was not long before Milton senior realized he was not up to the task of serving as the principal teacher for his learned son.

What the brilliant child needed was a tutor, and fortunately, in this age when universities were expanding rapidly, there were more than enough candidates at hand. Some decades later Thomas Hobbes was to say that these underemployed intellectuals, unable to find appropriate jobs, were a major source of the discontent that led to England's civil war. Milton's tutor, a Scotsman named Thomas Young, seemed to have no such difficulties—he ended up as the master of a Cambridge college—and he was a godsend for his talented pupil. Expert guidance was exactly what John needed, to channel his eagerness to learn, to be stretched, to achieve new masteries. He even relished the drudgery of ploughing through, and memorizing, the Latin classics that were the essence of Renaissance education. What he especially appreciated, though, was Young's gift for languages. By the time the tutoring was over, and Milton had completed a brief stint at London's most famous school, St. Paul's, he was at home in Latin, Greek, Hebrew, and Italian.

The next step was university, and in 1625 the sixteen-year-old entered Christ's College, Cambridge. Here the prodigy received the classic training that the seventeenth century offered: a solid grounding in Christian belief, wide reading in Latin and English literature, and thorough studies of the ancient Greeks and Romans. It was not an easy time for him, because he was always an autodidact as much as a pupil, and he had little respect for his teachers. But he stuck it out, with interruptions, for nearly eight years, and when he finally left Cambridge with his M.A., at the age of twenty-three, to go home to his parents, he had at least decided that a career in the clergy—the normal expectation for someone of his skills—was not for him. He had already begun writing verse, and in the Nativity Ode, "L'Allegro," and "Il Penseroso" he had already created his early masterpieces. As he asked himself, ironically, in the Nativity Ode:

> Say heavenly Muse, shall not this sacred vein
> Afford a present to the infant God?
> Hast thou no verse, no hymn, or solemn strain,
> To welcome him to this his new abode?

The answer was clear: his vocation was to be the life of the writer.

Soon after his return home, a musician friend of his father's obtained for Milton a commission to write the verse for a musical performance that was being prepared for an aristocratic family. These entertainments, known as masques, were lighter versions of the operas that were then appearing for the first time in Europe, and the commission (for an elegant pastoral narrative named for one of the characters, Comus, god of revelry, who was played by Milton himself) might have been the beginning of a career under noble patronage. Milton certainly had mastered the grace the form required:

> How charming is divine philosophy!
> Not harsh, and crabbed as dull fools suppose,
> But musical as is Apollo's lute,
> And a perpetual feast of nectared sweets.

But circumstances, above all the civil wars that were soon to engulf England, cut short the possibility of a courtly life, though it is hard, in retrospect, to imagine Milton fully at home in such surroundings.

Supported by the commission, but mainly by his parents, the poet spent the five years following Cambridge in further study, primarily of Greek and Latin authors, and also in new areas such as mathematics and music. His voraciousness extended to all of knowledge, and was to make his poetry the most erudite ever written in the English language. But in these youthful days, even as the political storms of the 1630s—growing religious and political repression at home, vicious wars abroad—gathered around him, his poems were glorious evocations of love and nature. Even the lament over the untimely death of his friend Lycidas ended with the poet moving on, his hopes still high:

Thus sang the uncouth swain to th'oaks and rills,
While the still morn went out with sandals gray;
He touch'd the tender stops of various quills,
With eager thought warbling his Dorick lay.
And now the sun had stretched out all the hills,
And now was dropt into the Western bay;
At last he rose, and twitch'd his mantle blue:
Tomorrow to fresh woods, and pastures new.

"Lycidas" was published in 1638, in Milton's thirtieth year, but still he did not consider his education complete. His mother had just died, and although his father was now seventy-five, the poet felt he needed to leave home for one more major experience before he could settle down. With his father's reluctant blessing, he set off to follow the path of the newly fashionable Grand Tour, which was coming to be seen as the perfect finishing touch in the education of those young Englishmen who could afford it. It offered an opportunity to see at first hand the relics of the classical age that filled their reading, and to encounter on the Continent the latest exponents of humanism, of the arts, of philosophy, scholarship, and literature. Milton's hope was to travel to Italy, Greece, and the Mediterranean, but in the event he turned back after little more than a year, when "the melancholy intelligence which I received of the civil commotions in England made me alter my purpose, for I thought it base to be travelling for amusement abroad, when my fellow-citizens were fighting for liberty at home."

Still, the months Milton spent in France, Switzerland, and Italy became a cherished experience, often recollected in later years. He was widely known for his poems in the international language of Latin, and his erudition opened all doors. The leading intellectual circles of Florence and Naples gave him a warm welcome; he spent an evening in Paris with the renowned philosopher Hugo Grotius; and in the little village of Arcetri, in the hills above Florence, he visited the blind Galileo, "grown old a prisoner to the Inquisition, for thinking in astronomy otherwise than the Franciscan and Dominican licensers thought." It was this encounter, with the bloody but unbowed prisoner, that left the deepest impression. The scientist, in his mid-seventies, was only a few years away from death, but he had just published his principal work on physics, *The Two New Sciences*, in the Netherlands, far from the reach of the Inquisition. The references to Galileo many years later, in *Paradise Lost*, testified to the profound impact of the meeting on Milton. And the focus on what the scientist had *seen* may also suggest the poet's sense, at the end of his life, of enduring a dissenter's fate (accompanied by a loss of eyesight) not unlike that of his hero.

> . . . like the moon, whose orb
> Through optic glass the Tuscan artist views
> At evening from the top of Fesolè,
> Or in Valdarno, to descry new lands,
> Rivers, or mountains, in her spotty globe.

And:

> As when by night the Glass
> Of *Galileo*, less assur'd, observes
> Imagined Lands and Regions in the Moon.

When Milton returned home in 1639, he brought his musician father a trunkload of the latest music from Venice, notably some works by the most exciting composer of the day, Claudio Monteverdi. But there was to be little time for quiet enjoyment of the news and ideas he had brought from the Continent. King Charles was already at war with his Scottish subjects over his attempt to standardize religious practices, and within three years there was to be civil war in England.

By then John, settled in London, had established a school in his house. One of his pupils, his nephew Edward, later praised "his excellent judgement and way of teaching, far above the pedantry of common public schools." And indeed, Milton made clear in his essay, "Of Education," that he was determined to clear away the "asinine feast of sowthistles and brambles" that was usually set before children of the "tenderest and most docible age," and focus instead on their "happy nurture." He wanted "a complete and generous education," which would go beyond the standard religious, Greek, and Roman texts to such subjects as anatomy, agriculture, gardening, music, and mathematics, and also promote physical skills. That Milton had impossible standards is obvious. He assumed that everyone loved learning as much as he did, and even expected his pupils to "have easily learned, at any odd hour, the Italian tongue."

In fact, though, there proved to be less and less time for these pursuits, let alone for his beloved poetry, over the next twenty years. As England became engulfed in the turmoil of civil war and revolution, Milton devoted much of the 1640s and 1650s to the writing of a series of prose works, all of them denouncing traditional repressions and demanding new standards of individual liberty. With orthodox authorities faltering, and accustomed controls weakening, he took advantage of a unique period of unrestrained expression to issue calls for an entire gamut of personal freedoms.

The stream of pamphlets that came from Milton's pen in these years, rejecting privilege and claiming egalitarian rights and tolerance for all manner of beliefs, have inspired revolutionaries ever since. Few have denounced restrictions on liberty with the eloquence of Milton. In scathing pages, he produced searing indictments of all forms of intolerance and repression. He defended the right of dissent and the right to hold personal religious beliefs. He advocated a broadening, a liberalization of the curriculum. And perhaps most radical of all, he argued in favor of divorce, free love, and even the ideal of platonic love between men and women.

Among the many issues Milton addressed, the one with which he is especially associated, as both pioneer and exemplar, is freedom of the press, championed in *Areopagitica: A Speech for the Liberty of Unlicensed Printing*, published in 1644. The title came from the Areopagus, a hill near the Acropolis on which an Athenian court had sat in ancient times. The court's main function was to supervise religious beliefs, but around the time of the Battle of Salamis, at the beginning of the Athenian golden age, it lost the right to censor an individual's ideas. Milton argued that the abolition of censorship promoted creativity, and he could see the analogy in personal terms, because the London book licensers (whose approval was required for every publication, and who were still trying to function amid civil war) had objected to his views about divorce as irreligious. His response was the first major defence of the freedom of the press in modern times. If occasionally he seemed prepared almost to forgo laws of libel or slander, his spirited argument has remained the foundation of all subsequent assaults on censorship and has become a cornerstone of the dissenter's claim to be heard.

The quotable passages are legion, but three will have to suffice:

> Books which are likely to taint life and doctrine cannot be suppressed without the fall of learning. A wise man can gather gold out of the drossest volume, and a fool will be a fool with the best book.

> He that can apprehend and consider vice, with all her baits and seeming pleasures, and yet abstain, and yet distinguish, and yet prefer that which is truly better, he is the true wayfaring Christian. I cannot praise a fugitive and cloistered virtue, unexercised and unbreathed, that never sallies out and sees her adversary, but slinks out of the race. Assuredly we bring not innocence into the world, we bring impurity much rather: that which purifies us is trial, and trial is by what is contrary.

> Where there is much desire to learn, there will be much arguing, many opinions. What some lament, we should rejoice at. Let Truth and Falsehood grapple; who ever knew Truth put to the worse, in a free and open encounter?

No stronger case has ever been made for the value of unorthodoxy —for the health it brings to society.

The struggles of the seventeenth century (like those of so many centuries) revolved around words, around the propaganda of clashing visions of human destiny. For a master of language like Milton it was almost second nature to throw himself into the issues of the day—to excoriate oppression by bishops, to justify the execution of King Charles, to attack tyrannical Presbyterians, to demand the suppression of Catholicism. He was the most famous publicist of the day, and it was thus entirely appropriate that the new government of

The first pictures of the execution of Charles I were published by the Dutch. This engraving shows with remarkable accuracy Inigo Jones's Banqueting House, which graces Whitehall in London to this day. Charles stepped through a window onto the specially built scaffold, and a huge throng watched as he was executed and his head, dripping blood, was displayed (on the far right of the platform). Many years later a statue of Charles was placed farther along Whitehall, and it shows him looking at this spot.

Oliver Cromwell, seeking a secretary to deal with foreign governments, should have chosen Milton. He had become the voice of all the freedoms the revolution stood for, and now he was to become its voice to the rest of Europe.

A few years earlier, in 1642, just as civil war was erupting, Milton, on a visit to Oxford, fell in love with the daughter of an old friend of his father's, a seventeen-year-old named Mary Powell, and within a month they were married. Just a couple of months later, however, the young wife was back with her parents, not to return to her husband for three years. Whether the separation was the result of the dangers of wartime, or of the incompatibility of a fiery, often solitary intellectual and a lively young girl, we do not know. What is clear is that there was recurrent tension with his in-laws, who were staunch royalists, and that Milton's acerbic views of the married state—couched in pleas for total freedom—suggest a less than perfect union.

When Mary finally returned, in 1645, the couple had a son and three daughters in seven years, but in the last of these childbirths the young mother died. Nor were his children much consolation. His son survived little more than a year, and the two older daughters complained bitterly of being forced to read to their father—who had gone blind in the early 1650s—in languages they did not understand. They seem, in general, to have felt ignored by the great man, and they had no compunction in selling off some of his books without his knowledge. When he remarried without even telling them, one daughter said: "That were no news, to hear of his wedding; but if she could hear of his death, that was something."

Despite the sorrows—and the misogyny that was evident in his writings on divorce, doubtless reinforced by a difficult marriage and the hostility of his daughters—he married twice more, had yet another daughter, and did gain some comfort from grandchildren in his old age. It was not that he was incapable of tender and loving feelings. In one of his sonnets the blind poet movingly recalls a dream in which his dead second wife appears to him:

> Her face was veiled, yet to my fancied sight,
> Love, sweetness, goodness in her person showed
> So clear, as in no face with more delight.
> But O as to embrace me she inclined
> I waked, she fled, and day brought back my night.

And yet it is clear that that was not where Milton's priorities lay. All his energies went into the lonely and time-consuming task of reading and writing. Like many a champion of humanity, he seems to have preferred words to people, ideas to individuals, and thus to have disappointed those who were closest to him.

The 1650s were an uneasy time for the poet, who felt increasingly burdened by domestic troubles and blindness. Even more dismaying than these personal difficulties, however, may have been his growing doubts about England's new rulers. Fearful of disorder, their leader, Oliver Cromwell, was taking on kinglike attributes, and was placing control of the country in the hands of his army. For all his loyalty to the cause, Milton's conscience would not let him remain silent about the new dangers of injustice as Cromwell's government began to display, quite alarmingly, the very indifference to the public good that had damned Charles. This might have been expected of church-men; indeed, Milton had complained that "new presbyter is but old priest writ large." But it was hard to fathom a betrayal by the rev-olutionaries themselves. Regardless of his admiration for his new employers, Milton had to be true to his dissenting instincts, and he had to protest:

> If the ability to devise the cleverest means of putting vast sums of money into the treasury, the power readily to equip land and sea forces, to deal shrewdly with ambassadors from abroad, and to contract judicious alliances and treaties has seemed to any of you greater, wiser, and more useful to the state than to administer incorrupt justice to the people, to help those harassed and oppressed, and to render to every man promptly his own deserts, too late will you discover how mistaken you have been. If you begin to slip into the same vices, to imitate those men, to seek the same goals, to clutch at the same vanities, you actually are royalists yourselves, at the mercy either of the same men who up to now have been your enemies, or of others in turn.

It was the credo of the eternal dissenter, sure that a new generation would arise to reprimand those who relapsed into the discredited policies of old.

As the aggravations multiplied, Milton turned for consolation to the stately, classical verse that had given him such joy in his youth. When blindness struck him in the early 1650s, and he feared that he could not keep up his "one talent," poetry, his response was a sonnet that is among the most moving ever written.

When I consider how my light is spent,
    Ere half my days, in this dark world and wide,
    And that one talent which is death to hide,
    Lodged with me useless, though my soul more bent
To serve therewith my maker, and present
    My true account, lest he returning chide,
    Doth God exact day-labour, light-denied,
    I fondly ask, But Patience to prevent
That murmur, soon replies, God doth not need
    Either man's work or his own gifts, who best
    Bear his mild yoke, they serve him best, his state
Is kingly. Thousands at his bidding speed
    And post o'er land and ocean without rest:
    They also serve who only stand and wait.

Increasingly, however, he was returning to a deeper and older ambition: to create in English verse an epic to match those that adorned the Greek, Latin, and Italian tongues. The result was to be *Paradise Lost*, written and revised over a number of years in the 1650s and 1660s—the first of three massive outpourings that were to demand comparison with the ancient achievements of Homer and Vergil. All three of the poems, which were to be Milton's crowning literary achievement—the others were *Paradise Regained* and *Samson Agonistes*—were published between 1667 and 1671, when Milton once again lived under a king: Charles II, son of the executed Charles I.

However sobered the monarchy had been by the revolution, and however much Parliament had been strengthened, the threat of repression often seemed as great now as it had been in the 1630s. The relaxed air of London under merry King Charles, with its bawdy theater, its fondness for elegant satire, and its wenching even among its bureaucrats, was deceptive. Unorthodox opinion was closely watched, and it was only the intervention of the favored poet of the new generation, John Dryden, that saved Milton from punishment. Thanks to his efforts, the blind old man was left to his own devices, and he could concentrate on writing his massive, stately, and dignified verse.

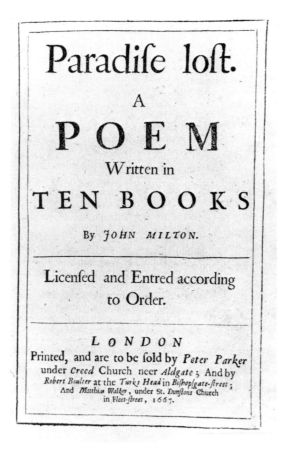

Paradiſe loſt.

A

POEM

Written in

TEN BOOKS

By JOHN MILTON.

Licenſed and Entred according
to Order.

LONDON

Printed, and are to be ſold by Peter Parker
under Creed Church neer Aldgate; And by
Robert Boulter at the Turks Head in Biſhopſgate-ſtreet;
And Matthias Walker, under St. Dunſtons Church
in Fleet-ſtreet, 1667.

The title page of the first edition of Milton's *Paradise Lost* has a simplicity that is an appropriate reflection of its disciplined and single-minded author.

In these masterpieces Milton looked back over the past and found consolation in faith, in poetry, and in the joy that he, like that other blind old man, Galileo, had found in an appreciation of life and nature. He explored the meaning of belief and, not surprisingly, the limitations of heroism. It was no wonder that the blind Samson, bereft of his former strength, should have inspired an allegorical lament for the failure of the true faith—the defeat of a revolutionary spirit that would, however, rise again.

Yet there was much more in these epics than political commentary. They laid out ideals that reflected Milton's abiding passion to improve the human condition, and his feeling that the love of

253

God—emerging from within, and never shaped or constrained by outside orthodoxy—was the essence of religious faith. If Satan at times seems almost heroic, that may be because he so ardently expressed the poet's own revolutionary instincts and fierce pursuit of unattainable goals. Only his challenge to God was unpardonable; in all other respects it was crucial for the individual to find his own way, undeterred by the dogmas of others. For what Milton sought to stimulate was above all a reformation in behavior and outlook, an unblinkered and determined quest for virtue that the angel describes for Adam as he leaves paradise, almost as the moral of the tale:

> This having learnt, thou hast attained the summe
> Of wisdom; hope no higher, though all the Starrs
> Thou knewst by name, and all th' ethereal Powers,
> All secrets of the deep, all Nature's works,
> Or works of God in Heav'n, Air, Earth, or Sea,
> And all the riches of this World enjoydst,
> And all the rule, one Empire; onely add
> Deeds to thy knowledge answerable, add Faith,
> Add Vertue, Patience, Temperance, add Love,
> By name to come call'd Charitie, the soul
> Of all the rest: then wilt thou not be loath
> To leave this Paradise, but shalt possess
> A Paradise within thee, happier farr.

In 1674, just a few years after these words were published, Milton died, sadly aware that the great moment of dissent was over. For a while the protest, the sense of injustice, that he embodied had helped shape the world. The tradition did not die, however, because a small, albeit grudging, place had been won—at least in England—for the tolerance of unorthodoxy that Milton had so ardently demanded. But the heroic days were over, drowned in an age of self-assurance and acquiescence, and they were not to return for over a century, when a new era of revolution dawned. Until that time came, Milton had at least pointed the way, and had shown that, when the public paradise faded, it was still possible to "possess a Paradise within thee, happier farr."

Afterword

CAN fifteen people exemplify an age three hundred years long? Do they even represent a significant cross section of the varied social types who made up Renaissance society? To the extent that they refused to sit back, satisfied and indifferent, while the world continued in its ways, they did embody the restlessness and struggle that marked these years. And they were also characteristic of their times in that they looked to the past for guidance and inspiration. If Petrarch had Augustine, Milton still had Vergil. But, however hard they looked backward, they brought about revolutions in almost every sphere of life, from architecture to astronomy, from statecraft to warfare. It was their vitality and exuberance, whatever cause they were pursuing, that gave them an appeal that has endured ever since.

Yet excitement and energy alone cannot account for the response they still evoke. What makes them speak to us, most of all, is their indeterminacy. Some of them—Hus, Teresa, Josselin—had answers, though they agonized long and hard before they found them. Most, however, felt that they could do no more than set out on the quest. Like Montaigne, though rarely to such an extent, they hesitated in the face of certainty and truth. Possibilities and opportunities seemed endless, and we honor their determination to keep them open. It was not just a Platter, a Ralegh, a Glückel, or a Galileo who never stopped

searching. The artists, the warriors, and the princes were equally caught up in the tireless campaign against closure, against a final definition of limits. It was an enterprise that distinguished these generations from their predecessors, and it binds them to ourselves in a crusade that is unsatisfied still.

Acknowledgments

For their comments on individual "lives," I wish to thank Christiane Andersson, Jodi Bilinkoff, Natalie Davis, Mary Garrard, Anthony Grafton, Thomas Kauffmann, Joseph Levine, Michael Mahoney, François Rigolot, and David Rosand. For his role in shaping the entire book, I am indebted to Dan Frank. My chief debt of gratitude, for help beyond measure, is to the dedicatee.

Illustration Credits

Black and White Illustrations

2 Portrait of Petrarch, Lombardo della Sala (Bibliothèque Nationale, Paris).

2 Portrait of Jan Hus, Artist Unknown (Princeton University Libraries).

9 View of Rome, from *The Nuremberg Chronicle* (Courtesy of the author).

23 The Last Supper, Albrecht Dürer (Princeton University Libraries).

30 Execution of Jan Hus, Artist Unknown (Martinitz Bible, Prague, 1434).

34 Self-Portrait, Titian (Museo del Prado, Madrid).

34 Self-Portrait (1498), Albrecht Dürer (Museo del Prado, Madrid).

41 Self-Portrait, Titian (Gemäldegalerie Staatliche Museen Preussischer Kultur-besitz, Berlin [West]).

43 Musculature, from Andreas Vesalius, *The Structure of the Human Body*, Titian's Studio (Princeton University Libraries).

47 Charles V at the Battle of Mühlberg, Titian (Museo del Prado, Madrid).

49 The Flaying of Marsyas, Titian (Kroměříž Museum, Czechoslovakia).

50 Pietà, Titian (Accademia, Venice. Scala/Art Resource, New York).

54 Gilt Silver Apple Cup (Germanisches National Museum, Nuremberg).

56 Four Horsemen of the Apocalypse, Albrecht Dürer (The Art Museum, Princeton University. Gift of Donald B. Watt).

58 Portrait of Willibald Pirckheimer, Albrecht Dürer (Kupferstichkabinett, Berlin).

59 Portrait of Agnes Dürer, Albrecht Dürer (Kupferstichkabinett, Berlin).

61 Venetian Lady and Nuremberg Lady, Albrecht Dürer (Städelsches Kunstinstitut, Frankfurt).

63 Proportions of a Female Body, from *Treatise on Human Proportions*, Albrecht Dürer (Princeton University Libraries).

65 Melencolia I, Albrecht Dürer (The Art Museum, Princeton University. Gift of J. Lionberger Davis).

68 The Four Apostles, Albrecht Dürer (Alte Pinakothek, Munich).

70 Design for a Monument to the Peasants' Revolt, Albrecht Dürer (Princeton University Libraries).

74 Portrait of Thomas Platter, Artist Unknown (Princeton University Libraries).

78 Contest Between Carnival and Lent (detail), Peter Brueghel the Elder (Kunsthistorisches Museum, Austria).

81 The Zurich Martyrs (detail), Hans Leu the Elder (Swiss National Museum, Zurich).

88 The Printer, from *The Book of Trades*, Jost Amman (Princeton University Libraries).

89 Skeleton, from Andreas Vesalius, *The Structure of the Human Body*, Titian's Studio (Princeton University Libraries).

94 Portrait of Teresa of Avila, Fray Juan de la Miseria (Convento de Carmelitas Descalzas de Santa Teresa, Seville. Courtesy of Archive Mas, Barcelona).

94 Portrait of Michel de Montaigne, Artist Unknown (Bibliothèque Nationale, Paris).

104 Ecstasy of St. Teresa, Gian Lorenzo Bernini (Santa Maria della Vittoria, Rome. Scala/Art Resource, New York).

111 Portrait of Michel de Montaigne, Artist Unknown (Musée Condé, Chantilly. Giraudon/Art Resource, New York).

120 Title page from Michel de Montaigne, *Essays* (Princeton University Libraries).

124 Portrait of Catherine de' Medici, François Clouet (Musée Condé, Chantilly, Giraudon/Art Resource, New York).

134 Massacre of Protestants, Artist Unknown (Princeton University Libraries).

140 Portrait of Walter Ralegh, Nicholas Hilliard (National Portrait Gallery, London).

140 Portrait of Galileo, Justus Sustermans (Uffizi, Florence. Scala/Art Resource, New York).

147 Town of Secota, John White (British Museum, London).

158 University of Padua, Artist Unknown (Princeton University Libraries).

165 The Copernican System, Galileo Galilei (Princeton University Libraries).

170 Frontispiece from Galileo Galilei, *Dialogue on the Two Chief World Systems* (Princeton University Libraries).

176 Self-Portrait, Artemisia Gentileschi (Royal Collection, St. James's Palace. © Her Majesty Queen Elizabeth II).

184 Madonna and Child, Artemisia Gentileschi (Corsini Gallery, Rome. Alinari/Art Resource, New York).

186 David and Bathsheba, Artemisia Gentileschi (Columbus Museum of Art, Ohio. Museum Purchase: Schumacher Fund).

189 The Queen's House, Greenwich, Inigo Jones (National Maritime Museum, London).

194 Portrait of Albrecht von Wallenstein, Van Dyck (Alte Pinakothek, Munich).

197 The Archdukes Albert and Isabella in a Collector's Cabinet, Jan Brueghel the Elder and Adriaen Stalbemt (Walters Art Gallery, Baltimore).

202 Garden and Loggia, Wallenstein Palace, Prague (Princeton University Libraries).

208 Execution, from *The Miseries of War*, Jacques Callot (Princeton University Libraries).

212 Portrait of Glückel of Hameln, Artist Unknown (The Israel Museum, Jerusalem).

216 The Jew, from *The Book of Trades*, Jost Amman (Princeton University Libraries).

217 Invasion of the Frankfurt Ghetto, Artist Unknown (Princeton University Libraries).

228 Portrait of Ralph Josselin, Artist Unknown (By kind permission of Lt. Col. Richard Probert and Geoffrey Probert, Esq., the owners).

228 Portrait of John Milton, William Faithorne (Princeton University Libraries).

239 Title Page from the Coverdale Bible (Princeton University Libraries, Scheide Collection).

249 Execution of Charles I, Artist Unknown (Princeton University Libraries).

253 Title Page from John Milton, *Paradise Lost* (Princeton University Libraries).

Color Plates

Between pages 16 and 17

I   Scene of the Life of Pius II: Aeneas Silvius Crowned Poet by Frederick III, Pinturicchio (Cathedral, Piccolomini Library, Siena. Scala/Art Resource, New York).

II   St. Augustine in His Study, Carpaccio (San Giorgio, Venice. Scala/Art Resource, New York).
     Execution of Jan Hus, Artist Unknown (Gradual of Leitmeritz, West Bohemia, 1517).
     Execution of Jan Hus, Artist Unknown (Gradual of Leitmeritz, West Bohemia, 1517).

III Assumption of the Virgin, Titian (Santa Maria dei Frari, Venice. Scala/Art Resource, New York).

IV   Portrait of Doge Andrea Gritti, Titian (Samuel H. Kress Collection. National Gallery of Art, Washington).
     The Vendramin Family, Titian (Reproduced by courtesy of the Trustees, The National Gallery, London).

Between pages 80 and 81

V   Venus with a Mirror, Titian (Andrew W. Mellon Collection. National Gallery of Art, Washington).

VI   Self-Portrait (1500), Albrecht Dürer (Alte Pinakothek, Munich).
Castle of Trent, Albrecht Dürer (British Museum, London).

VII The Schoolmaster, Ambrosius Holbein (Offentliche Kunstsammlung, Kunstmuseum, Basel).
Parable of the Blind, Peter Brueghel the Elder (Capodimonte, Naples. Alinari/Art Resource, New York).

VIII Resurrection of Christ, El Greco (Museo del Prado, Madrid).

Between pages 128 and 129

IX   Valois Tapestry, Festival with Tournament (Uffizi, Florence. Scala/Art Resource, New York).

X   Portrait of Walter Ralegh and Son, Artist Unknown (By courtesy of The National Portrait Gallery, London).

XI   Galileo's Telescope (Museo della Scienze, Florence. Scala/Art Resource, New York).
The Supper at Emmaus, Caravaggio (Reproduced by courtesy of the Trustees, The National Gallery, London).

XII Judith Slaying Holofernes, Artemisia Gentileschi (Uffizi, Florence. Scala/Art Resource, New York).

Between pages 224 and 225

XIII Judith and Her Maidservant with the Head of Holofernes, Artemisia Gentileschi (The Detroit Institute of Arts. Gift of Mr. Leslie H. Green).

XIV Rudolf II as Vertumnus, Giuseppe Arcimboldo (Skoklosters Slott, Stockholm).
Siege of Ostend, Sebastian Vrancz (Museo del Prado, Madrid).

XV Travelers, Hendrick Avercamp (Historisches Museum, Frankfurt).
Portuguese Synagogue in Amsterdam, Emmanuel de Witte (The Israel Museum, Jerusalem).

XVI The Saltonstall Family, David des Granges (Tate Gallery, London. Art Resource, New York).
Interior of the St. Odolphus Church in Assandelft, P. J. Saenredam (Rijksmuseum, Amsterdam).

About the Author

THEODORE K. RABB is Professor of History at Princeton University, where he has taught Renaissance and early modern European history since 1967. He has also taught at Stanford, Northwestern, Harvard, and Johns Hopkins universities. The author of numerous articles and reviews, and the editor of *The Journal of Interdisciplinary History* since its foundation, he has written or edited a number of books, including *The Struggle for Stability in Early Modern Europe* and *The New History*. His latest major undertaking has been to serve as the principal historical advisor to the PBS television series *Renaissance*.

Howard Menken

THEODORE K. RABB is Professor of History at
Princeton University, where he has taught Renais-
sance and early modern European history since 1967.
He has also taught at Stanford, Northwestern, Har-
vard, and Johns Hopkins universities. The author of
numerous articles and reviews, and the editor of *The
Journal of Interdisciplinary History* since its foundation,
he has written or edited a number of books, including
The Struggle for Stability in Early Modern Europe and
The New History. His latest major undertaking has
been to serve as the principal historical advisor to the
PBS television series *Renaissance.*